WOMEN'S SPIRITUALITY

Contemporary Feminist Approaches to Judaism, Christianity, Islam and Goddess Worship

WOMEN'S SPIRITUALITY

Contemporary Feminist Approaches to Judaism, Christianity, Islam and Goddess Worship

JOHANNA H. STUCKEY

INANNA PUBLICATIONS AND EDUCATION INC.

Canada Council for the Arts   Conseil des Arts du Canada

We gratefully acknowledge the support of the Canada Council for the Arts and the Ontario Arts Council for our publishing pr

We are also grateful for the support received from an Anonymous Fund at The Calgary Foundation.

Cover design: Val Fullard
Interior design: Luciana Ricciutelli

Library and Archives Canada Cataloguing in Publication

Stuckey, Johanna H., 1933-
Women's spirituality : contemporary feminist approaches to Judaism, Christianity, Islam and goddess worship / Johanna H. Stuckey.

Includes bibliographical references and index.
ISBN 978-1-926708-02-7

1. Feminist spirituality. 2. Women--Religious life. I. Title.

BV4527.S78 2010   248.8'43   C2010-901804-4

Printed and bound in Canada

Inanna Publications and Education Inc.
210 Founders College, York University
4700 Keele Street
Toronto, Ontario, Canada M3J 1P3
Telephone: (416) 736-5356 Fax (416) 736-5765
Email: inanna@yorku.ca
Website: www.yorku.ca/inanna

To the memory of my mother,
Mary

TABLE OF CONTENTS

ACKNOWLEDGEMENTS

NANCY MANDELL, FRIEND, colleague, and former Director of the Centre for Feminist Research, York University, has my gratitude for asking me to write the "Women and Religion" chapter for *Feminist Issues*, for thinking I could make it into a book, and for then arranging for the publication of the first edition. Little did she know to what her initiative would lead!

I also owe a great debt to Naomi Black, whose critical eye and sound judgment have been enormously helpful; her willingness to read successive versions of the book went beyond the bounds of friendship. My thanks go also to Jordan Paper and Li Chuang Paper for their encouragement, their willingness to listen, and their sound and stimulating advice.

Thanks also go to York University, where I was a member of faculty for over thirty years, and to its Women's Studies and Religious Studies Programmes, as well as to York's stimulating students. I am extremely grateful for the opportunity to develop and teach courses on ancient goddesses and on female spirituality and for invaluable sabbatical and research leaves.

The School of Continuing Studies at the University of Toronto and its students also deserve credit for letting me try out ideas in courses I devised and taught there for about a decade.

I should also like to thank for encouragement, help, and advice Amila Buturovic, Charlotte Caron, the Centre for Feminist Research at York University, Don Cole, Beth Cutts, Frances Devlin-Glass, Vicky Drummond and the staff of York University's Nellie Langford Rowell Library, Aviva Goldberg, John Alan Lee, Oana Petrica,

Luciana Ricciutelli, Jane Robin, the staff of York University's Scott Library, and, last but not least, Clara Thomas.

Of course, I take full responsibility for any mistakes or misinterpretations that may occur in this book.

FOREWORD

THIS BOOK BEGAN as a chapter for the second edition of the Women's Studies text *Feminist Issues* (Mandell 1997). Hence, its intended readership was originally first- and second-year university students. After finishing that chapter for *Feminist Issues*, I expanded it to produce an earlier version of this book.[1] For this edition, I have revised and updated both the text and bibliography to reflect the enormous increase in research and publications in the area since 1997-1998.[2] I have also added an index. I hope that, despite its inadequacies, this book will be useful to anyone unfamiliar with the work of feminists within any or all of the three monotheistic traditions that have been so crucial to shaping Western attitudes to and treatment of women. The book also undertakes to describe one of the fastest-growing new forms of feminist spirituality in the West: Feminist Goddess Worship.[3]

It is not my aim here to be comprehensive, but to summarize and explicate. The bibliography should assist readers in pursuing further their concerns and interests with respect to various forms of feminist spirituality. To give readers a start on researching women's and feminist spirituality in those traditions I was unable to discuss here, I include, at the end of the bibliography, brief lists of some pertinent works arranged alphabetically by religion: African, African American, Buddhist, Chinese, Hindu, Japanese, Korean, and Native American.

My sources for this text were, for the most part, books and articles that practitioners themselves and women inside the traditions have written. The feminist-theology sections of this book are heavily bibliographical, for I envision students and other readers using these sections as guides to their own studies. As to method, I decided at the outset that I would try to present each form of spiritual expression, as much as possible, from the point of view of insiders. Nonetheless, as a feminist I have felt the necessity to point out what I perceive as limitations, contradictions, and such like in what my sources present. In addition, some women inside the traditions I discuss may object to my assigning feminist-theological stances to four categories: Revisionist, Renovationist,[4] Revolutionary, and Rejectionist. However, I understand these categories to apply to attitudes and interpretations, not people; often feminist theologians use a mixture of positions in one piece of writing or shift from one stance to another over time.

Notes

[1]Since my original contribution to the second edition of *Feminist Issues,* I have revised Chapter 12 four times. The fifth edition appeared in 2009.

[2]We have also changed the title to provide a more nearly accurate description of the book. The earlier version was called *Feminist Spirituality: An Introduction to Feminist Theology in Judaism, Christianity, Islam, and Feminist Goddess Worship* (1998).

[3]This is my own term for the several, slightly different versions of the religion. I decided on it after considering the widely employed "Feminist Spirituality" (e.g., Gross 1996; Christ 1997) and "Modern Goddess Worship." The latter term would not work because it also applies to goddess worship in Chinese, Hindu, and other polytheistic traditions today. The fact that many women in the three monotheistic traditions are definitely practicing spirituality that is feminist made me abandon the other term.

[4]Originally, I called this category "Reformist," but found that "Reformist" became confusing when I was discussing "Reform" Judaism.

1.
WOMEN'S SPIRITUALITY

As we move forward in this new millennium, women's interest in goddesses and women's spirituality seems to be increasing. When, over thirty years ago, I first began to do scholarly work on ancient goddesses and their worship,[1] as well as women's spirituality in general, I had no inkling of how popular these topics were to become or that I would one day be describing the development of a new form of spirituality—Feminist Goddess Worship. When I first began investigating and teaching about goddesses, I quickly found out that what I was researching and teaching was not a very popular topic among my university colleagues. Luckily, however, I never lacked for students, many of whom turned out to be modern Pagans and Witches in search of information. Over the last three decades, women's desire to learn about goddesses and to develop their own spirituality has become overwhelming. Any popular book with the words "goddess" or "women's spirituality" in the title is usually an immediate best seller, classes on the topics are always full, and I cannot keep track of all the pertinent talks and workshops available in my home town, Toronto, Canada.

Women's spirituality and women's commitment to religion should be a very important focus of feminist concern and no longer considered to be peripheral to the feminist agenda. However, many academic and feminists continue to dismiss or ignore religion and spirituality (King 2000: 219-220). According to Ursula King, the word "spirituality" usually brings to people's minds religious associations or even ascetic ones suggesting renunciation of the world. However, spirituality is not separate from everyday, secular endeavours. Quite the contrary—it is a force that informs all human experience. It is "integral, holistic and dynamic," and it promotes development and change not only in individuals, but in society as well (1998: 5-6).

One dictionary defines "spiritual" as follows: "of, pertaining to, or consisting of spirit; incorporeal" (Webster's 1996). It proceeds to list a number of sub-definitions that distinguish the spiritual from the physical; designate it as related to the supernatural, the moral, and the religious; and situate it in the realm of the sacred. This definition takes for granted that the physical, material world and the body are separate from the soul/spirit/mind, the supernatural; thus, the world of the sacred is quite different from the world of everyday. This attitude is a very Western and Christian one, though not exclusively so (Bowker 1997: 106-107, 915-916).

In an attempt to develop a definition of the "spiritual" that avoids the soul/mind-body split, Tom Driver says that the spiritual involves, "yet surpasses the physical." That is, the spiritual is "the very act" of transcending the everyday world, while not leaving it out"(1998: 175). However, many non-Western cultures are "spiritual" without an idea of the supernatural, of transcendence, of a division between secular and sacred, and so on. Further, such cultures often focus on doing "ritual acts" rather than on believing (Paper 1997: 8).

Obviously, arriving at a satisfactory definition of "spirituality" is a difficult task. Writers who deal with the subject usually try not to define it. Further, they often use the word "spirituality" to avoid using the term "religion," which they understand as problematic because of the Western assumptions that go with it. Here I will follow suit and speak of spirituality without defining it precisely, except to say that spirituality is very personal and usually involves a person's taking an holistic view of the world. It can include everything from our sense of awe at observing a spectacular sunset or our emotional reaction to the denouement of a tragedy to our overwhelming response to organ music swelling and echoing through a cavernous building or our trance-like involvement in a well-loved ritual (Christ 1997; Paper 1997: 8).

Feminist issues in women's spirituality, as well as in spirituality in general, touch on and affect a number of areas in modern life.

Feminists exploring women's spirituality are deeply involved in examining sexual politics, and they often use research from such areas as anthropology, archaeology, psychology, and sociology, for example, Anne Baring and Jules Cashford (1991), Jean Bolen (1984), Naomi Goldenberg (1979), and Merlin Stone (1977). Many are committed to investigating and combating all forms of oppression, from sexism and racism to heterosexism and other "isms." Therefore, rather than withdrawing from society as a result of their spirituality, many feel the need for political action (Reed 1989; Reuther 1983; Starhawk 2002, 1989a, 1987a).

Many feminists who are exploring spirituality are also concerned with humano-centrism and ecology and seek to halt and, if possible, repair the damage that they accuse Western male-centred, linear, and hierarchical thinking of having done to the world we both live in and are part of. These feminists criticise the ways in which many male-centred religions have not only limited and excluded women, but also devalued and diminished nature and the non-human. Indeed, they argue that such religions have supported, and even promoted, courses of action that are fast leading to ecological disaster. Therefore, they are turning to alternative forms of spirituality (Adams 1993; Gaard 1993; Reuther 1992).

WOMEN'S SPIRITUALITY AND FEMINISM

Early in second-wave feminism, the feminism that began in the 1960s, American feminist theologian Mary Daly wrote that the Women's Movement, as long as it remains "true to its own essential dynamics," is a "spiritual revolution...." She further argued that the Women's Movement would "transform human consciousness"(1974: 6). Although her prediction about the effect of the Women's Movement on humanity has yet to come true, the spirituality she saw as inherent in the Women's Movement has certainly manifested itself in feminist theology and Feminist Goddess Worship. As a result, some feminist scholars of religious studies are investigating women's spirituality in general.

The Importance of Women's Spirituality

Many feminists and feminist theorists have denounced religion as irredeemably patriarchal and think feminist spirituality at best a form of eccentricity and at worst a real danger (Heschel 2004: 585; Magee 2000: 101; Beattie 1999). So why be concerned with female spirituality? Why take seriously women's roles in religions?

In addition to the fact that it is of burning interest to large numbers of women, there are many pressing reasons why feminists should be interested in women's spirituality. First, for feminists to omit from our thinking consideration of women's spirituality is to ignore what, for millions of the world's women, is central to their lives. Feminist commitment to addressing diversity entails our taking into account, indeed accepting and honouring, the multiple ways that women express their spirituality. I agree with Ursula King when she says that we need to engage with and examine the spiritual experience of women in "a positive way" (King 1989: xii).

Second, as second-wave feminists used to say, 'the personal is political,' and what could be more personal than spirituality, which is often at the centre of women's (people's) being? Spiritual concerns can be involved in shaping our view of the world, and they often influence political behaviour. Yet our feminist analyses usually ignore spirituality (King 2000: 219-220; King 1989: 207).

Third, the study of spirituality and its manifestation in world religions can reveal to us one of the main methods by which male-dominated polities have sustained, and still sustain, their control over women (and, of course, men as well). In a number of countries, indeed, religion is *the* major control mechanism. Further, gendered religious symbols both reflect and influence our political and cultural assumptions.

Fourth, as feminists we must refuse to divide women's (people's) selves and lives into separate compartments. Today we know that mind and body are not distinct entities; the same is true for other dichotomies, such as one that our culture generally accepts, but rarely names, rationality and spirituality.

Fifth, especially in the West, research into and discussion of religions has until very recently focused on the study of male involvement in them: male symbols and roles and male spiritual understandings. It is as if the female has not existed for many, if not all of religious-studies scholars.

Sixth, feminist theology is about change, and about change in women's lives. Feminist theology begins whenever women realise that the `universal spiritual truth' they have been accepting comes from the experiences of males. Its importance lies in the fact that it affords feminists another way to change "mind, heart, and ways of living and judging" (Finson 1995: 2).

There are, of course, other reasons why women's spirituality should be integral to our feminist endeavour, many of which will become apparent in the following discussion.

Examples of Women's Spirituality in Various Cultures

Though this book concentrates on feminist examinations and criticisms of the Western monotheistic religious traditions, women's spirituality flourishes in all traditions, however male dominated they may be. Somehow, women find, or make, space in which they can express their deepest spiritual feelings and thoughts. Some spiritual traditions, however, do not force women into separate spaces or make them manipulate the system in order to pursue their spirituality. They include religions with complementary female/male roles and religions dominated by women.

RELIGIONS WITH COMPLEMENTARY FEMALE/MALE ROLES

In religions with complementary female/male roles, such as most Native Australian ones, women practise rituals separately from men, and men from women, though sometimes women and men take part in each other's rituals. In such cultures, women and men undergo initiation in same-sex rituals, through which they each reach adulthood "as sacred beings within the ... community." Both sexes understand that the rites women perform and the rites men perform are equally necessary to the maintenance of the land/society's well-being (Bell 1993: 23, 37, 205ff.; Gross 1989: 258-59).

In what scholars trying to avoid the term "primitive" have called "primal" or non-literate cultures, knowledge, myth, and spiritual lore are oral and usually passed on through storytelling, art, dancing, and singing, all of which are ritualised. Through their separate rituals, women and men pass on to the next generation the traditional lore appropriate to their sex. Among Native Australians, for example, women have a "vital and complementary role ... in maintaining the [Dreaming/Dreamtime] heritage ..." (Bell 1993: 182ff., 205ff., 230).

In some non-literate cultures, however, women and men take complementary roles in joint rituals. In traditions such as many of the Native American ones, according to Jordan Paper, participants in rituals make offerings "equally to female and male spirits, to both the Grandmothers and the Grandfathers ..." (Paper 1997: 236). At most rituals, both females and males are necessary to the rituals' success. And women, as well as men, hold important, often complementary spiritual leadership roles. Indeed, Native Americans traditionally understood female and male as balancing powers. Many of the highly diverse African religions also follow a similar pattern and express in rituals "the distinctness yet complementarity" of the two sexes. Women in such traditions feel validated in their spiritual roles and usually have high self-esteem (Johnson, M. 1997; Carmody 1989: 21, 28; Shimony 1989).

We can also find complementarity of female and male in the religions of a number of literate societies, most of which were politically male dominated. For instance, complementarity was the way of life of the South American Inca civilization, which followed "gender parallel descent and leadership" (Paper 1997: 126). The deities also came in opposite-sex pairs. Contrary to the generally accepted view that a male king, who descended from the Sun, was the monarch of the Incan empire, a female-male couple ruled together. She was the descendent of the female Moon, he of the male Sun. The female Inca presided over the realm's women, the male Inca over its men. She made sacrifices to the Moon, and he to the Sun (Silverblatt 1987).

Ancient Sumerian religion was also primarily complementary, with paired female-male deities and priests, as was its successor, Akkadian-Babylonian religion, though both societies were male dominated politically. Chinese religions also demonstrate an understanding that Earth/female and Sky/male are complementary. In traditional China, the two sexes were understood as "equal and utterly essential to each other," and contemporary Chinese women embody "*yin* power, different from but equal to the *yang* power of males" (Paper 1997: 37, 94; Stuckey 1997).

RELIGIONS "DOMINATED" BY WOMEN

In some spiritual traditions, according to Susan Sered, women actually dominate at present, or have done so in the past, even if the society in which they function is otherwise male dominated. In *Priestess, Mother, Sacred Sister*, Sered includes examples from North America and Europe, Africa, Asia, and South America and the Caribbean (1994: 289-292).

All of the woman-dominated religions Sered discusses treat men and women as "essentially different," and many hold views of the meaning of sex difference that Western feminists would judge sexist. Nevertheless, a number consider that a significant element in women's difference from men is their greater proclivity for spiritual experience and activity. In some of these religions, these positions lead to complementarity, in others tensions and even conflict (Sered 1994: 197).

None of these traditions worships a sole, all-powerful, male deity as supreme, and none of them sees women as inferior by nature. On the contrary, they often understand women as better suited for spiritual leadership roles than men. Nonetheless, they all think that both women and men are needed in the world. These traditions usually have an internal hierarchy and strongly resist both doctrines that are "institutionalized" and centralisation. Moral behaviour is focused on inter-personal relationships, but seen as having community implications. In addition, these women's traditions support the secular needs and interests of the women involved. Finally, there is no "forcible conversion" and no concept of "holy war" (Sered 1994: 285).

Sered concludes that most of the spiritual patterns she describes are the result of women's mothering role, for in those societies motherhood gains a woman both recognised authority in the societal structure and considerable esteem. The woman-dominated religions, then, validate and elaborate the various aspects of motherhood (1994: 283, 286).

WOMEN'S SPIRITUAL SPACE IN MALE-DOMINATED RELIGIONS

Despite often extreme male dominance in religion, most women manage to express their spirituality in ways with which they report satisfaction. In Islam, for instance, women have always worshipped at home and, in most countries, if they want to, in a special area in mosques. They have ways, such as making religious vows, for getting access to family resources to pay for spiritually based, usually all-female celebrations at home; they also make visits or all-female pilgrimages to the shrines of saints, where they find other women with whom to worship.

Hindu women also make religious vows and go on all-female pilgrimages; at home they perform female-only rituals for childbirth and other domestic events. In addition, they can openly worship a variety of powerful goddesses who may, in a number of ways, validate them to themselves as women, but who normally do not help improve their social status. Finally, they sometimes become possessed by deities or spirits, a process that can be both societally acceptable and individually empowering. In these societies, then, women can manage, together and separately, to achieve, in Ursula King's words, "self-affirmation, strength, and spiritual power" (King 1989: 116; see also Shirali 1997; Betteridge 1989; Freeman 1989; Jacobson 1989; Kinsley 1989: Chaps.1, 3, 5; Mernissi 1989; Wadley 1989).

The fact that most women do cope with the spiritual restrictions imposed by male-dominated religions does not, of course, suggest that their spiritual lives are better, or even good, under religious male dominance than under another kind of religious system. However, many women seem content with what Western feminists would almost certainly regard as limited spiritual opportunities. Indeed, surprisingly, there seems at present a trend for women to join or return to religions that would, on the surface, appear unfriendly to women. Indeed, religious fundamentalism has been on the rise for some years, and it seems to be particularly attractive to women. Why would this be so?

WOMEN AND FUNDAMENTALISM

Fundamentalism[2] occurs in many religious traditions, including Christianity, Judaism, Hinduism, Buddhism, and Islam, and there seems to be "renewed conservatism in all world religions" (Haker,

Ross, and Wacker 2006: 7). Fundamentalists understand themselves to be committed to the basic and core "truths and practices" of their religion (Ruthven 2004: 34). In defining fundamentalism, Janet Bauer says that it is "narrow faithfulness to a particular set of beliefs" (1997: 247, n.3).[3] Often those to whom others apply the term, for example, "Islamic fundamentalists," resent being so described, mainly because the term has usually designated those Christians who argue for literal acceptance of the contents of the Bible. Christian fundamentalists usually prefer the description "Conservative Evangelicals" (Haker, Ross, and Wacker 2006: 7-11; see also Manning 1999: ix; Bowker 1997: 360-361, 1082; Marty and Appleby 1991).

Many scholars attribute the attraction of fundamentalism in religions to a desire to go back to a "Golden Age," when men and women were happy and knew their roles in life and things were generally much better—the "Good Old Days." For instance, today's Islamists, a term meaning Muslim fundamentalists, see themselves as "revivalists" who are going back to the origins of Islam "to regain a purified vision" (Ruthven 2004: 34; see also Brink and Mencher 1997: 6; Afshar 1996: 198).

Christian evangelical traditions are fundamentalist. They emphasise the authority of the Scriptures, the importance of preaching as opposed to ritual, and, above all, achieving salvation of the soul through personal conversion and belief in the atoning sacrifice of Jesus. Though it is often classed as evangelical and fundamentalist, Pentecostalist Christianity is spiritually egalitarian. It focuses on possession by the Holy Spirit. Since the Holy Spirit does not observe sex-role divisions and women are just as likely as men to receive the Spirit, in Pentecostalism women often have spiritual leadership roles (Bowker 1997: 326, 744).

Though there are various forms of fundamentalism, among the elements they usually share is an insistence that women perform domestic roles and restrict their public roles. According to Gita Sahgal and Nira Yuval-Davis, all fundamentalism concentrates on women, and all feminism should oppose fundamentalism (1992: 1; see also Winter 2001: 10). However, in recent times, women have been seeking out, or returning to, such religions in significant numbers (Manning 1999; Brink and Mencher 1997: 2).

Why do women remain in, return to, or join such religions? Writings on the topic explain the phenomenon in a number of ways. Aside from those who stay because they know no alternative, women members of fundamentalist religions are often alienated from the modern, secular world and need a sense of belonging to a community. Often they feel powerless to effect change in the larger society and so decide to focus on interpersonal relationships in tightly knit families and communities. Sometimes, particularly in developing countries, women's economic difficulties lead them to prefer dependence on a fundamentalist husband to coping on their own. Some women expect that conversion will increase their chances of marrying, and it may indeed do so. Others are drawn to the possibility of creating spiritual spaces where a little autonomy is possible for them; in some cases, they can even achieve limited public roles. Muslim women who embrace fundamentalism often do so to show their opposition to colonialism and to express their own nationalism; for many, wearing the veil is "the symbol of Islamisation" (Afshar 1996: 201). Other women, mainly Christians, belong to fundamentalist branches of religions because they think that strict adherence to a certain set of beliefs will lead to the salvation of their souls from an eternity in Hell.

Involvement in fundamental religions seems to be empowering for many women, because, among other things, it can allow them to seek personal identity, or find comfort and respite in personal or social terms, make up for limited educational choices and limited status, or experience their spirituality in a structured, often female environment (Manning 1999; Brink and Mencher 1997: 221ff.; Hawley 1994; Sahgal and Yuval-Davis 1992; Davidman 1991; Kaufman 1991; Frankiel 1990; Greenberg 1981).

AIMS AND SCOPE OF THIS BOOK

The aims of this book are to acquaint readers briefly with the range of expressions of women's spirituality; to give an accessible report on feminist theology, the theology that takes into account women's experiences; and, in particular, to examine how feminist theologians treat the central issues in three old traditions and one new one.

Though my parents were Christian and, as a child, I attended Protestant Sunday Schools, I am not today a follower of any of the forms of spirituality discussed here. Consequently, I write as an outsider. I have, however, asked various scholars of my acquaintance to read the text carefully, and I have tried to incorporate their comments and criticisms.

In addition, I am white, English speaking, and Canadian. My British-born parents, though in origin working class and lower middle class, aspired to improve their status and eventually did so. I was the first member of my family to have access to higher education, and I have spent most of my adult life as a middle-class student and professor in Canadian, British, and American universities. Thus, I am a woman whose age (Pagans would describe me as a crone), background, and experience distance me from many whose spirituality I discuss in this work.

It would be impossible for anyone to present even a cursory overview of all the world's religious traditions in a short book like this. Consequently, it focuses on the traditions that seem to have had the most impact in the West: Christianity, Judaism, and Islam. They are, of course, all monotheistic. As a scholar of goddess worship, I also wanted to include consideration of one of the fastest-growing new forms of spirituality in the West today: Feminist Goddess Worship.

The bibliography, though extensive, by no means encompasses everything published in a field that grows daily; the list does, however, include all the material that I consulted in the preparation of this book. The last section of the bibliography consists of short samplings of books on spiritual traditions not covered in this book. They are arranged alphabetically by tradition. The list should assist readers to begin to explore women's and feminist spirituality in those traditions.

Notes

[1]For a taste of my work on ancient goddesses, readers might visit the web magazine *Matrifocus* <www.matrifocus.com>, for which I have been writing four articles a year for the last six years. Previous pieces are available on the site through "Archives."

[2]It has been suggested that a more appropriate term would be "fanaticism."

[3]Another definition describes fundamentalism "a 'religious way of being'" in which group members, feeling under attack, try to protect "their distinctive identity" against "modernism and secularization" (Ruthven 2004: 8).

2.
FEMINIST THEOLOGY

THE USUAL DICTIONARY definition of theology goes something like this: "the field of study and analysis that treats of God and of God's attributes and relations to the universe; the study of divine things or religious truth" (*Webster's* 1996). In addition, the definition implies, though it does not specifically say so, that theology is the pursuit of professionals. Feminist theologian Sheila Collins disputes this idea: "Theologizing can be done by anyone, with or without theological degrees" (1974: 10). For our purposes, the term "theologian" includes anyone developing theology—professionals, religious functionaries, and worshippers.

Concentration on ideas about God, usually understood as theology, is, as Ursula King says, typical of monotheistic religions.[1] However, as she explains, theology, simply defined, is "the intellectual reflection on the experience of faith," and followers of all religious traditions formulate abstractions about their experience. Thus, she chooses to understand theology as a search for "ultimate meaning" (1989: 162).[2]

Collins insists: "Theology must come out of experience" (1974: 10). Theology results when people contemplate their spiritual experiences and develop ideas, concepts, and intellectual theories about them. Both women and men have had the sorts of experiences, both transformative and revelatory, that can produce theology. The problem for contemporary feminists is that women's experiences did not and usually do not make their way into traditional theologies. Thus, most feminists dismiss traditional theologies as neither meaningful for women, nor universal, despite their presenting themselves as such (King 1989: 162).

For example, Rosemary Reuther states that feminist theology not only demonstrates that female experience has been for the most part omitted from past theological thinking, but also uses women's experience to expose "classical theology, including codified traditions," as founded in the experience of men, and not universal at all (1983: 13). Contemporary women's stories of their own experiences of faith have made women the subject of a new form of theologising, no longer just "the object" of theology. Therefore, feminist theology is not only "experiential" but also experimental (King 1989: 163).

In criticising theologies based in male experience, feminist theologians appeared to be arguing that the addition of "women's experience" or "female experience" would make theology universal. However, these feminist theologians initially talked about "women's experience" as if there were only one form of "women's experience." In the mid-eighties, African American feminist theologians pointed out that the "women's experience" to which white middle-class feminist theologians were appealing was their own experience and not *all* women's experience. Feminist theology now has a number of branches as feminist theologians try to develop theologies that include the women's experiences relevant to their own contexts (Reuther 1983: 13).

All feminist theologians, whether working in or outside an established religion, agree, to varying degrees, that Western religious traditions have certainly devalued or undervalued women; some insist that they have betrayed women. Nevertheless, they would also accept the validity and meaningfulness of the spiritual (Heschel 2004: 585). This latter position represents a change from the late 1960s and early 1970s, when most second-wave feminists, myself included, dismissed religion not only as irretrievably male centred and sexist, but also as of no importance in the feminist agenda. Even today, secular feminists sometimes term feminists who are interested in spirituality "soft feminists" (King 1989: 16). Gradually such views are beginning to alter: most feminists now accept that women need to explore their spirituality in a feminist context and their feminism in a spiritual context (Goldenberg 2007).

Feminist theology consists mainly of the ideas and writings of women (and men) who, from insider positions, work to alter male-dominated religions to make them more hospitable to women (Reuther 2001). However, some, like Mary Daly and Carol Christ, do feminist theology outside of an established tradition. Feminist theologians have shown that, in the past, theologians almost totally dismissed or ignored women's spiritual experiences. They have also employed those experiences to demonstrate that what theologians and holy books have presented as universal experience was actually only male experience (Isherwood and McEwan 2001: 9; Reuther 1983: 13). Christian feminists in the United States of America were probably the earliest second-wave feminists to produce feminist theology, with American Jewish feminists not far behind. Muslim feminists have recently been quickly catching up. Nonetheless, Christian feminist theologians seem to be the most prolific writers in the field.

The criticism of religion by second-wave feminist theologians began with close reading of traditional texts for sexism; noting, and arguing against, the exclusion of women from priesthood and rabbinate; and examining of doctrines referring to women, such as those on marriage and the family.

Most scholars credit Mary Daly, who was from the Roman Catholic tradition, with beginning second-wave feminist theology. Daly's *The Church and the Second Sex*, which appeared in 1968, presented a detailed critique of the Roman Catholic Church and male domination in religion. Daly followed it in 1973 with *Beyond God the Father*, in which she coined what later became a motto for feminists interested in the subject of religion: " if God is male, then the male is God" (1974: 19; see also Finson 1995: 12; King 1989: 164; Christ and Plaskow 1979: 22).

In 1974 another Roman Catholic, Rosemary Radford Reuther, edited a ground-breaking collection of essays, *Religion and Sexism*. Containing articles by Christian and Jewish feminist theologians who were soon to become well known, the book dealt with many of the topics that were to involve the field, in North America at least, for the next forty or so years.

Feminist theologians tend to focus on a number of connected issues: for instance, the sexism they denounce as embedded in both sacred books and the attitudes and structures of organised religions; the difficulties resulting for women from scriptural and liturgical language and images that present God as male; and the underrepresentation of women in leadership roles in religious institutions (Green-McCreight 2000). Although they may not address them head on, most religious traditions have been affected by, and have had to pay at least some attention to, comments and criticisms of feminist theologians (Jushka 2001; Sawyer and Collier 1999; Russell and Clarkson 1996).

CATEGORIES OF FEMINIST THEOLOGY

In her 1983 essay "Symbols of Goddess and God in Feminist Theology," Carol Christ suggested that there were three main feminist-theological attitudes to the sexism of traditional religions and that they entailed three different solutions:

> (1) correct interpretation will isolate and clarify in a tradition the vision that is basically non-sexist;
> (2 a tradition does, indeed, contain "elements of an essentially sexist vision." While interpreters should emphasise the non-sexist vision as "revelation," they must repudiate the sexist vision "on the basis of the non-sexist vision" and also the contemporary understanding that women are fully human;
> (3) since a tradition is essentially sexist and is therefore irremediable, we must develop new visions out of our experience today and "nonbiblical religion" (1983: 238).

Since 1983, however, there have been developments in feminist theology that necessitate a change in Christ's categories from three to four.

The four categories that I have adapted from Christ's three are in practice not at all as distinct as they seem in the following descriptions, and they regularly shade into one another. However, for purposes of discussion, I find the following categories very useful:

> (1) *Revisionist*, Christ's type 1. The Revisionist position is the least extreme of the four categories, for it argues that

correct interpretation will reveal the liberating message at the core of a tradition. Some Revisionist thinking in some traditions also advocates the replacing of male-centred language in, for instance, liturgy, with sex-neutral language.

(2) *Renovationist*, Christ's type 2. The Renovationist position argues that, to rid a tradition of sexism, it is not enough for interpreters merely to uncover its liberating core, but they must also point out, and deny, the parts of a tradition that are sexist. Further, many Renovationist arguments insist on change in language and symbols of deity, as well as liturgical language, to include female imagery.

(3) *Revolutionary*, my addition to Christ's categories. The term "Revolutionary" describes the feminist theological position that advocates forcing a tradition to its limits. Some Revolutionary arguments suggest importing language and imagery from other traditions or from outside tradition. Those who take a Revolutionary position in ritual are occasionally influenced by other traditions or from outside tradition. Goddess spirituality is often such a source.

(4) *Rejectionist*, Christ's type 3. Those who take this stance have decided that a tradition is "intrinsically inimical to women" (Harrison 2007: 145). They usually have left it and set about creating new spiritual traditions.

In the practice of feminist theologians, the first three of these categories tend to overlap.

FIRST-WAVE FEMINISM AND RELIGION

Most early feminists in North America and Britain had their spiritual roots in the Christian tradition, and many, especially Quakers, were active in both the Anti-Slavery and the Woman Movements. Some first-wave feminists repudiated religion entirely, while others attacked religion as anti-woman. Still others, often very critical of their religion and of the Bible's views on women,

Sarah Grimké (1792-1873), woodcut, date unknown.
Photo: Women's Rights National Historical Park, U.S.

nonetheless remained devout and based their feminism in their religious convictions.

The American Quaker sisters, Sarah and Angelina Grimké, are a case in point. Sarah Grimké's writings of the 1830s make clear that she was unwilling to dismiss the Christian tradition, but that she was fully aware of what she saw as anti-woman passages in the Bible. She blamed the sexism she found in the Bible on male mistranslation or misinterpretation and insisted that, if the Bible's real meaning were known, it would prove to be an egalitarian document. Her views were clearly Revisionist (see Clark and Richardson 1977: 210).

American suffrage leader Elizabeth Cady Stanton, whose spiritual heritage was Protestant (Presbyterian), was much more non-conformist than Sarah Grimké; she was of the opinion that religion impeded women from reaching their full potential. Although she was not an atheist, Stanton would have nothing to do with the teachings of the Christian churches. Indeed, so incensed did she become with Christianity that, in the 1890s, she convened a group of thirty American and British feminists and scholars, some of whom were competent in Latin and Greek, as well as Hebrew; they prepared a women's commentary on the Bible (see Clark and Richardson 1977: 215ff; see also Finson 1995: 28).

A significant work of criticism, re-interpretation, and occasionally dismissal, *The Woman's Bible* appeared in two volumes in the late 1890s, and it puts Stanton into the Renovationist category. It was an early condemnation of the sexism of the Judaeo-Christian religious tradition and a courageous statement of the position that the subordination of women has roots that go deeply into religion. Nonetheless, most of Stanton's associates in the Woman Movement wanted nothing to do with *The Woman's Bible*. In 1896, the twenty-eighth annual convention of the National American Woman Suffrage Association, of which Stanton had been joint founder, voted to disclaim any involvement with the book. The result was its effectual disappearance until feminist scholars of the 1970s rediscovered it; it did not appear in print again until 1974 (Stanton 1974: 215-217; see also Christ and Plaskow 1979: 19).

In the nineteenth century, women in Europe and North America started to organise into groups to push for social change. Such organisations were often motivated by religious convictions. For instance, Christian views constituted, as their names indicate, an important part of the rationale of the Young Women's Christian Association and the Woman's Christian Temperance Union (Prentice et al. 1996: 198; Black 1989: 15).

Many of Canada's early women's groups, like their American counterparts, were also galvanised by religious, usually Christian

Cyril Jessop, "Nellie McClung at her writing desk," c. 1905-1922, Gladstone, Manitoba. Library and Archives Canada ref. no. PA-030212. Used by permission CC-SA.

convictions, whether they were Roman Catholic lay women in Quebec or Protestant social reformers in other provinces (Prentice et al. 1996: 189). For example, the Young Women's Christian Association and the Woman's Christian Temperance Union took a maternal- or social-feminist position that was deeply coloured by Protestant morality. The Canadian Woman's Christian Temperance Union was, indeed, the first large women's organization to support woman's suffrage. A Quebec example, the *Fédération nationale Saint-Jean Baptiste*, founded in 1907, pulled together the few associations of French-speaking laywomen (Prentice et al. 1996: 198-199, 206).

At the end of the nineteenth century and beginning of the twentieth, the Protestant "Social Gospel" movement drew women in large numbers. It supported equality, including woman's suffrage, and its adherents believed that, as Ramsay Cook puts it, "someday, somehow, the Kingdom of God would be established on earth" (1974: xvii-xviii). Canada's most famous early feminist Nellie McClung (1873-1951) was a part of this movement (Prentice et al. 1996: 164; Warne 1993).

Nellie McClung, a Methodist, was a social or maternal feminist. Her feminism is shot through with the view of evangelical social reform that the world need saving, redeeming. In 1897 she became a member of the Woman's Christian Temperance Union, and she was not the only one who found out first, at a temperance convention, what a good orator she was (Prentice et al. 1996: 225; see also Strong-Boag 1972). Like many of her American counterparts, McClung considered religion to be responsible for much of the inequality she saw in society. Nevertheless, she remained a devout Christian, and, after the creation of the United Church of Canada in 1925, she devoted considerable time to advocating women's ordination (Prentice et al. 1996: 316). However, even though her best-known book, *In Times Like These*, included a chapter "Women and the Church," McClung was by no means as critical of Christianity as Stanton. Indeed, she appealed to what she understood as original and true Christian values to support her arguments on behalf of women. In so doing, she showed herself to be essentially Revisionist in her views, a stance typical of most first-wave feminists.

SECOND-WAVE FEMINISM AND FEMINIST THEOLOGY

Just before the second wave of feminism began in the mid 1960s, an American female theology student, Valerie Saiving, published in 1960 an article that anticipated current efforts in feminist theology by at least ten years. It begins: "I am a student of theology; I am also a woman" (1979: 24). Saiving goes on to point out that a person's experience affects a person's theological ideas. However, like Stanton's feminist Bible, Saiving's article, though it saw print a second time, soon sank into twenty years of oblivion.

During most of the 1960s, the topic of "Women and Religion" drew scant attention. Carol P. Christ and Judith Plaskow comment that, when, in the late 1960s, they started graduate studies in theology at Yale, they heard nothing in their classes about "feminist or even feminine theology" (1979: 21). They had both read Valerie Saiving's article and were agreed that the texts they were reading for courses both omitted and demeaned their "experience as women." In the spring of 1970 at Yale, they heard Rosemary Radford Reuther expound the theory of the interrelationship of sexism and dualism, and for them a miracle had occurred: "an articulate woman" had outlined the difficulties that Western theology and Western society had got into as a result of seeing only with male eyes. Feminist theology was now a reality.

Like feminism, feminist theology is global, coming from Australia, Asia, Africa, and Latin America, indeed, from all over the world. Today feminist theology is on the curriculum at many North American universities, and the *Journal of Feminist Studies in Religion*, a scholarly publication, features a good deal of feminist theology. By 1975, feminist theologians were working in Great Britain and European countries, such as Germany, the Netherlands, Russia, Switzerland. By the 1990s they had made some headway in European universities (Haker, Ross, and Wacker 2006: 58). However, despite the foundation in 1986 of the European Society of Women in Theological Research, feminist theologians often had to keep in touch with one another through "loose networks" (Finson 1995: 8, 17-19). With respect to Great Britain, Ursula King commented in her 1989 book that feminist theology had made little headway in the "official theological establishment" (161, 163-164).

In her 1995 bibliographical essay, Canadian Shelley Finson presents a very useful historical overview of what she calls "Feminist Liberation Theology."

Notes

[1]For a theology of polytheistic religions, see Jordan Paper's *The Deities Are Many: A Polytheistic Theology*. Albany: State University of New York, 2005.

[2]At a Roundtable discussion organised by *Journal of Feminist Studies and Religion* (Gross 2000), there was considerable discussion about whether the Christian term "theology" was the right one for what all feminists working on religion were doing. Naomi Goldenberg prefers to call it "religious studies" (cited in Gross 2000: 116).

John Collier, "Lilith," oil on canvas, 1887. The Atkinson Art Gallery, Southport, England.

3.
JUDAISM, FEMINISM AND FEMINIST THEOLOGY

JUDAISM IS THE earliest of the three monotheistic religious traditions[1] that have had an enormous influence on Western culture. Although Judaism as we know it today developed fully only after the Roman destruction of the Temple in Jerusalem in the first century of our era, it traces its origins back to the time of Biblical patriarchs Abraham, Isaac, and Jacob (Hayes and Miller 1977: 93ff.). Scholars usually date this period to the early second millennium BCE (Before Common Era). The religion is firmly monotheistic and recognises only one god. Observant Jews do not pronounce God's name, but, when reading the sacred texts, conventionally substitute for it the words *ha-shem*, "the Name," or *adonai*, "my Lord" (Bowker 1997: 20, 412, 513).

Over the last forty years, Jewish feminists have been increasingly involved "in naming and shaping Jewish tradition." They have, above all, been questioning male dominance in their religion and its conception of the divinity as male (Plaskow 1990: vii). Answering both questions involves, as Alice Shalvi says, "revisioning and revising" the basic beliefs and understandings that have underpinned Judaism for over three thousand years (1995: 232). Judaism is, however, rooted much more deeply in the past than three millennia.

BACKGROUND

According to the Hebrew Bible, Jewish women's heritage goes back at least to the times of Sarah, Rebecca, Leah, and Rachel, that is, about four thousand years. However, Judaism, as we know it today, does not go back that far; many scholars agree that it actually began to take its present form after the Diaspora, the dispersal of the people from Jerusalem in the year 70 of our era, when the Romans destroyed the Second Temple and the Holy City. The famous Western Wall ("Wailing Wall") is a remnant of the foundations of the Second Temple. Post-Diaspora Judaism, of course, had its origins in the ever-changing religion of a people who had, in all likelihood, been living in and moving as semi-nomads across the land of Canaan (modern Israel) for at least two thousand years.

Covenant, Exodus, Conquest, and Kingdom

In the Hebrew Bible, the story of Abram, later Abraham, begins in Haran in northern Mesopotamia, probably his family's original home (Genesis 24: 4, 40). According to the Hebrew Bible, Abram's father Terah and his extended family had made their way to Haran from Ur, one of the biggest and most important of the cities of ancient Mesopotamia. Some have suggested that the family exodus from "Ur of the Chaldees" (Genesis 11: 31) probably took place around 1960 BCE when invading Elamites destroyed the great city. In Haran, Terah died, and God told Abram to leave everything and set out for another land, where his descendants would become "great nation" (Genesis 12: 1-2). So Abram, his wife Sarai, later Sarah, and their people, living as semi-nomads, made the journey to the land of Canaan (Genesis 12: 4-6). However, as the Bible tells us, Abram and Sarah were old and had no children (Epstein 1990: 11-12, 17, note2).

Following a custom which Savina Teubal argues came from Mesopotamia (1990; 1984: 33), Sarai asked Abram to take her Egyptian slave Hagar as concubine, so that barren Sarai could have children through her (Genesis 16: 2). Hagar's son Ishmael was also to become the ancestor of "a great nation" (Genesis 17: 20). After Ishmael's birth, God made a Covenant with Abram to give him and his descendants the land of Canaan, and God changed his name to Abraham, meaning "father of a multitude." The mark of the Covenant was to be the circumcision of Abram, his sons, and all the males among his dependents and descendants (Genesis 17: 1-14). Then God promised the now very elderly Abraham that his equally

Adriaen van der Werff, "Sarah presenting Hagar to Abraham," oil on canvas, 76.3 x 61 cm., 1699. Staatsgalerie, Schleissheim, Austria.

elderly wife would also bear a son. When the son was born, they named him Isaac (Genesis 17: 15; 21: 2-3) (Epstein 1990: 14).

God re-affirmed the Covenant with Abraham's grandson Jacob, to whom He gave the name Israel (Genesis 35: 9-12). Jacob had twelve sons, the ancestors of the Twelve Tribes of Israel. Jacob's favourite wife Rachel was mother of two, Joseph and Benjamin, Jacob's youngest (Genesis 36: 23-26). Jealous of Joseph, who was his father's favourite, the older sons sold him into slavery in Egypt (Genesis 37: 28, 36). Through fortuitous circumstances, Joseph managed to attain a position of power in the Egyptian court and was able to help the members of his family when, during a famine, they went to Egypt to buy grain (Genesis 42-45). At the king of Egypt's invitation, Joseph's family settled in Egypt and multiplied (Genesis 45: 17-47: 11; Exodus 1: 7).

Many years after Joseph's era, one of the Egyptian kings made the Israelites into slaves to build cities for him (Exodus 1: 8-11). Through Moses, to whom God appeared in the Burning Bush (Exodus 3), God procured the Israelites' freedom by sending plagues against the Egyptians (Exodus 6-11). The last affliction caused the death of all the first-born sons of the Egyptians, but "passed over" the houses of the Israelites (Exodus 12: 1-30). After this demonstration of God's power, the Egyptians let the Israelites go (Exodus 12: 31-33).

A few months after the people left Egypt on the Exodus, Moses ascended Mount Sinai, where he received from God the Ten Commandments, as well as other rules (Exodus 19-23). God then renewed the Covenant He had made with Abraham (Exodus 24: 7-8). An essential element in this Covenant was the designation of the Israelites as "a kingdom of priests, and a holy nation" (Exodus 19: 6; Epstein 1990: 20).

It took the Israelites forty years, however, before they could undertake the Conquest of the land of Canaan. The victorious Israelites divided the land among their tribes (Book of Joshua). For about two hundred years, while they were settling in the land, the Israelites were ruled through an informal system of "judges," among them the female prophet Deborah (Joshua, Judges, and I Samuel 1-8). After most of the Canaanites were subdued, the warlike Philistines began to invade the territory of the Israelites (Epstein 1990: 32, 34).

Eventually, the Israelites asked for a king to lead them against the Philistines, and their chief priest Samuel selected Saul, who was not a success as monarch (I Samuel 8-10). After Saul's death, David (c.1012-972 BCE), the youngest son of Jesse of Bethlehem, became king (I Samuel 16: 13; II Samuel 5: 3). With David and his "house," God re-affirmed the Covenant once more (II Samuel

7). David captured the last citadel of the Canaanites, Jerusalem, as his capital (II Samuel 5: 6-9) (Epstein 1990: 35).

David's successor was his son Solomon, who was noted for his wisdom. It was he who had the first Temple built in Jerusalem (I Kings 6). After Solomon died in 931 BCE, the kingdom of Israel split into two parts, Israel in the north and Judah in the south (II Kings 12). In 721 BCE, the Assyrians destroyed the northern kingdom Israel and exiled its people to the far reaches of their empire (II Kings 17: 23-24). The southern kingdom Judah survived until, in 586 BCE, the Babylonians forced the people of Judah into exile and burned Jerusalem and Solomon's great Temple (II Kings 25). Epstein comments: "Out of the crucible of exile and affliction," Judah became "a new people—the Jews" (1990: 45, 54).

In 538 BCE, the Persian king Cyrus allowed the people of Judah to return from exile; and, by 516 BCE, they had rebuilt the Temple (Ezra 3: 8; 6: 15). However, from the Persian Period to 70 CE, when the Romans destroyed Jerusalem and the Second Temple, Judah, later the Roman province of Judea, was a theocratic state ruled by the High Priest of the Temple (Epstein 1990: 81). Further, it was almost always under the domination of foreign rulers (Epstein 1990: Chaps. 10-11).

THE HEBREW BIBLE

Biblical scholars are in general agreement that the Hebrew Bible was composed in the land of Canaan over a period stretching from around the eleventh century BCE to around the second century BCE, but that the oral traditions of the book are considerably older than that. The contents include, among other things, historical accounts, prophecies, poems, and law codes. These texts were written down, edited, and re-edited by numerous writers, until the Hebrew Bible reached its final form around 200 BCE. The book as we know it today is therefore a late compilation or edition of this variety of materials from a variety of times and places. The early books of the Hebrew Bible contain material that is mythic and legendary, but, from the narratives about the Monarchy on, the Bible's account becomes increasingly historically accurate (Laffey 1988: 2; Friedman 1987; Halpern 1983: 3).

Lucas Cranach the Elder, "Adam and Eve" Beech wood, c. 1533.
Bode-Museum, Berlin.

The Hebrew Bible consists of three parts: the Law or Torah, the Prophets, and the Writings. Later Christian translations order the contents differently from the original. Before the advent of Christianity, the Hebrew Bible had already been translated twice. The first part, rendered into Greek, was the Torah, and it was translated in the first half of the third century BCE for the Jewish community of Alexandria, whose members no longer understood Hebrew. Translation of the rest of the books was finished over the next two hundred years. Called the Septuagint (Bowker 1997: 875-876), it was this translation that the early Christians used. The second translation was into Aramaic (Bowker 1997: 84). In the final few centuries BCE, very few people still understood Hebrew, and the language of Jerusalem and many areas of the land the Romans called Palestine was Aramaic. An Aramaic *targum*, "translation," was essential to allow people to follow the reading of the sacred texts in Hebrew (Bowker 1997: 954; Jewish Publication Society 1985: xv, xxiv).

The Hebrew Bible and Women

The Hebrew Bible, unlike the Qur'an, the sacred book of Islam, does not have a specific section on women (Bowker 1997: 1042). Nevertheless, it does refer to women often throughout the text, and from these references we can come to some conclusions about the text's view of role and status of women.

As Carol Meyers points out, the Hebrew Bible is "male-centered in its subject matter, its authorship, and its perspectives." She cautions us, therefore, not to assume that Biblical material is useful as a source of information about real women's lives in Biblical times (1992: 245). Nonetheless, later interpreters took at face value what the Hebrew Bible said or did not say about women and often justified treating women as inferior by appealing to scripture. A case in point is the story of Adam and Eve in Genesis 2-3.

God created the first woman, Eve, to be a "helper" or "companion" to man (Genesis 2: 23-24). As punishment for her part in human disobedience to God's instructions, Eve was to be ruled by her husband and have pain in childbirth. Childbearing, especially of sons, would be woman's main responsibility, with barrenness a

Raffaello Sanzio, Detail, "Adam and Eve," fresco, 1508. Stanza della Segnatura, Vatican. Later Christian beliefs saw Lilith depicted as temptress, as seen above. Photo: The Yorck Project: 10,000 Meisterwerke der Malerei. Used by permission GNU free documentation licence.

great disaster, and honour would come to her as a fruitful and good mother. Praise would be hers if she also proved to be a productive and obedient wife (Proverbs 31: 28).

The Hebrew Bible (Christian Old Testament) contains perhaps one mention of Lilith (Isaiah 34:14), a fascinating topic much explored by the rabbis of Talmudic times (second-fifth centuries CE).[2] She it was who caused women to be barren and men to be impotent. She also stole children (Patai 1990: 225). Her name was often connected to layla ("night" in Hebrew), and so Lilith was understood to be a demon of the dark. Later Jewish legend saw Lilith as having flowing locks and wings. She was Adam's first spouse. She disputed Adam's claim to sexual superiority ("Why should you be on top when we are equals?"). Enraged, Lilith spoke God's magic name and took flight to the Red Sea region. There she gave birth to thousands of demonic offspring and set about her evil activities (Patai 1990: 223-224). To keep her at bay, people used amulets and chanted spells.

Finally, the mystical (Kabalistic) tradition, which started in the Mediaeval Period, exalted Lilith as "queenly consort at God's side" (Patai 1990: 221). However, Jewish popular religion in the Middle Ages considered Lilith as the devil's grandmother or the devil himself (Patai 1990: 221-254).

In only a very few matters were women and men equal; for instance, adulterers of either sex suffered the same punishment. However, in most situations, women were men's inferiors, for God had decreed that men should rule over women (Genesis 3: 16). In the Hebrew Bible, most women had no names, being referred to only as daughters of their fathers or wives of their husbands. Women's marriages were arranged between the male heads of families, and women had very limited access to divorce. The Bible also describes menstrual and birth taboos and other rules to do with pollution that affected women (Troyer et al. 2003; Frymer-Kensky 1992: 52-62; Meyers 1992: 245; Wegner 1992: 36-44).

ARRIVAL IN CANAAN

Scholars are in general agreement that the Exodus from Egypt, whatever its form, took place around 1200 BCE and that the people who became the Israelites settled in the land of Canaan at a time of great social upheaval throughout the Eastern Mediterranean area. They established themselves peacefully in the sparsely populated Judaean hill country, the very area where, just two hundred years later, an Israelite monarchy developed. Thus, the story of the "Conquest" as it appears in the Bible is, according to many archaeologists, largely unfounded (Dever 2003). It is highly unlikely, therefore, that they practised the genocide the Bible describes in the Book of Joshua (Silberman 1992; Finkelstein 1988: 16).

Feminist writings about goddesses and "Goddess Cultures" sometimes present interpretations of the Biblical "Conquest" narrative; in particular, they see the Bible and archaeology as demonstrating that the male-dominated Israelites destroyed the Canaanite religion, one dominated by goddesses and so woman centred. The invaders replaced the Canaanite Goddess religion with their own monotheistic, religious and ethical system, which was male dominated and virulently anti-woman (Eisler 1987: 44-5, 94-5; Stone 1977: 46: Davis 1972: 141). However, whatever form the "Conquest" took, around 1200 BCE Canaanite religion was not a "goddess religion," although undoubtedly goddess worship was still very strong in the land. On the contrary, the religion and culture of Bronze Age Canaan was male dominated. Thus the future Israelites certainly could not have destroyed a Goddess culture or a Goddess religion (Sanday 1981: 215ff.; Plaskow 1980).

Canaanite Religion

The Levant or Syro-Canaan, as scholars call the area from Syria in the north to Israel in the South, was quite uniform in culture in the Bronze Age (Aharoni 1982: 89). In the Late Bronze Age (c.1550-c.1200 BCE), the area was dotted with small city-states ruled by kings (Tubb 1998: 35ff.). Further, for a good two thousand years or more *before* "the Israelites" entered their land, the Canaanites had worshipped a male-dominated pantheon of deities.

In the Late Bronze Age, one of these male-dominated cities was ancient Ugarit, a flourishing Canaanite port on the sea coast of what is now Syria (Tubb 1998: 72-75). Excavators have found there masses of written material, a large amount of which concerns the religion of Ugarit. Both city and religion were male dominated. However, in the abundant mythic texts, independent or truly influential female deities, Asherah and Anat, still played important and central roles (Patai 1990).

Syro-Canaan has also provided us with other evidence about the female element in Canaanite religion. Numerous female figurines, probably representing goddesses, were found all over the area in the remains of private houses, public buildings, palaces, and graves, as well as shrines and temples. The enormous number and wide-spread distribution of the figurines suggest that, despite the fact that the official religion was male dominated, veneration of goddesses might have been popular. According to Raphael Patai, around three hundred "terra cotta figurines and plaques representing a nude female figure" had been found in Syro-Canaan by the 1940s (1990: 58); many, many more have been unearthed in the area since. It is likely, then, that, although Canaanite religion was male dominated in the Bronze Age, goddesses continued to be worshipped by ordinary people as well as by large numbers of the elite (Holladay 1987: 265ff.).

ISRAELITE RELIGION

The Bible and other evidence suggest that the early hill- country settlers who would become the Israelites—and later the Jews—were not monotheists, for they did not deny the existence of other deities (Books of Joshua and Judges). However the deity who, in the Hebrew Bible, gives His name as *Y-H-W-H* appears to have been their most important god; scholars usually pronounce and write this name as "Yahweh" (Halpern 1983: 247). What Yahweh wanted the Israelites to do was to honour Him before all the other gods.Eventually, the worship of Yahweh became the main religion of the land of Canaan. However, archaeological and other evidence indicates that the worship of goddesses continued to be popular throughout the two hundred years when the Israelites were consolidating themselves in the land of Canaan (c.1200-1000 BCE) and during the period of the Monarchy (c.1000-586 BCE) (Dever 2005: 252ff.; Olyan 1988: Chap. 3; Patai 1990).

The spiritual role of Israelite women is difficult to deduce from the Biblical texts. As Carol Meyers (1979) says, there were no "public temple buildings" in the villages of the Israelites. Consequently, it seems likely that festivals and rituals occurred in family situations. Indeed, from passages in the Bible, we learn that households had their own shrines and sacred objects, which probably included images, and it is likely that women took religious roles in domestic worship. There are also examples of Israelite women's filling public religious roles.

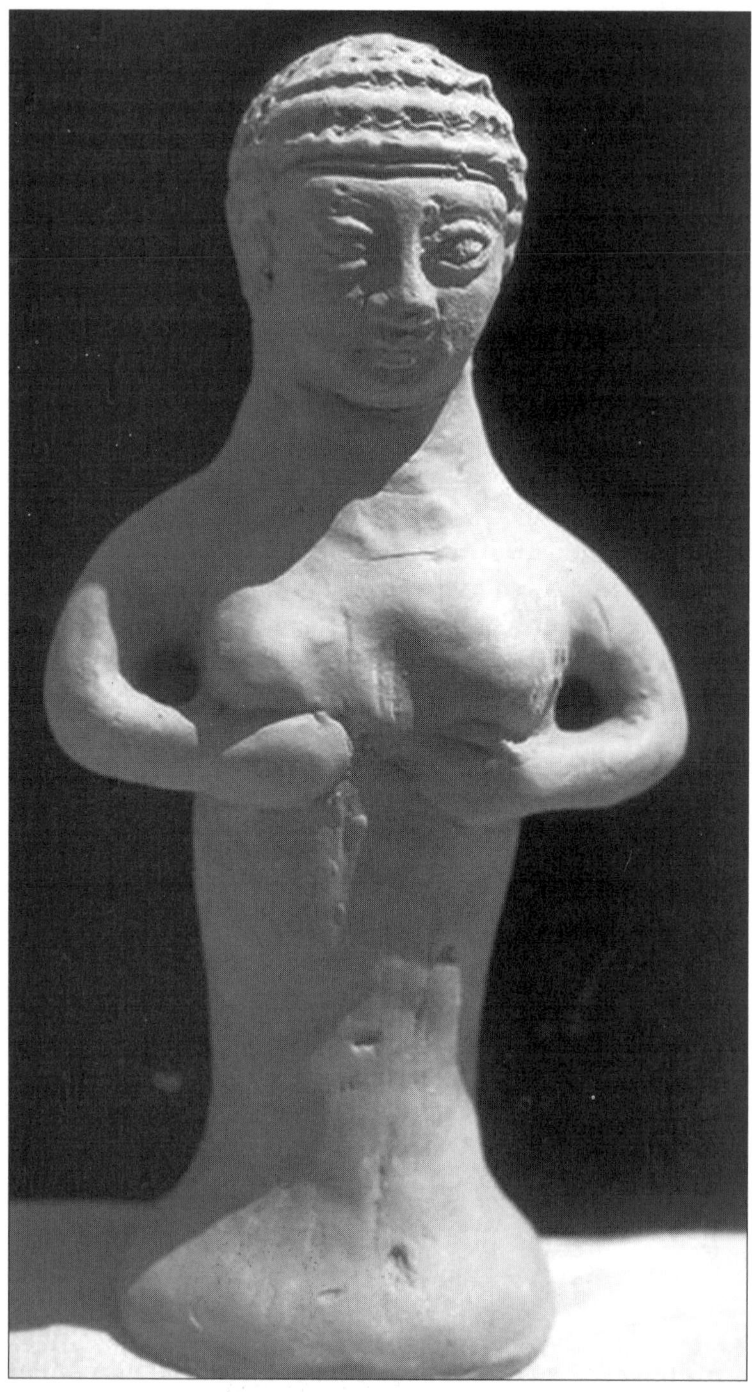

A clay figurine, possibly of the goddess Asherah. Used with permission CC-SA.

After 1000 BCE, "public, male-dominated institutions," along with monarchy and priesthood, took over from the domestic world as the centre of "organized community life," and bureaucracies developed to support them both. The result was that women became almost invisible in public religious life. However, they seem still to have taken part in rituals in the home and in what scholars call "popular," as distinct from state or officially recognised worship (Meyers 1988: 159-160).

Popular religion consists of the rites and spiritual observations that ordinary people perform today as in the past. For instance, as they go about their daily lives, they might place an offering or say a prayer at a shrine in a field or at a street corner; today such a shrine would likely be dedicated to the Virgin Mary. Modern women in Crete, grateful for an easy birth, tie pieces of coloured ribbon to trees in a grove once sacred to a pagan goddess, now presided over by a Christian saint. Women in contemporary Eleusis in Greece take cakes to the ruins of the sanctuary of the Goddess Demeter in hope of becoming pregnant; Demeter's temple is now dominated from a height by a chapel to Panagia, the "All Holy One," the Virgin Mary.

Religion During the Period of Monarchy

In Monarchic times, the Israelite god Yahweh probably had a consort, the goddess Asherah (Dever 2005). A scholar who studied the issue concluded that Asherah and "her cult symbol" were not only worshipped in popular religion, but also approved by "the official cult as well" (Olyan 1988: 74). According to Raphael Patai, an image of Asherah stood in the Solomonic temple for close to 236 years, that is, at least two-thirds of that temple's existence (1990: 50, 52-53). Further, Asherah seems to have been a very attractive deity, especially to women (Dever 2005: 236-246).

Excavators of sites dating to the Monarchy and situated all over the land of Canaan have unearthed amazingly large numbers of small, terracotta figurines of semi-nude females (Kletter 1996). Raphael Patai thinks they represent the Goddess Asherah (1990: 39). Other scholars interpret them as human females, perhaps "expressing the quest for human fertility." Since these figurines come mainly from domestic contexts and no "analogous male figures" have come to light, they may represent evidence of female spiritual life (Meyers 1988: 162-163).

Some female figurines have come from sites other than domestic ones, for example, a cave just outside Jerusalem. University of Toronto archaeologist John Holladay, Jr., excavated the cave, which, he thinks, people visited frequently during the Monarchic Period. Objects he found there included sixteen female figurines, most of which Holladay thinks probably represented Asherah. He concludes that, along with one or two other sites, the Jerusalem Cave provides evidence of a completely different kind of spirituality from that of the state religion; further, he thinks that the state must have tolerated it. In all likelihood, women would have been regular worshippers at the cave (Holladay 1987: 259ff.).

The Temple and its Destruction

After Solomon had the Temple constructed, official religion, as the Hebrew Bible makes clear, increasingly focused on the Temple and its male priesthood. As long as the Temple existed in Jerusalem and the devout could reach it reasonably easily, all living in the united kingdom (consisting of Israel and Judah) were expected to pay tithes to the Temple and to make certain sacrifices there. Further, it was a religious duty to celebrate the major festivals in Jerusalem.

After the division of the kingdom into northern Israel and southern Judah in the tenth century BCE and the Assyrian destruction of Israel in 721 BCE, Judah's religious observance continued to centre on the Jerusalem Temple. Disaster fell on the kingdom of Judah in 586 BCE, with the destruction of the Solomonic Temple and the subsequent "Babylonian Captivity or Exile." These events caused the first of a number of changes in the thinking of the Judaites, as the "eternal" dynasty founded by King David came to an end and the "invulnerable" temple was destroyed. Cut off from the Temple, Judaite exiles in Babylon and elsewhere were forced to worship in temples and small shrines (Runesson 2001: 165; Hayes and Miller 1977: 479).

Under the auspices of the Persian king Cyrus, a large number of Judaites returned to Jerusalem. Eventually, the Temple was re-built. Many of the exiles, however, did not return to Judah, and so the

Babylonian Exile constituted a kind of first Diaspora. For the exiles, the Temple, though holy, became "a remote and unimportant place" (Epstein 1990: 80; Hayes and Miller 1977: 666).

The Persian Period (539 BCE-331 BCE) was a time when the exiles started to develop new ways of existing as separate and autonomous religious communities inside a "universal" empire (Runesson 2001: 396). While priests were still sacrificing according to Biblical precepts in the re-built Temple, the lives of exiles began to centre on the Torah and what became the synagogue, from Greek *synagogue*, "assembly"; that is, it was a special place where Jews gathered together for worship, festivals, community functions, and instruction. The word "synagogue" can also mean "congregation" and even the totality of a Jewish community as a political and social entity (Kraemer 1993: 118; Pritchard 1991: 122; Epstein 1990: 79, 82, 86, 112).

The leader of a synagogue was a rabbi, who was understood as a "teacher." A rabbi got authority from a congregation's recognition that he was "an authentic receiver and transmitter" of the Law (Runesson 2001: 397). These early rabbis began a process that was continued by rabbis in the later Diaspora proper. This rabbinical process was eventually to alter the spiritual focus of the religion and make it independent of the Temple. Thus, for the exiles, who were now focusing their religious and social lives on synagogues, the Romans' destruction of Jerusalem, along with the Second Temple, in 70 CE made little difference (Runesson 2001: 475; Hayes and Miller 1977: 538).

Over time, the rabbis worked out the concept of the *minyan*, an all-male prayer quorum: wherever ten adult male Jews gathered to pray, God would be there also. They also constructed a basic liturgy in prayer books. Though prayer books could be added to, they nonetheless provided a fixed order of service for the widespread Jewish population (Epstein 1990: 251, note11).

THE SYNAGOGUE IN THE DIASPORA

With the burning of the Temple in 70 CE, Temple rituals and sacrifices ceased completely, with most of the people of Jerusalem and many of Judah dispersed widely across the Roman world, the scattering known as the Diaspora. Now the Jews all needed to replace the Temple cult with another form of spiritual community, one based in the Torah and in the rabbinic tradition: the rabbi was the equivalent of priest, Torah study the equivalent of ritual, and "deeds of loving kindness the new sacrifice ." For the Jews of the Diaspora, the synagogue replaced the Temple as the hub of their community (Runesson 2001: 476; Pritchard 1991: 122; Hayes and Miller 1977: 676).

Women's Leadership in the Early Synagogue

That women attended synagogues and were deeply involved in synagogue life is clear from a wide range of evidence from the Greco-Roman period. Numerous inscriptions document women's roles as synagogue patrons; they financed the construction of synagogues and paid for their enhancement. As a result, some female patrons received the title "Mother of the Synagogue." In addition, a number of women functioned as synagogue officers and leaders. Ancient evidence demonstrates that women held the offices of elder, and they also served as heads of synagogues (Kraemer 1993: 106, 120-121; Brooten 1982: 27-55).

Further, it is not at all certain that seating was sex segregated in ancient synagogues of the Greco-Roman period, nor do we have evidence, apart from rabbinical writings, that women at that time had special religious obligations that did not apply to men. Some Jewish women may have been prophets and ecstatics, although nothing suggests that such experience increased Jewish women's chances of attaining to leadership, as it seems to have done in early Christianity. In addition, there is extant an account of a Jewish monastery in Egypt that received educated contemplatives, both female and male. Like Christian nuns, most of the Jewish women who joined the community were celibate (Kraemer 1993: 106-107, 109, 113-117, 123).

It is significant that rabbinic reports of women's roles and spirituality for the Greco-Roman period differ markedly from the evidence scholars have gleaned from inscriptions, archaeological research, and Greek literary texts. In contradiction of the latter material, rabbinical sources imply that Jewish women were kept in seclusion and had little access to the spiritual life of the synagogue.

This important observation suggests that the rabbinical sources were indulging in a kind of wish-fulfilment in their views on Jewish women. It also warns us that we should always read with caution the statements of religious functionaries about the practices of their religions with regard to women (Kraemer 1993: 93).

JEWISH LAW AND WOMEN

As Kraemer says, the terms "the rabbis" and "rabbinical sources" are short forms for the great diversity of people, communities, and points of view that went into producing the considerable "literature collectively called rabbinic" (Kraemer 1993: 93-94). The development of Judaism as we know it began with the rabbis of the Greco-Roman world and continued during the Middle Ages. Indeed, Judaism in the Medieval Period was effectively controlled by the rabbis and their Talmud. Further, rabbinical elaboration of Judaism did not stop with the entry of Judaism into the modern world. Thus, Judaism can still be considered a developing tradition (Plaskow 1991: 108; Epstein 1990: Chap.20; Carmody 1989: 134).

In the first and second centuries CE, the most distinguished rabbis of the time started compiling earlier materials about issues in religious law that eventually became the *Mishnah*, "the code of Jewish law." This code and commentaries on it make up the Talmud. By about 500 CE, the Talmud had achieved very much the form it has today. From then on, it was the Talmud which served as the guide for living as a Jew (Kraemer 1993: 94; Epstein 1990: Chaps. 14, 15, 16; Jewish Publication Society 1985: xxiii).

The *Mishnah* devotes one of its six sections to women. It makes clear that woman's place is inside marriage and that a woman in transition, not yet married or, for whatever reason, exiting a marriage, is dangerous: as Carmody puts it, "women on the loose, unplaced, are likely to be loose women" (1989: 145). Nonetheless, the Talmud praises women as wives and mothers, for they make it possible for their husbands and sons to study the Torah. That is, as well as having responsibility for housework and child care, women were also expected to be the breadwinners.

If the Talmud waxes almost lyrical in its praise of the good wife and mother, it is also quite specific on a wife's right to financial support, health care, sexual satisfaction, and an allowance as a widow or divorcee. In return, a wife is to provide her husband with food and rest, sexual satisfaction, and time to study the Torah. Though only sons inherit, it is understood that a man will provide for his daughters. The greatest sorrow for a woman is to be barren, her greatest joy to have many children, particularly sons (Carmody 1989: 146-147; Hauptman 1974: 194-196).

Only a man can terminate a marriage. In order to remarry, a woman has to have a *get*, proof of divorce. Today, a major problem for a growing number of observant Jewish women is that men can use their power to refuse a woman a *get*, and thus she becomes an *agunah*, "one who is anchored or chained." Though she can acquire a civil divorce, she cannot remarry in a religious ceremony. Further, if she nonetheless remarried and had children, Jewish law would consider them *mamzerim* "bastards." Jewish women can, of course, appeal to a rabbinical court for help in dealing with various marital circumstances. However, the women "in chains," the *agunot*, have had little help from the rabbinical courts, which no longer have any power to enforce their decisions (Rosenberg 1996: 69; Hauptman 1974: 189-190).

Rabbinical interpretation of the Torah, as well as the rest of the Hebrew Bible, and of the Talmud, continued throughout the Middle Ages, the Renaissance, and into the modern world. Over time, the rabbis produced *halakhah*, meaning "the path" or "walking" (a reference to Exodus 18: 20). *Halakhah* is rabbinic law, which rabbis interpreted and added to by means of new judgments (Epstein 1990: 114, 125).

JEWISH MYSTICISM

In the first half of the eighteenth century, a revivalist movement began in Eastern Europe. The members of the movement observed rabbinic law, *halakhah*, strictly, but they were even more devoted to ecstatic experience. Founded by Israel "Baal Shem Tov" Besht (1700-1760), the movement was called Hasidism, from Hebrew *hasid* meaning "pious." The most important woman in Hasidism is Oudil, the daughter of the movement's founder. It is clear that she was a mystic in her own right. In the late eighteenth and nineteenth centuries, Hasidic groups made their ways back to Palestine and, in so doing, paved the way for the Zionist Movement and eventually the state of Israel. Today Hasidic Jews live in small communities and try to follow rabbinic laws as much as is possible in the modern world (Epstein 1990: 271, 277; Carmody 1989: 150; Harris 1985).

Eighteenth-century Hasidism developed out of a tradition of Jewish mysticism going back to the eleventh, twelfth, and thirteenth centuries. Known as the Kabbalah, "receiving or tradition," the movement was based on even earlier Jewish mystical traditions. One of its streams began in the south of France at the end of the twelfth century. The Kabbalah's most important text, the monumental *Sefer ha-Zohar, the Book of Radiance*, usually called the *Zohar*, appeared around 1300. Jewish mystics quickly adopted the *Zohar* as their text, and, next to the Talmud, it has had "the profoundest influence" on Judaism. Jewish women mystics probably existed, but, if they did, little or no hint of them remains (Matt 1995: 2, 4-6, 15-16; Epstein 1990: 223, 229-30, 234).

The Kabbalah did, however, develop the rabbinic idea of "*Shekhinah*, divine immanence," until it became "the feminine half of God." Thus, the Kabbalah bequeathed to Jewish women a powerful image of the femaleness of divinity, an image which many women today find empowering (Gottlieb 1995; Matt 1995: 1; Epstein 1990: 137, 238).

LATER DEVELOPMENTS

For most of our era, the majority of Jews have lived as minorities in Christian and Muslim societies. In Christian societies especially, Jews were often subject to persecution. As a result, Judaism had to concentrate on tradition and the preservation of Jewish identity. To that end, rabbinic interpretations of the Bible and the Talmud emphasised a strong Jewish family, kept together by a devout wife and mother, as a hedge against assimilation. Until the nineteenth century, most Jews lived traditional lives (Carmody 1989: 135, 147-150; Glückel 1977).

From the eighteenth century on and especially after the French Revolution, Jews saw the possibility of getting citizenship in lands that had previously confined them to ghettoes. By the nineteenth century, with its concepts of democracy, pluralism, and nationalism, many Jews had started re-consider the separateness that had been a survival strategy in previous centuries. In response to the demands of the modern world, many Jews began to question traditional Judaism, with its numerous strict, rabbinical laws (Epstein 1990: 290-292; Carmody 1989: 135).

Finally, in Germany, some of them developed what became Reform Judaism; it sprang from the attempt to reconfigure Judaism "in modern terms." These reformers declared that a large number of the rules in the Torah and Talmud were no longer applicable in the modern world, and they called their synagogues "temples" to show that they no longer looked forward to a time when the Jerusalem Temple would rise again (Kaplan 2003; Epstein 1990: 291-294; Carmody 1989: 152).

At this time, traditional Judaism acquired the name "Orthodox Judaism." Gradually, as a result of further attempts to adjust the tradition to the modern world, two other distinct streams of Judaism came into existence: Conservative Judaism and Reconstructionist Judaism (Epstein 1990: 295-298).

In the West, all this revolutionary turmoil led many Jews to leave the tradition all together. However, in Eastern Europe the Russian Tsars did not permit such change in status. Thus, Eastern European Jews remained traditionalist. However, it was among them that, in the late nineteenth century, a movement originated that advocated the return of Jews to the Jewish homeland: Zionism. In 1895, Theodore Herzl (1860-1904) published his classic pamphlet *The Jewish State*. Zionism shifted from being "a philanthropic religious movement" to operating as a world-wide political organisation. The small Zionist groups that braved the difficulties of settling in the southern part of Syria paved the way for the establishment of the state of Israel in 1948 (Epstein 1990: 277, 291, 309-310).

Unquestionably, the major event of the twentieth century for all Jews was the Holocaust. During World War II (1939-1945), Nazi Germany exterminated an estimated six million Jews in death camps like Auschwitz and Belsen and destroyed the long-established Jewish communities of Europe. It was largely in response to the Holocaust that the Jewish state of Israel came into existence in 1948 (Bowker 1997: 436-438).

For all Jewish women, the Holocaust is the single most significant historical event. The Nazis recognised Jewish women as the principal carriers of "communal and religious continuity" and so, for sending to the death camps, targeted them particularly. Certainly, the Nazis put women in "double jeopardy" as victims of both women hatred and anti-Semitism (Raphael 2003: 1). For secular Jewish feminists, the Holocaust is a major ingredient of their identity, while observant women have had to come to terms with what is for all observant Jews a major theological problem, God's apparent reneging on His portion of the Covenant. To answer the question "Where was God?" Melissa Raphael produced a Jewish feminist theology of the Holocaust (2003). The developing tradition of Jewish feminist spirituality is in large part a response to the way in which the Holocaust nullified both the interest in assimilation and the trend to secularism in the modern period (Bowker 1997: 436-437).

JUDAISM TODAY

To be a Jew, a person, male or female, must have been born from a Jewish mother or formally converted to Judaism. In Jewish Law, descent follows the female line. A person born from a Jewish mother who does not observe the obligations of a Jew is, nonetheless, considered a full Jew. Judaism is not now a proselytising religion, but it does accept converts. Conversion entails study and complicated ritual, with ritual immersion and, for men, circumcision. For many Jews, there is no problem with being both agnostic/atheist and Jewish. Thus, like Islam, Judaism can be a faith, an ideology, or a sign of group and individual identity, or all three at once (Bowker 1997: 236, 500; Ruthven 1997: 3).

In early times, Jews became divided into two main communities: the Sephardi and the Ashkenazi. This distinction manifests itself today in differences in liturgy, religious customs, and pronunciation of Hebrew. The *Sephardim*, from Hebrew *Sepharad*, "Spain," are descendants of Jews who, in the Diaspora, lived primarily in Spain and Portugal (Bowker 1997: 875). After their expulsion from those countries in 1492, they scattered throughout the world, settling in, among other places, North Africa (especially Morocco), Western Europe, the Balkans and Greece, Asia Minor (Turkey), India, and China, where they set up distinct communities. They spoke *Ladino*, a dialect based on Castilian Spanish. Another group often included with the Sephardim name themselves *Mizrahi(m)* (Crespin and Jacobus 1997-1998: 6). The Hebrew term *mizrahi* means "eastern," and the Mizrahi are descended from Jews who remained in the Middle East and North Africa throughout Jewish history. They usually speak Arabic or "Judeo-Arabic." Most Mizrahi from, for example, Tunisia, Algeria, Morocco, Egypt, Lebanon, Syria, and Turkey, have emigrated to Israel. The *Ashkenazim* are descendants of Jews who, in the Diaspora, settled in eastern, northern, and central Europe (Bowker 1997: 98-99). They spoke, and some still speak, a dialect based primarily in German, now called Yiddish.

According to 2007 figures, the world-wide Jewish population numbers about 13.2 million, about 41 percent of whom live in Israel (estimate by the Jewish People Policy Planning Institute and published on Wikipedia [www.wikipedia.com]). Other estimates have put the population at between 12 and 18 million. Jews of Ashkenazi origin make up the largest number. The Jews of Ethiopia, the Falashas, believe themselves to have been Jews since the time of Solomon (Bowker 1997: 334-335). There are also very old Jewish communities in other places, for instance, China and India. In the United States there are several congregations of African-American Jews (Chafets 2009: 34-39).

Central Tenets

Judaism is, first and foremost, a monotheistic religion. God, the creator of the universe, is the only god. The *Shema*, Hebrew for "Hear," is its classic statement and age-old "confession of faith": "Hear, O Israel! The Lord is our God, the Lord alone" (Deuteronomy 6: 4). The other central tenet is that God has chosen the people of Israel "to be the bearers of this belief." Thus, God is both leader and protector of His people and active in the world (Epstein

1990: 134-135, 162; Jewish Publication Society 1985: 284).

God's Law appears in the Hebrew Bible, particularly in the Torah, its first five books, the "Books of Moses." The people's adherence to the Law as set out in the Torah can lead to improvement in their lives, and eventually the arrival of the Messiah, who will be both Davidic king, restorer of political Israel, and this-worldly saviour; he will come to usher in a time of peace and plenty and a time of righteousness, an earthly paradise (Epstein 1990: 62).

The two pivotal events of Judaism are Exodus and Covenant. The Book of Exodus in the Torah tells how, under the leadership of Moses, the Israelites fled from slavery in Egypt. During the long years of wandering, Israel accepted the Torah as its law. The Exodus symbolises God's caring for the people of Israel and His liberating nature and function. Closely connected to the Exodus is the Covenant, originally an agreement between God and Abraham on behalf of the people and re-affirmed under Moses. In return for God's attention to them as His special concern and His giving them the land of Canaan, the Israelites, later the Jews, were to obey the Ten Commandments and the other laws of God as set out in the Torah. Judaism normally construes the teachings in the Talmud as elaboration of the Torah and interpretation of the Covenant in the light of new circumstances. It is, at least in part, for this reason that Judith Plaskow can describe Judaism as an "evolving tradition" (1991: 108).

However, as Plaskow points out, behaviours not beliefs are the central defining characteristics of Judaism, and behaviours are elaborated in *halakhah* (Jewish rabbinic law), a system that deals with all facets of life. Today, though some forms of Orthodox Judaism understand that Jewish law is binding, other forms of Judaism do not consider it so, and in general it is not enforced (1994: 63).

Rituals

For observant Jews, whatever branch of Judaism they adhere to, spiritual life focuses first on the family and then on the synagogue. Rituals, prayers, and blessings occur in both locations (Epstein 1990: 166, 169). However, according to Orthodox feminist Blu

Greenberg, communal spiritual experience is the preferred form, and, as a result, women's responsibilities and rights are less (Greenberg 1981: 7).

Jewish rabbinic law, *halakhah*, ideally demands that observant Jews obey a number of commandments, or *mitzvot*; traditionally, there are 613 in all. The Talmudic rabbis decreed that adult males who were free, not slaves, were obligated to obey all of them. Further, both men and women must fulfil all the negative commandments, the ones that forbid an act. However, the rabbis decided that women were obligated to obey only those others that were not "time-bound," that is, for which there is no set time. For instance, the rabbis exempted women from the obligation to pray communally three times daily and also excused them from fulfilling the commandment to study. In addition, the Talmud denied women the privilege of reading from Torah at a prayer service, because of "the dignity of the congregation." The Talmud does not give reasons for these exemptions, but the demands of women's domestic role would almost certainly have caused women difficulty in obeying most of them. In addition, a taboo about menstruation may have been the reason why the rabbis denied them access to the Torah scroll. Isidore Epstein argues that women were exempted because womanhood is so sacred that it demands all of a woman's attention, and therefore nothing, not even other religious duties, should interfere with "her special tasks" (1990: 169). Judith Baskin, on the other hand, thinks it likely that the rabbis did not think women "capable of any direct experience of the divine" (Baskin 1985: 3; Hauptman 1974: 190-193).

Certain commandments were called "women's commandments," because it was the responsibility of women to see that they were fulfilled. The enforcement in the home of dietary laws (*kashrut*, kosher) fall into this category. Observing all the rules about the proper handling of fish, birds, animals, and their products devolves on women only after a trained and licensed slaughterer, a *shohet*, has killed the creatures in ritually correct way. However, the dietary laws are extremely complicated, and their observation very time consuming (Bowker 1997: 281-282; Epstein 1990: 161; Hauptman in Reuther 1974: 192).

Three commandments in particular became women's obligations:

challah, breaking bread dough at Sabbath; *hadlik ner*, lighting Sabbath candles; and *niddah*, observing laws of family purity. The latter commandment enjoins women to practise sexual abstinence during menstruation and for seven days after it ends. Then, before resuming sexual relations with their husbands, women must immerse themselves in a ritual bath, a *mikveh* (Barclay and Jaeger 2004; Frankiel 1990: 74-85; Harris 1985: 147-148).

Some rabbis construed these women's obligations as punishment for Eve's sin and warned that a woman's neglect of these commandments would result in her death in childbed. Ross Kraemer suggests that these commandments directed to women were intended to facilitate men's fulfilment of their obligations under the Covenant (1993: 95, 100). In any case, as Judith Hauptman observes, the end result of such exemptions has been that men have taken over the synagogues and the academies. Prayer and study in the Jewish tradition require immense amounts of time and learned skill. Because of their ascribed role, women can neither pray regularly, nor explore the tradition. Thus, two of Judaism's "essentially spiritual experiences" cannot become "part of a woman's religious experiences" (Hauptman 1974: 193).

One act that observant Jewish men perform every morning is not strictly a commandment, but a blessing. Men say the following prayer: "Blessed be God, King of the universe, for not making me a woman." Dating back to the second century CE, the blessing has been interpreted to mean that a man thanks God for giving him greater opportunities to obey commandments than a woman has. Another view has him expressing gratitude for being what he is (Hauptman in Reuther 1974: 196).

The ritual which has been the building-block of Judaism's continuity and continuance over the millennia is the Sabbath, which observant Jewish households celebrate weekly, from dusk on Friday to dusk on Saturday. We could also class the Sabbath as a weekly festival. For this ritual, the woman preparing Sabbath bread (*challah*) is obligated to break off and burn a symbolic piece of dough before she bakes it. A woman, usually the mother, performs the ritual of lighting the Sabbath candles at dusk (*hadlik ner*), and the family, usually led by its male head, the father, welcomes the Sabbath as "Queen." It is usually the father who says *kiddush*, "sanctification," the blessing over the cup of wine to consecrate it, and the food too is blessed before the family eats it. In traditional households, no one works on the Sabbath, so that women must prepare all Sabbath food the day before (Kraemer 1993: 95; Epstein 1990: 170-171, 187).

Judaism has always marked main events in an individual life-cycle with ritual:

(1) a boy's circumcision, *berit* or *bris milah*, "covenant of circumcision," when he is eight days old. At the *bris*, the child is given a name. He is thus received into "the covenant of Abraham" and into the community. This ritual is conducted by a *mohel*, an expert in Jewish law, as well as the medical facts of the operation. The *mohel* was always male, until recently, when Reform Judaism has begun certifying women to perform the ritual. The *mohel* included the father, but not the mother in the naming and blessing ritual. In traditional Judaism, there is no equivalent rite for a girl (*The Toronto Star* 1998, August 1: L10; Bowker 1997: 224; Epstein 1990: 168; Plaskow 1979: 179).

(2) when a boy reaches thirteen years of age, a *bar mitzvah*, meaning "son of the commandment." The boy is called to the front of the synagogue and reads from Torah as an adult member of the community. From then on, he must perform the religious obligations (*mitzvot*) of an adult male. In traditional Judaism, there is no equivalent ritual for a girl, who, in religious terms, comes of age at twelve (Epstein 1990: 168-169).

(3) marriage, on the day before which bride and groom ritually purify themselves and pray and the groom inspects the *ketubah*, the marriage contract, which he has had drawn up. At the wedding, before the whole community, the couple share a glass of sanctified wine under the *huppah*, the wedding canopy; the rabbi reads the terms of the *ketubah*; and the groom shatters the wine glass underfoot. Though religiously sanctioned, marriage is not a sacrament, as it is in Christianity (Epstein 1990: 166-167).

(4) death, with burial taking place within twenty-four hours and then a week of ritualised mourning at home, "sitting *shiva*," when kin of the deceased sit near to the ground; men do not shave; friends and relatives visit; and a rabbi regularly leads the prayer for the dead (*kaddish*). For eleven months, sons go daily

to the communal service in the synagogue to recite *kaddish*. For some Jewish women, their being denied the right to say *kaddish* in the synagogue was the trigger for their becoming feminists and beginning to work to change the role of women in Judaism (Heschel 2003: 145). After eleven months have passed, the ritual dedication of the tombstone officially ends the mourning period (Epstein 1990: 178).

Festivals

Passover, *Pesach*, a major festival for Jews, lasts eight days among Jews of the Diaspora and seven in Israel. In a week of symbolic feasts, Jews recall, in accordance with God's instructions (Exodus 12; Numbers 9), the events before, during, and after the Exodus from Egypt. For women, Passover entails an enormous amount of work, not only inordinate amounts of cooking, but meticulous cleaning for sometimes over a month before the festival. Some years ago, I was in Jerusalem for an extended period. During the week before Passover, I remember taking my clothes to a near-by laundromat to wash them. On previous occasions, the facility had not been at all busy, but on that day the place was humming, and there was a line-up of women and children carrying bags of bedding, comforters, curtains, table linens, and so forth. The attendant told me that, for several weeks, the women had been in the throes of preparing for Passover. I discovered later that, not only were they washing all their household linen, but they were also doing an extremely thorough spring cleaning of their living quarters. They were spending days and days preparing all the food necessary for the festival, as well as seeing to it that cutlery and dishes were ritually correct for the occasion. It was not unusual for women to organise the repainting of their kitchens and sometimes their whole houses. The significance of all the cleaning was that it was the responsibility of the women to make sure that their rooms were free of every *hametz*, impurity, and thus to make it possible for their men and children to observe Jewish law during the festival (Toronto *Globe and Mail*, 10 April 1998: A13; Sered 1992: 80-85).

On the eve of Passover, a Jewish family gathers at home for *seder*, meaning "order," the main ritual of commemoration, and they follow the ritual set out in the *Haggadah*, the order of service for Passover. In a traditional family, the ritual leaders and participants are all male, the father and the sons of the family. The *seder* includes eating a number of symbolic foods and a festive meal, all prepared by the woman of the house. Jews of the Diaspora normally celebrate another *seder* on the second night of the Passover period. During Passover, Jews eat unleavened bread, *matzah*, in memory of the fact that the people fleeing Egypt could not wait for bread to rise (Epstein 1990: 171-172).

The High Holy Days of Judaism occur in the Fall and last for ten days. They begin with the sounding of the *shofar*, the ram's horn, at Rosh Hashanah, the New Year's festival. Ten days later, the High Holy Days end with Yom Kippur, the Day of Atonement, when, from dawn to dusk, most Jews fast and pray. At the end of the day, the sounding of the *shofar* signals the closing of the period for another year (Epstein 1990: 173-176).

Women's Ritual Roles

Observant Jewish women have to be ritual specialists. Not only are they responsible for the preparation of kosher food and special foods for festival occasions and for the purity of living quarters for Passover, but they perform other ritual duties that are crucial to the maintenance of Jewish life. Normally, however, most observers of Judaism, as well as most participants in it, dismiss what women do ritually on a day-to-day basis as not central to the religion. Typically, they recognise and value only what men do ritually.

In her study of the religious lives of elderly Jewish women in Jerusalem, Sered points out that the women she studied consider themselves as "spiritual guardians" of their families, the link between generations and to ancestors. To make contact with ancestors and solicit their support, they regularly perform rituals, both at home and at graves and sacred tombs. At Passover, women are ritual experts *par excellence*, and many of them know it. Passover sacralises the world of women, "the domain of sinks, buckets, mops, and rags." Food preparation is also a ritual act, which women themselves understand as "a sacred task" (Sered 1992: 18-19, 85, 88; Sered 1988).

TYPES OF JUDAISM

In the contemporary world, Orthodox, Conservative, Reform, and Reconstructionist Judaism often overlap in tenets and practices. Individual synagogues are autonomous, and rituals vary widely from synagogue to synagogue, even when they understand themselves to belong to the same branch of Judaism. In addition, there are a number of contemporary movements.

Orthodox Judaism

Today there are many varieties of Orthodox Judaism, ranging from Ultra-Orthodox to Traditional Orthodox to Modern and even "Egalitarian" Orthodox, each differing in tenets and practice. Not all Orthodox Jews keep every rabbinic law of the past. As in other branches of Judaism, *halakhah* is generally no longer enforced. Most Orthodox Jews do, however, consider Torah binding. Extremely traditional Jews, *haredim* "those who tremble," still exist (Longman 2007), and today they are normally called the "Ultra-Orthodox"; the *Hasidim* "pious ones," among whom there are many variations, fall into this category. Orthodox Jewish men cover their heads at all times, usually with a skull cap (*yarmulkah*). Male worshippers wear a fringed prayer shawl (*tallit*), and they also wrap around their arms and forehead leather straps with phylacteries (*tefillin* "prayer"), tiny black boxes containing Biblical verses. Hebrew, which traditionally women do not study, is the language of prayer and liturgy, and the *minyan* is all male (Epstein 1990: 161-163, 270-281; Neudel 1989: 179; Harris 1985).

Orthodox synagogues segregate men and women with a partition or provide women with a gallery or other such place from which to observe services. Women remain exempt from daily communal prayer, but nonetheless they can, and some do, attend. Most Orthodox Jewish women fulfil the three *halakhic* commandments pertaining to them, and rabbinic marriage and divorce laws still apply to them. In general, Orthodox Judaism sees women as having "a separate and powerful role" in the private, domestic sphere, but they have had "no access to the public domain" (Schulman 1996: 312).

Regina Jonas (1902-1944). Photograph presumed to be taken after 1939. Stiftung "Neue Synagoge Berlin – Centrum Judaicum," Berlin.

Reform Judaism

Reform Jews do not consider Torah binding, but they do follow its ethical content. *Halakhah* is binding on neither men nor women. From its beginnings, Reform Judaism "abolished most of the ritual functions unique to men," such as the prayer quorum. In synagogue men do not wear the phylacteries with their leather straps or the prayer shawl, nor is the skull cap necessary, though many men put one on when entering the synagogue. Women and men sit together during services. Often the prayers are in the vernacular, not Hebrew. From its earliest years, the Reform branch abolished the *bar mitzvah* and "instituted confirmation as a coming-of-age ritual for [both] boys and girls." Reform Judaism celebrates the major festivals and emphasises ethical teachings. In Susannah Heschel's view, Reform Judaism preserves the essence of Judaism (1983: xliv; Neudel in Falk and Gross 1989: 180).

Well ahead of its time, Reform Judaism's Breslau Conference in 1846 concluded with a call for "sexual equality in all areas of religion," but there was little response. In the 1890s, however, a Jewish feminist, Henrietta Szold, worked for equality and was founder of the international women's Zionist organization Hadassah. In 1903 she attended the Jewish Theological Seminary in New York on condition that she not seek ordination (Heschel 2003: 147). She ended her days in Palestine, where she founded the health-care system, out of which modern Israel's Hadassah Medical Organization developed. Before 1940, Reform Judaism had ordained at least two female rabbis, one of them in the U.S. However, the first one, Regina Jonas, was ordained in Germany in 1934 and died in Auschwitz in 1944 (Klapheck 2006: 20; Goldstein 2000: 27; Nadell 1998; Carmody 1989: 152; Neudel 1989: 180).

Conservative Judaism

Conservative Judaism has the largest number of adherents in the United States today, and its goal is to confront the challenge of integrating tradition with modernity. When it started, however, the Conservative movement "rejected virtually all Reform innovation," except seating women and men together. Use of the vernacular occurs in some Conservative services. Conservative

Judaism understands *halakhah* as binding on its members, but does not enforce it (Epstein 1990: 296-297; Neudel in Falk and Gross 1989: 180).

In 1886 the Jewish Theological Seminary was founded in New York City, and its ordained rabbis then constituted the Rabbinical Assembly of Conservative Judaism. The Assembly set up a twenty-five member Committee on Jewish Law and Standards to advise on *halakhic* interpretation, but its decisions are not binding. Member synagogues can accept them or reject them (Schulman 1996: 314). In 1973, in the U.S., the committee of the Rabbinical Assembly that interprets *halakhic* matters pronounced that women could participate in a *minyan*. In 1983, the Conservative movement decided that women could attend the seminary and be ordained rabbis. By the middle of the first decade of the twenty-first century, 40 percent of the students at the Jewish Theological Seminary were women (Keller and Reuther 2006). Interestingly, in 1983, feminist Susannah Heschel had argued that Conservative Judaism had no basis for changing the status of its women (1983: xlvi; see also Schwartz 2007; Schulman 1996: 314;).

Reconstructionist Judaism

Reconstructionist Judaism developed within the Conservative movement. Mordecai Kaplan (1881-1982), the founder of the branch, was one of the promoters of women's equality in Judaism (Alpert and Milgram 1996: 291). A motion of a Reconstructionist conference in 1967 set up the Reconstructionist Rabbinical College in Philadelphia. The Reconstructionist Rabbinical Association and the Federation of Reconstructionist Congregations govern the movement (Epstein 1990: 297).

Reconstructionist Jews think that *halakhah* is a sacred, but non-binding tradition and that it needs to take into account contemporary ethical standards. The movement also stresses "humanistic values" and downplays revelation. According to Rebecca Alpert and Goldie Milgram, Reconstructionist Judaism conceives of God as a power, not a person, and understands God as having no sex or gender. The stream is also egalitarian and non-hierarchical. Therefore, it has managed to effect important changes (1996: 291-292). However, critics point out that Reconstructionist Judaism puts its emphasis not on effecting changes in Judaism, but on maintaining that Judaism is a civilization and that religion is just "one of the many forms in which [the] civilization expresses itself" (Epstein 1990: 297; Heschel 1983: xlviii; Carmody 1989: 152).

WOMEN AND RELIGIOUS LEADERSHIP

Orthodox Judaism still opposes the ordination of women as rabbis (Joseph 2007). However, as Rabbi Elyse Goldstein points out, there are and have been great female Orthodox Jewish teachers and scholars (2000: 34). In addition, one Orthodox feminist describes being a *madricha ruchanit* "religious mentor" doing much of the work of a rabbi but not being ordained. She says that, in terms of *halakhah*, women can perform all but five percent of "rabbinic functions" (Hurwitz 2009: 145). Though pressure for the ordination of women in Conservative Judaism began in the early 1970s, there were no female Conservative rabbis until the early 1980s (Schwartz 2007). By the early 1980s, there were fourteen female Reconstructionist rabbis, almost twenty percent of all rabbis ordained since the establishment of the Reconstructionist Rabbinical College in 1968 (Moore and Bush 2007). The first female American Reform rabbi was not ordained until 1972; today there are considerably more (Goldman 2007).

Rabbi Isaac Mayer Wise, the founder of Hebrew Union College, a Reform seminary in Cincinnati, encouraged women to study at the school. In 1921 the College's faculty voted to allow women to study for ordination as rabbis, but the Board did not approve. It was not until 1956 that the Board agreed to ordain any women who managed to achieve the requirements. Nonetheless, it was not until 1972 that the Hebrew Union College ordained its first female Reform rabbi, Sally Preisand (Carmody 1989: 152; Preisand 1975).

Recently, Reform Judaism has begun certifying women to perform circumcision ceremonies. There are at present twenty-four women in North America who can function as *mohelet*, feminine of *mohel*, ritual circumciser; two of them are in Canada. Orthodox Judaism does not accept that Reform *mohel*s, even when male, are properly qualified (*The Toronto Star* 1998, August 1: L10).

CONTEMPORARY MOVEMENTS

As in other religious traditions, especially in the West, Judaism has its share of seekers for an authentic Jewish spirituality. They are trying various techniques of meditation, investigating Jewish mysticism, attending small prayer groups, and joining renewal movements. For "the vast majority," their search does not take them into synagogues.

In the United States, responding to this situation, some rabbis are taking meditation workshops, and one Conservative rabbi in New York City has been testing out meditation and "wordless humming" in his daily services. In addition, he holds meditation services for an hour before morning service on the Sabbath. Rabbis are also taking part in conferences on how to make "the synagogue a spiritual place."

Recently, the United Jewish Appeal's Santa Monica conference on "prayer and spirituality" drew more than five hundred people under the age of forty five. A Berkeley conference on Jewish meditation attracted over 550 participants. Originally a network of prayer groups, ALEPH: Alliance for Jewish Renewal is expanding rapidly and has 37 affiliated communities in North America, as well as several abroad. To date over 100 rabbis have completed the ALEPH: Rabbinical Program. The Association of Rabbis for Jewish Renewal, founded by Rabbi Zalman Schachter and others, held in 2004 a conference on exploring the "feminine divine." Jewish Renewal emphasises spirituality and "experiential relationship with the divine." It combines tradition and innovation, and it welcomes women with "its feminist prayer language" (Weissler 2007: 51-81; Kamenetz 1997).

JEWISH FEMINISM AND FEMINIST THEOLOGY

In the introduction to her important book, *Standing Again at Sinai* (1997), Judith Plaskow observed that, in the last twenty years, "non-Orthodox" Judaism had changed. It had eliminated most of the religious and civil disadvantages for women. However, she noted that Judaism had not as a result become feminist. Instead, women had become "participants in, teachers, and preservers of a male religion." What Plaskow wanted, and still wants and works for, is that, through a total alteration of the religion, the tradition should take women's experience into account. It would then be a "post-patriarchal Judaism" (1990: xiv-xv; Millen 2007: 28).

Since the early 1970s, Plaskow has been one of the leading Jewish feminists and feminist theologians in the United States of America. She was among the scholars who, in 1974, published articles in Rosemary Reuther's edited book *Religion and Sexism*; at the time she was a doctoral candidate at Yale University and research associate at Harvard Divinity School, just beginning her academic career. So, at the beginning of the 1990s, after twenty years of working to change Judaism, she could see little of the change she had hoped for. Nonetheless, the movement's achievements by then and afterwards are many and significant (Heschel 2003: 148; Reuther 1974: 12, 341-343). A conference in May 2004 on "The Changing Role of Women in American Jewish Life" produced one of the first assessments of these achievements (Prell 2007: ix).

Over the past four decades, Jewish feminists and feminist theologians have been asking what Judaism would be like if it allowed not only the full involvement of women, but also recognized their experiences and point of view (Plaskow 2005: 66). Thus they have developed "a feminist vision" of a religion in which women and men are equal as actors. Consequently, they have been and are challenging "the assumptions" underlying Judaism, that is, "traditional authority" (Prell 2007: 5, 11). In the process, they have focused on, among other things, the fight for the right of women to take part in public ritual and to fill leadership roles (ordination)(Nadell 1998), the analysis of sacred and legal texts (Levine 2001), and broad issues of the relationship of feminist theory and Judaism (Plaskow 2005: 65-80).

Today, in the non-Orthodox streams of Judaism, there are a number of women rabbis, even in Conservative Judaism (Blohm 2005; Keller and Reuther 2006; Nadell 1998; King 1989: 1989: 43). Nonetheless, a Conservative survey of the impact of female leadership carried out in 2004 showed that problems still existed: among other things, there were no women leaders in the largest Conservative synagogues and, in general, the salaries of women rabbis were lower than those of men (Goldman 2007: 128, 130).

In Conservative, Reform, and Reconstructionist Judaism, women can read from Torah in public; and, even in Conservative Judaism, they can form part of the *minyan*, the formerly all-male prayer quorum of ten adults (Prell 2007; Elwell 1996; King 1989: 43).

Alice Shalvi comments that all this Jewish feminist activity was influenced by parallel work in other traditions: Judith Plaskow's *Standing Again at Sinai* was, she maintains, made possible by Mary Daly (1983: 232). While Susannah Heschel does not put it quite so strongly, she does agree that Daly's exposure and analysis of the sexism in Christianity did help to shape Jewish feminism (Heschel 1983: xxi).

In 1994, Plaskow, writing about Jewish feminist theology, first explored the issue of whether there is such a thing as Jewish theology and concluded that, if she defined theology broadly, she could describe the Jews as "closet theologians." What these closet theologians have reflected on is not the nature of God, but "the experiences and categories of a particular religious tradition" and the world from the point of view of the tradition. Jewish feminist theology also deals with the tradition, but from the viewpoint of women's experiences, the "substance" of their daily lives, their reality, which is by no means uniform. Jewish feminist theology starts with a critique of the sexism in Judaism and presents a vision of what it would mean for the religion if women were full participants in Jewish life. It asks what sort of a religion Judaism would be if it incorporated the experiences and viewpoints of women (1994: 64-65, 81; 1990: 11-12).

The positions of Jewish feminist theologians fit, roughly, into the categories Revisionist, Renovationist, and Revolutionary, though the stances they take in their work often overlap categories.

Revisionist Views

The earliest Jewish feminist work was, understandably, Revisionist; a good deal of it concentrated on recovering lost women and their contributions (Plaskow 2005: 66; Henry and Taitz 1990). Many Jewish feminist historians have been doing such recovery work, for example, Ellen Umansky and Diana Ashton (1992) and, to some extent, Tikva Frymer-Kensky (1992), who had as one of her concerns to show that Israel developed male dominance in an already male-dominated Eastern Mediterranean context. Other studies have explored women's roles in the early synagogue (Brooten 1982), Jewish women's history from 600 BCE to 1900 CE (Taitz, Henry, and Tallan 2003), women in rabbinic literature (Baskin 2002), and women in the history of American Judaism (Nadell and Sarna 2001).

Orthodox Jewish feminist Judith Antonelli, whose writing also takes a Revisionist position, has concluded that Torah is not basically sexist, but that sexism in Judaism comes from society (1995: xxviii). In addition, the ideas of many of the thousand or so women who attended the First International Conference on Orthodoxy and Feminism in New York in February 1997 also belonged in the Revisionist category. Well-known Orthodox feminist theologian and founder of the Jewish Orthodox Feminist Alliance (1997) Blu Greenberg was present and gave a talk (Joseph 2007: 199). According to reporter Debra Cohen, the women at the conference described themselves as "modern or centrist Orthodox." The conference discussed such issues as ways of effecting changes in *halakhah*; the problem of the *agunot*, women whose husbands refuse to give them a *get*, a religious divorce that only men can grant; and the ordination of women as rabbis. The conference heard that some Orthodox women were already performing all rabbinic roles except those in public ritual; it learned that a group of modern Orthodox rabbis had formed a new religious court to deal with the *agunot* problem and that it has already managed to finds ways *inside Jewish law* to annul the marriages of six women. Most important, one speaker after another insisted that rabbis could interpret *halakhah* in ways that would let Orthodox women take a more active part in their own religious lives (Cohen 1997; Greenberg 1981). The Jewish Orthodox Feminist Alliance was founded in 1997 (Hartman 2007: xi).

Over the past twenty years, Orthodox women have been gradually expanding their areas of religious expression, for instance, celebrating revived women's rites like Rosh Hodesh, a monthly new-moon gathering (Feldman 2003). They are also meeting in women's prayer groups, which many rabbis have seen as "subversive." According to Norma Joseph, these prayer groups, about sixty of which are now in existence around the world, are "the cutting edge of the Jewish women's movement within Orthodoxy" (2007: 193, 196, 201). Often they celebrate a *bat mitzvah*, a coming-of-age ceremony for a girl, parallel to a boy's *bar mitzvah*. Some groups even call it a *bat mitzvot*, the plural *mitzvot* signifying the girl's right to observe all duties of an adult Jew, not just those called women's *mitzvot*. Many Orthodox synagogues also depart from long-standing tradition by encouraging women to touch the Torah scroll: after the men have read from the Torah scroll in public, they pass it behind the screen separating the women from the men for the women to touch (Ross 2004; Cohen 1997; Umansky 1995: xii; Adelman 1994: 155).

Most Orthodox feminists, such as most of those at the 1997 conference in New York and feminist theologian Tamar Frankiel, intend to observe fully "the bounds of generally accepted halacha [sic]" (Frankiel 1990: xiii, xi; Joseph 2007: 183). From that position, they want to reveal the liberating core of the tradition and the power and influence women have in their families and their communities. Thus, their stance is clearly Revisionist. In the 1990s, Orthodox Judaism had considerable difficulty with a small, but vocal feminist group that wanted more drastic change. Members of this group argued that women should be able to study the Talmud, wanted women to form their own *minyan*, and asked women to "observe *mitzvot* that have been traditionally left to men." Nevertheless, these women insisted on remaining Orthodox Jews, though they were "a serious threat to the status quo." Needless to say, other Orthodox Jews have been "severely" critical of them (Myers and Litman 1995: 69). Despite their insistence on remaining Orthodox, we should perhaps class their demands as Renovationist.

In 2007 the Jewish feminist journal *Nashim* published a thorough and enlightening exchange between Orthodox feminist theologian Tamar Ross and Judith Plaskow. In an up-to-date discussion, the two women examined most of the main gender issues (Ross and Plaskow 2007).

Feminist theologians working inside Conservative Judaism, also take, for the most part, Revisionist stances (Schwartz 2007: 153-179). Judith Plaskow argues that the opportunities, educational and otherwise, now available to women in the Conservative tradition lead only to contradictions. She cites as an example the *bat mitzvah*, which represents a girl's *final* participation in the congregation, not the beginning, as the parallel ritual is for a boy (1990: ix). However, under feminist pressure, there have been improvements for women even in this stream of Judaism.

Starting in 1972, the Conservative Jewish Women's Group began requesting changes that would eventually lead to women's full involvement in education for the rabbinate. Women were finally admitted to Conservative Judaism's Jewish Theological Seminary in 1983. However, the Seminary accepted women provided that they voluntarily undertook to fulfil all the obligations. Some female rabbinical students report that they have problems with this logic. They argue that it implies that women as women are not acceptable, that they have to become quasi-males. As one woman student said, a woman has to "overcome her fixed female nature" in order to be equal to a man (Schulman 1996: 315-316). From May 1985 to May 1993, the Jewish Theological Seminary ordained fifty-two female rabbis. Most of the women who were interviewed at the time of their ordination were by no means radical; they explained that, in becoming rabbis, they were seeking "personal authenticity and equality of obligation and authority within the system" (Schulman 1996: 327-328). Usually women do not occupy leadership positions in the largest Conservative synagogues, and as a rule they receive lower pay than men (Goldman 2007: 128). Most Conservative Jewish feminist theology is also Revisionist.

Conservative Judaism in Toronto, with the biggest Jewish population in Canada, is less liberal than its counterparts in the United States. Almost all Conservative congregations in Toronto bar women from reading the Torah aloud at services, except during their *Bat Mitzvah*s, nor do they permit women to approach the Torah "to present blessings." In addition, in 1997 Toronto still had no Conservative female rabbis (Goldberg 1997: 23).

Renovationist Views

The work of many feminists and feminist theologians who consider themselves to be Reform Jews is essentially Renovationist, though, occasionally, the ideas of a few of them push the tradition to its limits and hover over the boundary between Renovationist and Revolutionary. For feminists in the Reconstructionist stream of Judaism, in principle, pushing the tradition to its limits should have been easy. The stream is egalitarian and sees the deity as gender neutral (Alpert and Milgram 1996: 292; Moore and Bush 2007). In fact, feminist endeavours inside Reconstructionist Judaism, though quite successful, seem to have been more Renovationist than Revolutionary.

Jewish feminist theologians taking the Renovationist position have been particularly successful in pushing the Reform branch of Judaism to ordain women as rabbis. Reform Judaism was the first to ordain women as rabbis (Preisand 1975). By 1982, there were sixty-one female Reform rabbis and by 1986 a total of 131 (King 1989: 43). Feminist pressure was paying off. By 1991, ten percent of all Reform rabbis were women, and forty to fifty percent of all applicants to the rabbinic programme at Hebrew Union College were female. Recent graduating classes at the College have been close to fifty percent female (Goldman 2007: 128; Marder 1996: 287).

In recent times, Reconstructionist women have also been very successful in attaining leadership roles. By the early 1980s, there were fourteen female Reconstructionist rabbis, almost twenty percent of all rabbis ordained since the establishment of the Reconstructionist Rabbinical College in 1968; in 1983 the College ordained forty-seven students, of whom twenty-three were women (Carmody 1989: 152-153).

Feminist theologians whose work is in the Renovationist category have been quick to attack the sexism in Judaism, in Torah and especially in *halakhah*. Judith Plaskow, who was raised in the "classical Reform" tradition (1990: vii), says that Jewish feminist aims have to involve rethinking the basis of Jewish life and that this entails developing a new interpretation of the Torah, because it is profoundly unjust (1983: 230; 1990: viii). Of course, *halakhah* is not binding for Reform Jews.

In any case, according to Plaskow, although *halakhah* has been the focus of feminist pressure for religious change and some feminists want to raise the status of women through it, to date feminists have challenged only specific laws, and not the basic assumptions of rabbinic law. Plaskow sees revolution in the legal system as possible, because the halakhic system stemmed from "revolutionary changes" that resulted from the destruction of the Second Temple. She is referring to the development of a new spiritual community to replace the Temple and its rituals, the synagogue with its rabbi, and to the rabbinic tradition which gave the Jews *halakhah* (Plaskow 1983: 224; 1990: 73).

Jewish feminist theologians commit themselves to a Renovationist position when they challenge the Jewish tradition's male-centred language and its imagery of God as male (Spiegel 1996: 126-127). Reconstructionist women rabbis, in particular, have also paid careful attention to the development of inclusive language and non-sexist names for God (Alpert and Milgram 1996: 309).

In an article published in 1979, feminist theologian and scholar Rita Gross pointed to the need for re-uniting the masculine and feminine sides of God and for the use of female language to refer to God. However, she considered female imagery to be more important than female language (1979: 167-168). It should come as no surprise that, in 1995, Rita Gross outlined steps toward developing in Judaism an imagery of God that was feminine: the use of female language, especially pronouns, "in *all* the familiar contexts," and the collection of female images of God from two main sources, inside the Jewish tradition and outside it. She argued the need for "Goddess," because She "completes" and makes whole the image of God. By advocating the addition of Goddess to Judaism, Gross seemed to be pushing the tradition beyond its limits, and her argument indicated that her ideas were becoming at least Revolutionary, if not Rejectionist. A year later she declared herself to have become "personally involved" in one of the important non-Western traditions (Gross 1996: 3; Gross 1983: 246; Lit(wo)man 1988; Starhawk 1987a).

Judith Plaskow also deals with language and imagery about God. She argues that, for women to be truly included in the Jewish community, there has to be a drastic change in Judaism's "religious language" in order to recognise the feminine side of God. Further, she insists that the tradition must accept Goddess as an element in God, thus, perhaps, demonstrating the Revolutionary tendencies in her work, but it does not yet go beyond the limits of the tradition. Plaskow is probably referring to the Kabbalistic concept of *Shekhinah*, which other feminists have also found both useful and empowering (1983: 229-230; see also Gottlieb 1995: Chaps. 3, 4, 5).

Jewish feminist theologians have also been examining liturgy from a Renovationist point of view. In particular, they have directed their attention at the *Haggadah*, the liturgy used at Passover, as well as various prayers and blessing formulae. They have revised *Haggadah* texts and also constructed various feminist and women's *Haggadah*s: they have added references to women from the Bible, legends, and history, and they often expanded the *Haggadah*'s focus on the oppression and liberation of the Israelites and the Jews to include women's oppression and their need for freedom (Elwell 1996: 333-334, 338-339; Cantor 1979; Goldman 2007: 124-127). They have changed the language in Sabbath prayers to make it inclusive of the female; and they have altered old and composed new blessing formulae and prayers (Klirs 1992; Janowitz and Wenig 1979: 174-178). Particularly notable in this regard is Marcia Falk, whose collection of feminist prayers and blessings is a rich resource (1996); many of her prayers are now part of ritual in liberal synagogues. In addition, some liberal synagogues make ritual use of music and liturgy by Debbie Freedman (2000).

Jewish feminist theologians have adopted a Renovationist view in attempting to recover old and develop new rituals for women (Orenstein 1994; Orenstein and Litman 1994; Spiegel 1996: 128ff.). They have created rituals to mark the passages in female life-cycle, for example, menarche and menopause (Adelman 1990; Fine 1988), and other important events, for instance, miscarriage, divorce, and rape. Judith Plaskow (1979) devised a ritual for the welcoming of a baby daughter into the Jewish community. Reconstructionist women rabbis have been especially involved in "the creation of rituals, stories, music, and theologies that have begun to give women's experience a voice in Judaism" (Alpert and Milgram 1996: 303).

In an article on ways to produce a feminist "people of Israel," first published in 1991, Judith Plaskow examines the implications of God's having chosen the Jews as His special people. She discusses "the communal nature of personhood" and insists that, when the Jewish community includes women as full persons, the very nature of that community will change drastically (Plaskow 1997).

Canadian Jewish feminist theologians, whose work generally fits into the Revisionist or Renovationist categories, have also been busy discussing the sexism in Judaism and working for change in their traditions. S. Medjuck's (1993) overview article discusses Jewish feminism in Canada. In addition, a memoir of a pioneer Jewish feminist activist, Minerva Davis, was published in Toronto in 1992. Another Canadian work, *Half the Kingdom*, edited by Francine Zuckerman, prints interviews with seven prominent Jewish feminists and feminist theologians, who were featured in the film of the same name by the National Film Board of Canada (1992). Among the seven women whose stories and reflections the film and book record are three Canadian lay women and a female rabbi: Norma Baumel Joseph, scholar, teacher, and feminist theologian from Montreal (2007); Michele Landsberg, a journalist from Toronto; Naomi Goldenberg, religious-studies professor and feminist theologian from Ottawa (2007, 1979); and Rabbi Elyse Goldstein, Director of Kolel, an Canadian egalitarian adult learning centre in Toronto, who every month greets menstruation with a blessing: "Blessed art Thou, Lord our God, Ruler of the Universe, who *has* made me a woman" (2009, 1990). The others interviewed are: Shulamit Aloni, one of the few women members of the Israeli parliament; Esther Broner, feminist theologian and writer from New York; and Alice Shalvi (1995), an Israeli academic and feminist activist.

Canadian feminist theologians have also been active in developing new Jewish rituals (Brin and Sharkey 1992). An account of how a group of women created a ritual appeared in the "Jewish Women" issue of the Canadian journal *Fireweed* in the Spring of 1992; one author is a rabbi. In 1996, a new women-led synagogue, *Shir Libeynu* "Song of Our Hearts," gathered in Toronto in September to celebrate the High Holy Days. One of the ritual leaders, Aviva Goldberg, informed me that it is an unaffiliated synagogue, an egalitarian, liberal congregation, which, after the success of September 1996, now meets once a month. The facilitators plan and hold High Holy Days services yearly (personal communication, May 19, 1997).

In 1996 *Canadian Woman Studies/Les cahiers de la femme* published an issue called "Jewish Women in Canada." It contains articles organised under the headings: "Speaking: Our/Selves," "Shechinah: Female Spirit," "Shifshvester: Sister Voyager," and "Recalling: Past

Lives." In addition, the 1997 issue of *Canadian Woman Studies* on "Female Spirituality" offered a few articles on Jewish topics.

Where should we place the Jewish Renewal Movement in our list of feminist theological views? Its vision "began over thirty years ago" (Goldberg 2002: 13), and it has developed and changed over time. Still the Movement still seems in some ways Renovationist, but some practices are clearly Revolutionary. Indeed, several writings appear quite Rejectionist, "albeit the authors tenuously hold to a Jewish ethos" (Goldberg 2002: 24). Liberal Jewish women find in the Movement a place to express their "spiritual understandings" in a context that welcomes feminist ideas (Goldberg 2002: iv). With its views on the Shekhinah, it is even open to ideas about goddesses (Weissler 2007: 58).

Revolutionary Views

Very few Jewish feminist theologians take fully Revolutionary stances in their work, though some do occasionally entertain Revolutionary ideas, that is, ideas that test the limits of the tradition. For instance, her argument that Judaism needs a goddess put Rita Gross's thinking on this matter in the Revolutionary category (1995). Further, with the drastic changes that she envisions, Judith Plaskow may also be approaching the Revolutionary position in some of her writing (2005, 1997, 1990). During the First International Jewish Feminist Conference in Israel in 1988, seventy or so women from several divisions of Judaism did a revolutionary act. They carried a Torah to the sacred West Wall ("Wailing Wall") of the destroyed Temple in Jerusalem in order to have "a halakhic women's prayer service" (Chesler and Haut 2003: xix). They were subjected to jeers and threats, but they completed the ritual. Despite the defiance of the act, it is unlikely that any of them would think of herself as revolutionary (Joseph 2007: 198-199; Zuckerman 1992). Although her spiritual history suggests that she has long held such views, Jewish feminist theologian Lynn Gottlieb did move her thinking into the Revolutionary category in her 1995 book. In what was clearly a radical decision, Lynn Gottlieb declared her intention of becoming a rabbi and began her studies in 1972 at Hebrew Union College, a Reform seminary. She soon withdrew, but continued learning with rabbis and scholars whom she persuaded to work with her. In 1973 she became leader of a synagogue for the deaf in New York City and directed a popular performance group which played all over the U.S. to enthusiastic audiences. By 1977, she was "something of a national Jewish phenomenon" (Umansky 1995: ix-xv).

In 1980, two male rabbis privately ordained Lynn Gottlieb, conferring on her the title of rabbi. The fact that Gottlieb did not receive public ordination as a result of years of seminary study harks back to the origin of the position of rabbi in the early synagogue. Then a rabbi was a teacher and leader of a synagogue as a result of his recognised authority as someone able both to receive and pass on the Law (Umansky 1995: xv). Lynn Gottlieb decided *not* to fight, as did many other Jewish feminists, for women's access to leadership roles or changes to rabbinic law, but rather, convinced that such changes would not help women gain equality within Judaism, she focused on the complete and radical change of the Jewish tradition (Umansky 1995: xiii).

In her book, *She Who Dwells Within*, Gottlieb centers her argument on the female "Presence of God," the Shekhinah (1995: 20). She borrows from other spiritual traditions, for example, Native American or ancient eastern Mediterranean ones; she revives and recasts parts of the Jewish tradition; and she taps her own vision for new material to use in rituals and prayers. What Gottlieb envisions would entail the "thoroughgoing transformation" that Judith Plaskow has spoken of. Gottlieb's work suggests that such a vision is a Revolutionary one (Gottlieb 1995; Plaskow 1990: xiv-xv).

Another Revolutionary is Jenny Kien, whose aim seems to be to uncover the goddesses "buried within Judaism" and to create "a practice" that will satisfy both men and women, yet to stay "within a Jewish context" (2000: iii). Her book discusses the history of the development of Judaism; explores the "Jewish goddess," particularly Asherah; examines why she disappeared from Judaism; and concludes with a chapter on "Reinstating the Divine Woman" (197-229).

MULTICULTURALISM AND DIFFERENCE

Almost all of the Jewish feminist theologians we have been discussing are Ashkenazic (Bowker 1997: 98-99). Ashkenazic women

"The Acacia Tree: Shekhinah of the Burning Bush"
Painting © 1999 by Sandra M. Stanton <www.goddessmyths.com>
for The Green World Oracle by Kathleen Jenks, Ph.D. Used with permission.

have been the subjects of most of the research, as well as being the researchers. However, the voices and theological thinking of Sephardic women (Bowker 1997: 875) and women of other origins are by no means absent from the record, but it is hard to find their work in North America. In the 1990s, articles by Sarah Taieb-Carlen (1997, 1996), Sandra Haar (1996), and Judith Cohen (1996); an anthology of Sephardic-American writings (Matza 1997); and special issues of *Canadian Woman Studies* ("Jewish Women in

Canada" 1996) and the Jewish feminist journal *Bridges* (Crespin and Jacobs 1997-1998) have partly remedied that situation.

Sephardic women point out that the placing of Ashkenazim in the centre of "a Jewish universe in which Sephardim are distantly orbiting planets" distorts and limits perceptions of Jewish identity; they add that the range of Jewish women's experience is amazing (Crespin and Jacobs 1997-98: 5). Recently Jewish feminists have joined other feminists in exploring multiculturalism and difference "without and within" (Brettscheider and Rose 2004; Plaskow 2003: 91), and the *Journal of Feminist Studies in Religion* devoted one of its 2003 issues to the topics; it featured articles by six Jewish feminist theologians (Brettschneider and Rose, Plaskow, Falk, Cohler-Esses, and Levine).

LESBIAN VOICES

Among the Jewish feminists who often take a Revolutionary feminist theological stance are a number of lesbians; they often have difficulty finding acceptance even in the liberal streams of Judaism (Eron 1993: 103-134; Alpert and Milgram 1996: 308). Increasingly, Jewish lesbians are creating their own rituals and supporting or even founding independent synagogues where they can openly worship as lesbians (Eron 1993: 126). For instance, in Toronto there is a Gay and lesbian synagogue which has about seventy members (Aviva Goldberg, personal communication, 14 May 1997). In 1997, Rebecca Alpert published a book on how these developments are transforming Judaism.

Although Judaism and *halakhah* view lesbian relationships as prohibited, the Hebrew Bible contains no explicit ban on same-sex relations between women (Riccetti 2005: 262). Further, the rabbis of the Talmud thought female homosexuality to be "a lesser sin" than male homosexuality; nonetheless rabbinic sources do not consider lesbian sexual behaviour as permissible (Bowker 1997: 440; Goldberg 1997: 36-37).

Thus, as we might expect, Orthodox Judaism today condemns homosexuality "as both disgusting and a sickness" (Goldberg 1997: 36-40). In 1993, an anonymous article discussed being both an Orthodox Jew and a lesbian.

On the other hand, Reform Judaism in the United States decided in 1996 that, while it objected to efforts by the government to ban homosexual marriages in civil law, it still did not approve of a rabbi officiating at them. Further, openly homosexual persons cannot gain admission to Reform seminaries. In 1992 the Conservative branch of Judaism had come to the same conclusions on both the matter of homosexual marriages and admission to seminaries. However, in 1995 a Conservative committee recommended that synagogues support civil protection for the rights of homosexuals and welcome them into their congregations (Goldberg 1997: 37-38).

As to the Reconstructionist branch of Judaism, it admits openly homosexual persons to its seminaries, and it encourages member synagogues to welcome homosexuals into their community and ritual life. Further, Rebecca Alpert mentions six openly lesbian Reconstructionist rabbis who assisted her when she was writing her recent work. There are also Reconstructionist rabbis in the U.S. who will perform commitment or marriage rites for persons of the same sex (Alpert 1997; Goldberg 1997: 38).

The Jewish lesbian publication, *Nice Jewish Girls*, contains essays, poetry, and stories about women's identity (Beck 1982). Also noteworthy is *Twice Blessed*, which contains a number of articles by Jewish lesbians (Balka and Rose 1989). Israeli lesbians are represented in *Lesbiot*, a collection of writings and interviews (Moore 1995). Two recent articles, one in *Jewish Quarterly*, the other in the Jewish feminist journal *Bridges*, discuss Jewish lesbians (Sarah 1993; Rogow 1990).

Many Jewish lesbians are developing rituals for themselves, especially "coming-out" rituals, in which they identify themselves publicly as lesbians. However, most synagogues do not permit lesbian coming-out ceremonies to be part of their services (Goldberg 1997: 55). There are available an increasing number of books on Jewish lesbian rituals, noteworthy among them being a collection of ceremonies for celebrating lesbian unions (Butler 1990) and a lesbian *Haggadah* (Stein 1984). In addition, a special issue of the American lesbian journal *Sinister Wisdom* was dedicated to discussing religion ("Lesbians and Religion" 1994-1995).

In the last decade or so, Jewish feminist theologians have increasingly considered and written about transgendered and bisexual women, and some Jewish lesbians have started to refer to themselves as "Queer," a postmodern description first employed by scholars (Schneer and Aviv 2002; Butler 2001: 629-647).

DISCUSSION

In early Israelite religion spiritual life seems to have been family centred. Households would have had their own shrines, and it is likely that women would have had central roles in domestic worship. Some women, it seems clear, also fulfilled public roles. After 1000 BCE, with the development of the Monarchy, religion became institutionalised, and any public religious roles for women disappeared. Archaeology shows that domestic worship was still important to women, though men probably valued it much less than they did official religion. This change in focus is very like what happened in early Christianity with the shift from "house church" to public basilica, which I discuss below (Meyers 1988: 159, 160).

During the Babylonian Exile and later in the early Diaspora, a similar situation probably existed. What eventually became the synagogue might have begun as small community groups meeting, perhaps in peoples' houses, though there is considerable evidence that, away from the Jerusalem Temple, temples also existed, some even in the Babylonian exile (Runesson 2001: 403, 427). However, we do know that, in the early synagogues, women often took leadership roles. The discrepancy concerning women's roles between the actual inscriptions of the early Diaspora period and the rabbinical texts might be the result of the latter's reflecting the practice of a few communities or, equally, the rabbinical texts may enshrine rabbinical wish-fulfilment. It is certainly entirely possible that the rabbinical stance on women might have issued from an unrelenting conviction of male superiority. On the other hand, the rabbinical texts might also have resulted from their authors' perception of what the people of the Diaspora needed to survive as a separate religion (Kraemer 1993: 93; Torjesen 1993: 14; Brooten 1982: 27-55).

It seems possible that the rabbis legislated a sexual division of labour aimed at having women's domestic and income-generating work sustain men's Torah study and sacrificed women's spiritual and educational needs to what they saw as the survival of the religion and the people. Certainly, throughout the Middle Ages and the early modern period, most Jewish women focused their lives on family, and most Jewish men focused theirs on synagogue (Carmody 1989: 145-146). Many Jewish women did support their husband and children economically, men did study and pass on the Torah and many of the Jewish traditions, and Judaism did survive persecution, forcible uprooting, and economic hardship.

Though there is some evidence for there having been female ecstatics in the early synagogue, there is no evidence that ecstatic experience led to leadership roles for Jewish women at the time, as it often did for Christian women (Kraemer 1993: 109, 123). In addition, it is very difficult to tell from the much later Kabbalistic writings whether there were Jewish female mystics and ecstatics or what, if any, their roles might have been. Further, there is little evidence that mysticism interfered with marriage, as in Christianity, or that the tradition gave anyone an alternative to marriage. A persecuted minority needing to ensure the survival of its culture and religion could not tolerate, let alone encourage asceticism and celibacy. Thus, for Jewish women of the Diaspora there were few, if any, alternatives to marriage, especially since the rabbis made family central to the Jewish life. For Jewish women, the family has always been the focus of spirituality and ritual, and, until very recently, women must also have expressed their personal spirituality in the company of other women. The monthly visit to the ritual bath (*mikveh*), for instance, is an all-female experience of "cleansing and renewal" for many Jewish women (Harris 1985: 147-148). Today, a growing number of Jewish women are getting together in prayer groups that meet in homes and occasionally have the support of the synagogue. Other are exploring the Jewish mystical tradition (the Kabbalah) and participating in the Jewish renewal movement (Kamenetz 1997). Jewish women are seeking new ways to develop their spirituality inside a religious tradition that is intimately linked to their sense of identity.

Secular feminists have recommended to spiritual feminists struggling with the sexism of their traditions that they leave their religious tradition either for a secular life or a non-sexist religion. While such a decision may be possible for Christian feminists, it appears to be almost impossible for Jewish feminists. In *Standing Again at Sinai*, Judith Plaskow discusses the dilemma that entertaining the thought of choosing between Judaism and feminism caused for her. She says that, "sundering Judaism and feminism would mean sundering [her] being." That is why many Jewish feminists echo Plaskow when she states that Judaism must change if it is to allow women to develop whole identities (1990: x, xi).

Jewish feminist theologians have already had an enormous influence on their traditions. Even Orthodox Judaism is now responding to pressures from feminist theologians inside the tradition, particularly with respect to Jewish law, and Orthodox women who do not wish to leave Orthodoxy are now increasingly able to articulate, in feminist terms, their reasons for staying (Ross 2004; Frankiel 1990; Greenberg 1981). Further, Reform, Conservative, and Reconstructionist feminist theologians continue to work on making their traditions more hospitable to women. One scholar says of the Jewish feminist movement, which includes feminist theologians, that it "rides a fine line between maintaining the meaningful components of tradition" and simultaneously striving "to transform the more oppressive elements of that tradition" (Rudavsky 1995: xiv).

The question still remains, however: Will Jewish feminist theologians be able to change their traditions enough to satisfy Judith Plaskow and other Jewish women? If they do, will the altered traditions still be Judaism?

Notes

[1]The three are often called the Abrahamic religions because they all trace their origin back to the Biblical patriarch Abraham.

[2]See my article in *Matrifocus* archives, vol. 4-4, Lammas 2005 <www.matrifocus.com>.

Jean Hey, "The Annunciation," Oil on panel, 72 x 50.2 cm, 1490/1495.
The Art Institute of Chicago, Mr and Mrs Martin A. Ryerson Collection.

4.
CHRISTIANITY, FEMINISM AND FEMINIST THEOLOGY

CHRISTIANITY IS CHRONOLOGICALLY the second of the monotheistic religions that we discuss in this book. It began in the Roman province of Judea in the first decades of our era with the mission and death by crucifixion of a Galilean Jew, Joshua ben Joseph, "Jesus son of Joseph." Christians consider Jesus to have been the long-awaited Messiah of the Jews; "Messiah" means "the Anointed One," *Christos* in Greek. However, Jews object to Jesus's being so designated since Jesus did not fulfil very many of "the biblical signs of the Messiah" (Bowker 1997: 637).

Christianity also sees itself as originating in the Covenants that God made with the people of Israel. For Christians, their God and the Jewish deity are the same, but, since Christians hold that Jesus was the Son of God and therefore divine Himself, they understand the nature of God to be a Trinity, God in three persons, the Father, the Son, and the Holy Spirit (Bowker 1997: 216, 990).

In North America, Christian feminists were the earliest to publish examinations of their tradition from the point of view of women. Galvanised by their increasing awareness of the male dominance of Christianity and their annoyance at its unwillingness to ordain women, Christian feminist theologians began critically to examine aspects of their tradition and to argue for sweeping changes. In particular, they undertook to investigate the history of their religion.

BACKGROUND

In the first century CE, after the crucifixion of Jesus of Nazareth in about 30 CE, Christianity began as a Jewish renewal movement. Christians believed that Jesus was the Messiah, a prophet and king anointed by God. The group that gathered around Jesus when he was alive and teaching in Palestine is often called "the Jesus Movement" to distinguish it from early Christianity, which developed after his death (Chadwick, H. 1993: 22-23; Kraemer 1993: 129, 138; Torjesen 1993: 11; Fiorenza 1992: 72).

The sources for Jesus's life and utterances are almost all later Christian ones, with one or two exceptions. Contrary the claims of Christian writers of the second century CE, there are no surviving Roman records of the trial of Jesus. Therefore, "the quest for the historical Jesus" has been a scholarly and sometimes not-so-scholarly endeavour fraught with difficulties which, nevertheless, have not deterred searchers. Although archaeology has been quite successful in uncovering and explaining sites that had connections to the New Testament stories of Jesus and His Apostles, so far it can add nothing concrete to the problem of "the historical Jesus" (Bowker 1997: 496-499; Smith 1993; McRay 1991; Pritchard 1991: 114-117, 124-127; Kee 1970).

The New Testament Story

According to the Christian scriptures, the New Testament, during His lifetime Jesus attracted a group of followers, called "disciples." Twelve of the men among them became the first "apostles," that is, missionaries (Mark 14-15). As the New Testament makes clear, the disciples included women, among them Mary Magdalene, who was also the first apostle (Mark 15: 41; Haskins 1993: 3-4, 5). The evening before His arrest, Jesus ate the Passover meal, the "Last Supper," with "the twelve disciples," all of whom were male. At the meal He blessed bread and wine and, giving them to the disciples to eat, He told them that the bread and wine were His body and blood (Matthew 26: 26-28).

On what is now called Good Friday, Jesus died the death of a Roman criminal—crucified on the Cross (Luke 23). During His agony, Jesus's women disciples, among them Mary Magdalene, waited within sight of the Cross, even after the male disciples had forsaken their master (Mark 15: 40, John 19: 25). Three days later, Jesus rose from the dead and showed Himself first to two female disciples, one of whom was Mary Magdalene (Matthew 28:

Alexander Ivanov, "The Appearance of Christ to Mary Magdalene," oil on canvas, 1834-1836. Russian Museum, St. Petersburg, Russia.

9-10; Mark 16; Kraemer 1993: 129-130). Later, He appeared to all the disciples and instructed them to include the non-Jewish in their missionary activities (Matthew 28: 18-20). Forty days after his Resurrection, His return to life, Jesus ascended into Heaven (Acts 1: 9-11).

We read in the Acts of the Apostles that, ten days after Jesus's Ascension, the Holy Spirit descended on the apostles (Acts 2). The event occurred at Pentecost, from Greek *pentecostos* "fifty," exactly fifty days after Jesus's Resurrection. On the day of Pentecost, as a result of the Apostle Peter's preaching, three thousand people received baptism, and then the first Christian community at Jerusalem was formed. Thus, the Christian Church began with ecstatic experiences, the early missionaries understanding themselves as prophets. Leadership based in ecstatic experience was usual in early Christianity (Fiorenza 1992: 198; Ware 1997: 12).

THE CHRISTIAN SCRIPTURES

Soon after the crucifixion of Jesus, oral material in Greek about

Jesus and his life began to accumulate. It consisted of the recollections of some of his disciples about his birth, life, miracles, death, and resurrection, as well as disciples' accounts of his teachings. Eventually, around the middle of the first century of our era, this material was written down in Greek and now constitutes the four Gospels. Soon the Acts of the Apostles and writings attributed to Paul and other apostles were added to the Gospels, and the collection was completed with the Revelation of John, the Apocalypse. These works form the sacred writings which Christians call the New Testament. For Christians the Hebrew Bible is the Old Testament, and the Old and New Testaments constitute the Christian Bible, from Greek *ta biblia*, "the books" (Bowker 1997: 147; Mack 1995; Chadwick, H. 1993: 31-34).

The first part of the Hebrew Bible to be translated into Greek was the Pentateuch or "five books" of Moses. The translation was probably completed by Jews for Jews in Alexandria between 200 and 250 CE. Translations into Greek of the rest of the Hebrew Bible followed over the next two centuries, and this version was soon taken over by the Christians. According to legend, this Greek translation, called the Septuagint, from Latin *septuaginta*, "seventy," was produced by seventy men in seventy days (Bowker 1997: 875; Chadwick, H. 1993: 35).

Between 390 and 405, the renowned scholar Jerome (c.340-420) learned Hebrew from a rabbi and translated the Hebrew Bible into Latin. St. Jerome's version is now called the Vulgate, from Latin *vulgus* "common people," and it remained *the* Bible for most Europeans until translations into other European languages became available in the sixteenth and seventeenth centuries (Chadwick, O. 1993: 360, 364).

The Christian Scriptures and Women

The New Testament is full of images of women, but it says very little about their daily lives. It does, however, suggest that their situations were very diverse. Still, they were, for the most part, embedded in the male-dominated household as everything from managers to slaves (Wordelman 1992: 390-396).

Some feminist scholars have argued that the Jesus of the New Testament was a feminist, in that He treated women as equals.

One feminist scholar takes issue with this view (Carley 2002). However, it seems clear that Early Christianity as presented in the New Testament began as an egalitarian movement. However, detailed feminist analysis of New Testament books reveals a varied and complex picture of women's role and status, and therefore it is difficult to generalise. It is indeed likely that at least part of the presentation of women as inferior had to do with the attempts of men to minimise or obscure women's vital role in the origins of Christianity (Newsom and Ringe 1992: 252-289).

On the one hand, the Gospels do not include women among Jesus's chosen Twelve Disciples, despite that fact that there were obviously influential women among His followers. Often, as in the Gospel of Luke, the New Testament presents as role models women who are silent, devout, and "supportive of male leadership." The mother of Jesus, the Virgin Mary, is mentioned only rarely in the Christian Bible (New Testament). However, by the second century CE, Mary was beginning to be very popular in the devotions of the common people. She provided a female and feminine influence that had earlier been lacking in Christianity (Warner 1976). On the other hand, the New Testament presents many women who had significant roles in events of Jesus's life and during the early period of Christianity: for example, Mary Magdalene, one of Jesus's disciples (Mark 15: 40-16: 8, 28: 9-10, John 20: 1-18); Lydia, the first convert in Europe (Acts 16: 11-40); Priscilla, an early missionary (Acts 18: 1-4, 18-28); and the deacon Phoebe, the apostle Junia, and other women prominent in Christian circles at Rome (Romans 16: 1-16) (Schaberg 1992: 275). The New Testament says that Jesus had "cast devils" out of Mary Magdalene (Mark 16:9; Luke 8:2; John 20). These comments, along with later identification of her with a female "sinner" who anointed Jesus's feet and dried them with her hair (Luke 7: 37-38), led to a story, which began in the sixth century CE, that the Magdalen had been a prostitute. Far from being a prostitute, Mary Magdalene was almost certainly an important disciple of Jesus and apostle of Christianity, as an apocryphal text "The Gospel of Mary," dating to the second century CE, makes clear. Another such writing, "The Gospel of Philip," hints that she might also have been Jesus's wife (Bowker 1997: 624-625; Haskins 1993: 40).

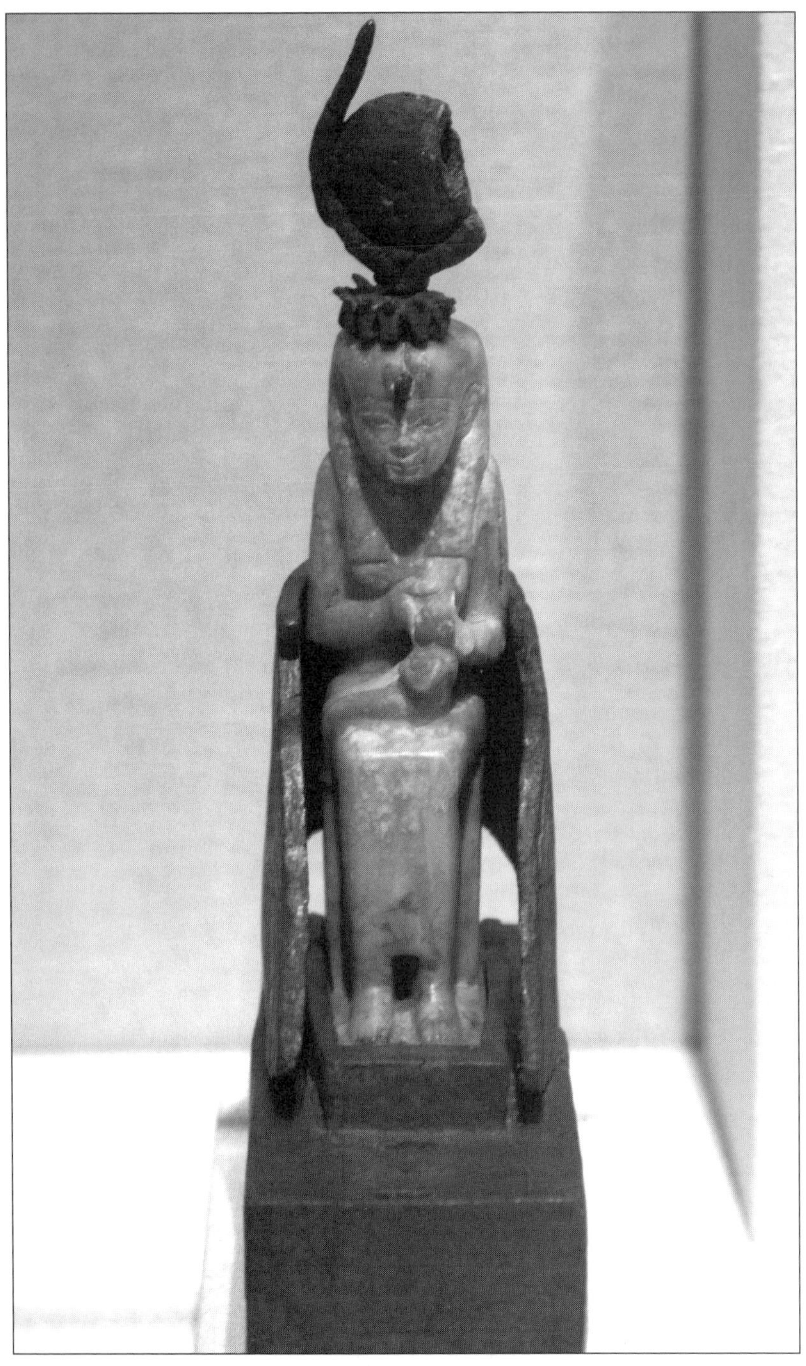

Isis Nursing Horus, ca. 712-525 B.C.E. Calcite and bronze.
Brooklyn Museum, Charles Edwin Wilbour Fund, 37.400E. Used with permission

Christianity also adopted and interpreted the Hebrew Bible and its attitudes to women, as well as taking over many of the predominantly patriarchal views of the Roman Empire and its various provinces (Wordelman 1992: 390-396).

The Apostolic Period

After his conversion from Judaism, Saul of Tarsus, now named Paul, and other apostles undertook the dissemination of the faith throughout the Roman Empire (Acts 9). It took an amazingly short time for small Christian groups to be established in all the major cities of the Roman Empire, and even outside its boundaries (Ware 1997: 12; Chadwick, H. 1993: 24-28).

In the early years, missionaries still considered themselves Jews, but Jews who had received the Messiah. Therefore, when apostles arrived in a town, they would go to the synagogue to teach. Many of the first converts were Jews. However, burgeoning Christianity was very soon recruiting primarily non-Jews, many of whom would have already had some acquaintance with the extremely popular "Mysteries" of the Greco-Roman world (Chadwick, H. 1993: 22; Torjesen 1993: 14-15, 31; Epstein 1990: 107).

THE MYSTERY RELIGIONS

The word "mystery" comes from Greek *mysteria*, "festival or rites of initiation." The Greek terms *mysteria* and *mystes*, "an initiate," were used in the Eleusinian Mysteries, which classical Athens celebrated yearly in honour of the goddesses Demeter and Persephone (Foley 1994: 66-67; Burkert 1987: 8-9).

Mystery traditions focused on initiation of devotees, who sought preferential treatment in the Underworld, as well as happiness and prosperity in this world. Though a myriad of people became initiates at Eleusis over its two thousand years of uninterrupted rites, the oath of secrecy was so binding that no *mystes* ever told what occurred in the core rituals. Initiates of the other Mystery traditions showed the same loyalty to their oaths (Foley 1994: 55, 68).

Scholars speculate that the rewards of initiation probably came from identification with a mediator deity like Persephone, Osiris, Attis, or Adonis. All of them, as "dying" and resurrected gods, could cross the barrier between earth and the Underworld, a boundary which neither mortals nor most deities could penetrate. One of the titles of such deities was "Saviour." The dominant deity in almost all the Mysteries was, however, a goddess—Isis, Cybele, Demeter, for instance—to whom the saviour deity, usually Her child, was subordinate. The Virgin Mary took over many of the titles of ancient goddesses, for instance, "Queen of Heaven" (Inanna/Ishtar of Mesopotamia) and Stella Maris "Star of the Sea" (Egyptian Isis). There is also some support for the assertion that the many statues of Isis with her son on her lap were models for the numerous Christian depictions of the Virgin and Child. In addition, many ancient goddesses were understood to be "virgins," but not in our sense of "sexually untouched." The word "virgin" in a number of ancient Mediterranean cultures denoted a nubile young woman who had not borne a child or was not dependant on a man (Warner 1976). Many Christians still worship Mary as a kind of goddess.

Undoubtedly, Christianity was deeply permeated with the atmosphere, language, and rituals of the Mysteries. Indeed, some scholars argue that, at first, Christianity was just one of a number of Mystery traditions (Rudhardt 1994: 203; Chadwick, H. 1993: 53; Burkert 1987: 3; Meyer 1987: 225-226).

EARLY CHRISTIANITY

The first followers of Jesus, then, were Jews, except that for them Jesus was the Messiah. Many converts in the first century CE were also Jews: their belief that Jesus was the Messiah did not result in their being cut off from Judaism. However, as Christians began to alter their concept of Jesus to make him more than human and eventually God, a rift was inevitable. In some places, the consequence was conflict between Jews and Christians. For example, because of "rivalries" between Jews and Christians, the authorities expelled the Jews from Rome in 45 CE. Soon, however, early Christian missionaries directed their efforts at pagans and very quickly attracted converts from among their numbers (Chadwick, H. 1993: 22; Kraemer 1993: 131; Torjesen 1993: 17, 31; Epstein 1990: 107).

The Acts of the Apostles and the writings of Paul make it clear that stipulations that all converts observe the Jewish laws about food (*kosher*) and that all men who converted had to be circumcised were fast becoming difficulties for non-Jewish converts. Early Christianity soon abandoned both circumcision and food laws (Romans 2: 25-29; Galatians 2: 11-13; Colossians 2: 16). It is not surprising that, by about 100 CE, early Christianity had cut all ties to Judaism, or vice versa. Nonetheless, Christianity owes much of its tradition to Judaism (Chadwick, H. 1993: 24; Kraemer 1993: 143; McManners 1993; Torjesen 1993).

The Only Official Religion

In 312 CE, before winning a crucial battle, Constantine, Roman Emperor since 306 CE, had a vision of the Christian Cross; from that point, he started to support Christianity. In 313 CE, he issued an edict that made toleration for all religions the law, but granted Christianity a special place as a privileged religion. Eventually, in 392 CE, Theodosius I passed edicts that, effectually, declared Christianity the exclusive religion of the state (Ware 1997: 16, 18; Chadwick, H. 1993: 64; Chuvin 1990: 24-25, 69-72).

In 324 CE, Constantine made a decision that was to have far-reaching effects on the later development of Christianity: he moved the capital of empire east to the site of the Greek city Byzantium, today Istanbul in Turkey. Constantine also called the first Ecumenical or General Council of Christianity. It took place at Nicaea, now Iznik in north-west Turkey; the year was 325 CE. Six more General Councils were convened over the following centuries. At these councils, male bishops dealt with issues relating to the organization of the Church and worked out what would be the Church's position on the basic doctrines of the religion. In effect, defining doctrine meant choosing between differing interpretations of, for example, the nature of Jesus. The early Church was deeply divided such issues. Councils met mainly to decide which views were orthodox and which heretical (Ware 1997: 19-31).

The "Fathers of the Church"

The era from the second to the fifth centuries CE, the Patristic Period (from Latin *pater*, "father"), "mediated between the end of the New Testament era and the early Middle Ages." The term "Fathers of the Church" usually refers to bishop-theologians who were all men. They preached and wrote on the numerous controversies of the developing Church (Carmody 1989: 161).

By the third century CE, early church Fathers such as Tertullian, Chrysostom, and Augustine of Hippo had started to elaborate a Christian tradition of misogyny and hostility to the body and sexuality. Most of them identified women with the body and the body's sexuality with sin (Chadwick, H. 1993: 41-44; Torjesen 1993: 155ff.; Borresen 1981; see Clark and Richardson 1977a: 69ff.; Prusak 1974: 89-116; Reuther 1974a: 150-183).

In the thirteenth century CE, perhaps the most influential medieval Church Father Thomas Aquinas (c.1225-1274) developed a male-centred theology that had enormous significance for the Catholic Church's attitudes to women. Starting from the Aristotelian position that women were defective men, he demonstrated that the inferior status of women was part of the structure of the world as God had created it (Johnson 1997: 24-25; Borresen 1981).

The Division of Christianity into Two Churches

In the early centuries CE, the Roman Empire was a political unity spanning the whole Mediterranean area. Educated people shared a common Greco-Roman culture, and most people understood either Greek or Latin or both. However, at the end of the third century CE, the Roman Empire separated into two parts, the Greek-speaking East and the Latin-speaking West, each with its own emperor. When Constantine founded Constantinople in 324 CE, he only made matters worse. By 450 CE, very few in the West were able to read Greek, let alone speak it, and by 600 CE, few in the East could speak Latin (Ware 1997: 46).

From the fifth century CE on, barbarian invaders began to divide up the Western Empire among them. Slowly, the East grew increasingly isolated from the West, until the rapid spread of Islam in the seventh and eighth centuries CE inserted the final wedge between the two Christian worlds. The Church also became divided: the Western or Roman Church, today known as the Roman Catholic Church, and the Eastern Churches, today known as the Eastern Orthodox Churches (Ware 1993: 151-154).

In the fifth and sixth centuries CE, however, another division in Christianity had already taken place: the Oriental Orthodox Churches became separated from the rest of Christianity. These Churches themselves fall into two groups: first, the Church of the East, mainly now in Iraq and Iran, the distancing of which occurred primarily from lack of contact, and, second, five Churches that separated for doctrinal reasons: the Syrian Church of Antioch, the Syrian Church in India, the Coptic Church in Egypt, the Armenian Church, and the Ethiopian Church (Ware 1997: 3-4, 313).

Over the course of seven General or Ecumenical Councils, from 327 CE to 787 CE, the still loosely unified Church had organised itself into five administrative regions. They were ranked according their claims to foundation by an Apostle; Rome was first, followed, in order, by Constantinople, Alexandria, Antioch, and Jerusalem. A bishop entitled "Patriarch" presided over each city, and among them the five Patriarchs had religious jurisdiction over the whole Christian world.

As a result of the chaotic situation in the West during and after the barbarian incursions, the Bishop of Rome emerged as the only focus of continuity and stabilising factor, both spiritually and politically. The Western Church then became increasingly centralised on Rome and its bishop, who followed in direct line from the Apostle Peter (42-67), the first Bishop of Rome. Gradually, in the West, the Bishop of Rome was able to assert supreme authority in spiritual matters. However, it was not until the reign of Martin II (882-4) that the bishop acquired the title "Pope" (Ware 1997: 20, 26-27, 47; Chadwick, H. 1993: 40; Mayr-Harting 1993: 128; Ware 1993: 153).

In the mid-eighth century CE, the beleaguered Bishopric of Rome sought support from Christianised barbarians, the Franks. Finally, in 800 CE, Leo III crowned the Frankish king Charlemagne (c.742-814) as "Holy Roman Emperor." The Eastern or Byzantine Empire and the Eastern Churches recognised neither the Holy Roman Empire nor its Emperor (McManners 1993: 115, 717).

By the early eleventh century CE, the churches of East and West were completely estranged, but the division did not have much effect on ordinary Christians in either area. The Crusades, on the other hand, did. These Western military expeditions, which took place from the late eleventh to the thirteenth centuries CE, were mounted against the Muslim forces occupying the Holy Land, today Israel; the Crusaders' aim was to re-capture the land where Jesus had lived. In 1204, Western forces of the Fourth Crusade ensured the complete alienation of the East by sacking Constantinople (Ware 1997: 45, 59-60).

For centuries, the Byzantine Empire had been under continuous threat from Islam. Finally, on May 29, 1453, Constantinople fell to the Turks. However, this event did not mean the end of Eastern Christianity, for Muslim teaching does not allow persecution of Christians, as long as they do not make trouble for their rulers (Ware 1997: 87-88).

After Eastern Christianity was cut off from Churches to the East and the West, it started to spread to the north. In the mid-ninth century, its missionaries began to teach the Slavs. Thus, Eastern Churches took root in, among other places, Greece, Russia, Serbia, Romania, Bulgaria, Georgia, and Cyprus, as well as in Poland and Albania (Ware 1993: 158-160).

WOMEN'S LEADERSHIP IN THE EARLY CHURCH

Like most of the Mysteries, early Christianity was egalitarian, and so it attracted converts from all walks of life, large numbers of whom were women. The New Testament makes no secret of the fact that female converts were deeply involved in the spread and development of the new spirituality (Kraemer 1993: 128, 174; Torjesen 1993: 5, 11; Parvey 1974: 117-149).

Neither the paganism nor the Judaism of the Greco-Roman world had any difficulty with women's taking leadership roles. In fact, it was normal for pagan women to occupy most offices in the religious sphere and, as religious functionaries, to serve deities of either sex. Jewish women attended synagogue, took full part in synagogue life, and even held synagogue offices. Consequently, women converts probably expected to function as leaders, and there is considerable evidence that they did (Kraemer 1993: 106, 191-192; Torjesen 1993: 11, 19ff.; Brooten 1982).

In early Christianity, women led congregations and functioned as prophets, apostles, evangelists, deacons, priests, and even bishops.

Often women's leadership resulted from their prophetic powers. However, according to Ross Kraemer, women's leadership became a contentious issue quite early in Christianity's development, and those arguing against it were probably reacting to the actual exercise of leadership by real women. Those arguments that date to the first and second centuries CE have as their main focus "women teaching men and baptizing anyone." Later, arguments include discussion of rituals that entailed functions that were considered priestly, particularly consecrating and distributing the bread and wine for Communion and forgiveness of sins. Kraemer concludes that, from quite early times, the real problem was women's having authority over men (Kraemer 1993: 177ff., 195; Torjesen 1993: 5, Chap. 1, 28-30).

To the Romans, early Christianity was primarily a troublesome superstition, but it was also a political problem because its adherents refused to worship the Roman emperor, worship of whom was one Roman way of assuring political stability. Thus, the lives of Christians during the first two centuries CE were, to say the least, precarious. In addition, the authorities and the populace in general believed that Christians celebrated immoral rituals, including incest and cannibalism. Christians were often victims of sporadic outbreaks of often local persecution, usually of short duration. In addition, Roman authorities sometimes used Christians as scapegoats. During the first three centuries CE, thousands of women and men became Christian martyrs. In such a dangerous world, early Christians had to meet in small groups and often in secrecy. They gathered mainly in homes, "house churches." This cellular organisation and decentralisation was one of the factors that promoted women's leadership in early Christianity (Torjesen 1993: 12-13, 76ff., 204; Fiorenza 1992: 175ff.).

Asceticism, particularly sexual asceticism, was significant in the development of Christianity. Many early Christians, and large numbers of them women, opted not to marry. By the early second century CE, there were two opposing positions on what constituted a Christian life: the first argued for "marriage, social conformity, hierarchy, and structure" and vehemently opposed women's leadership, whereas the second promoted asceticism, refused to follow social conventions, saw no value in the hierarchy of the day, and was firm in its belief that women, as well as men, could perform baptism and teach. As the Church became increasingly institutionalised, the first position won out, particularly on the matter of women's leadership; the second, considerably modified, found an approved, but separate place in the Christian world: monasticism (Kraemer 1993: 146, 154).

By the early fourth century CE, Christian asceticism began to manifest itself in withdrawal from the world. From the outset, women were just as likely as men to become involved in the monastic movement. In the Middle Ages, monasticism offered women a reputable alternative to marriage. Further, as abbesses, a few women could exercise considerable authority. Normally, however, men controlled the lives of nuns; they were either their superiors in the monastic order they belonged to or bishops of the regions in which their convents were located. Nonetheless, there is little doubt that monastic life gave some exceptional women opportunities to explore their talents in a way that marriage and motherhood would not have done (see Clark and Richardson 1977b: 56ff.)

FROM "HOUSE CHURCH" TO BASILICA

Over the course of the third century, with increase in membership, Christianity started its development toward becoming a public religion. As it moved from the private realm of the "house church," hierarchy and male dominance increased. Opponents of women's leadership gained ascendency, and eventually the Church declared most branches of early Christianity in which women were prominent to be heretical (Kraemer 1993: 157; Torjesen 1993: 37).

The word "bishop" had come originally from the Greek secular and domestic word *episcopos*, "overseer," and it was the title of women leaders of early Christian "house churches." During the late third and the early fourth centuries CE, however, Christians began to conceive of the office of bishop in monarchical terms. The fourth century CE saw the building of Christian churches modelled on the Roman basilica, the Roman public court of law and government reception hall. In the Christian basilica, the bishop's throne stood in a prominent place before the congregation. Christian leadership was now public and began to take its models from Roman public life, from which Roman women were excluded. Thus, growing institutionalisation and male dominance, which began as early as the second century CE, along with the development of the public church, eventually led to the exclusion of women from leadership roles (Chadwick, H. 1993: 37; Torjesen 1993: 5, 157; Fiorenza 1992: 294, 309).

CHRISTIAN MYSTICISM

Another way in which women could achieve some authority in the Church was as a result of their ecstatic and prophetic powers. For many women mystics of the Middle Ages, the combination of two august Christian traditions, ecstatic experience and asceticism, provided status in an otherwise severely male-dominated world (Bova 1997: 22).

There were many revered female mystics of the period, St. Teresa of Avila being perhaps the best known. Saint Teresa (1515-1582) was a Spanish nun whose mystical experiences culminated with her "spiritual marriage" with the deity (Bowker 1997: 965). Hildegard von Bingen (1098-1179), an aristocrat who became a nun and an abbess, succeeded in her fight for the Church's authentication of her powerful visions. The Church's acceptance of Hildegard's ecstatic experiences as genuine may have contributed to the proliferation of mystical writings by women in Germany and the Lowlands in the twelfth and thirteenth centuries (Garay 1997: 18).

Another famous mystic, Julian of Norwich, was a fourteenth-century English celibate hermit. In her works, Julian described Jesus as the "Working Mother" of the Trinity, likened Jesus's blood to mother's milk, and thought of God as Mother. Although the theology that she expressed was quite subversive, her celibacy and retreat from the world apparently protected her (Bova 1997: 22).

Yet another female mystic was not so lucky. Marguerite Porete, who lived in the thirteenth century in France, had her book of visions burnt in the town square in 1306, and she herself was burned at the stake in 1310. She was not a hermit or, as far as we know, a nun. She was a "beguine," part of a loosely organised group of devout lay women. Beguines either lived in a kind of

Gianlorenzo Bernini, "The Ecstasy of St. Theresa," 1652. Left transept of Santa Maria della Vittoria, Rome. Photo: Jastrow 2006. Used with permission by CC-BY.

cloister or wandered out in the world. Unprotected by a societally or religiously accepted female role, Marguerite de Porete died as heretic (Garay 1997: 18).

THE REFORMATION IN THE WEST

Toward the end of the fifteenth century, change was in the air. The "Hundred Years' War" between England and France, which had begun in the mid-fourteenth century, was finally over. Feudal relationships, which had for so long kept people firmly tied to the land and their roles in the hierarchy, were weakening; peasants were being uprooted; and a new merchant class was starting to make its presence felt. Italy was already experiencing the Renaissance, with its new attitudes to humans and their place in the world. The printing press had been invented, and literacy was on the increase. Most important, criticism of the Church and society was widespread.

At the end of the fifteenth century, the monk-theologian who precipitated the Reformation Martin Luther (1483-1546) was born in what is now Germany. By that time, grievances about the Church were increasing, a major one being about its wealth. The sale of "indulgences" was especially annoying. For a fee, a penitent gained an indulgence, a pardon for sins, and thus could escape punishment in the Afterlife. After much study and thought, Luther concluded that forgiveness of sins was God's free gift and that no one could buy it; furthermore, he insisted that the salvation of the soul came not through deeds, but only through faith (Collinson 1993: 255-256).

In his numerous lectures on these and other subjects, Luther became a strong advocate of Church reform. Soon he was criticising not only the sale of indulgences, but also the veneration of saints. On October 31, 1517, Luther posted on a door of the Castle Church of Wittenberg his "ninety-five theses," summarising his views on indulgences. In a matter of months his ideas were circulating all over Europe (Collinson 1993: 255).

The Reformation seemed unstoppable. Soon the north of Germany, parts of Austria, Hungary and Poland, Scandinavia, and England were in its grip. Reformers caused problems even in France and Italy. However, the Church of Rome stemmed the tide by launching the "Counter-Reformation," and in 1545 its Council of Trent reached agreement on major reforms. The followers of Luther were not called Protestants until 1529, when the term was applied to the German cities and princes that "protested" a 1529 edict to eliminate the Lutheran movement. For about one hundred years, Europe suffered religious turmoil and even wars, as other Protestant spokesmen, like John Calvin (1509-1564) and his disciple John Knox (1505-1572), gained followers (Collinson 1993: 25-255, 268).

There is some disagreement among scholars about the effect the Reformation had on women and the status of women. Some argue that the Reformation afforded women increased freedom and responsibility, while other insist that the leaders of the Reformation basically did little to alter women's second-class status (Bowker 1997: 1043; Carmody 1979: 174-176; see Clark and Richardson 1977c: 130ff.; Douglass 1974: 292-318).

In this regard, it is significant that, contrary to popular belief, the infamous witch hunts of Europe and America did not take place in the Middle Ages, but in the sixteenth and seventeenth centuries, around the same time as the Renaissance and the Reformation. In almost every part of Europe, the accused and executed witches included many more women than men: women made up 80 percent of the accused and 85 percent of the executed. However, both Protestants and Roman Catholics thought witches existed and took action against them (Barstow 1994: 23, 60; Kramer and Sprenger 1971).

The Reformation should have led to improvement in women's status, as a result of Protestantism's insistence on individual access to God and on the importance of individual conscience, and in some ways it did. However, increasing emphasis on literal reading of Biblical texts tended to affect women adversely. Some Protestant groups, especially those that emphasised prophecy and ecstatic experiences, did allow women to take leadership roles. Most Protestantism, like Roman Catholicism and Eastern Orthodoxy, considered women as second class in both church organisation and in spirituality (Bowker 1997: 1043; McManners 1993: 307-308).

CHRISTIANITY TODAY

Normally, the designation "Christian" is "strictly confessional"; that is, a Christian "confesses" belief in God, Jesus's saving sacrifice on the Cross, his Resurrection, and the inevitability of the Last Judgment. Thus, the phrase "Christian atheist" would, to most Christians, seem like a contradiction in terms. For many Christians, proselytising is an imperative, since they believe that their religion is the only route to Salvation (John 14: 6). Indeed, members of certain Protestant traditions have an obligation to seek to convert others. In the past, there were undoubtedly forcible conversions of the heathen; today, however, conversion is understood to be voluntary. For most Christian traditions, conversion minimally entails baptism (Bowker 1997: 236; Ruthven 1997: 3).

Christianity consists of four main blocks: the Orthodox Churches, Oriental Orthodox Churches, Roman Catholicism, and Protestantism. Protestantism includes numerous branches and sub-branches. According to 1987 calculations, Christianity is the religion of about a third of the world's population, almost 1.6 billion people. By 2006 that number had reached 2.1 billion, 33 percent of the world's population, half of whom were Roman Catholic (Crandall 2006: xiii). Estimates published in 1987 put the membership of the Eastern Orthodox Churches at 158-160 million. Roman Catholics number about 900 million, and the Protestant denominations claim around 550 million members. Except in East Asia, which has only 75 million Christians, Christianity is "highly visible" all over the globe (Carmody 1989: 163; Fargis and Bykofsky 1989: 191, 194).

Central Tenets

Contemporary Christians are monotheists. Nevertheless, most agree that the one divinity takes the form of the Trinity, "God in Three Persons": God the Creator, Jesus Christ the Son, and the Holy Spirit. Most Christians accept that Jesus is both divine and human. They believe that, when He died on the Cross, He took upon Himself the sins of the world. Hence, He is the "Saviour." For Christians, the Crucifixion and Jesus's subsequent return to life, the Resurrection, together constitute the main revelation of God's love. Most also agree that, at the end of time, there will be a "Last Judgment" of all souls.

Many Christians accept that a virgin, Mary, conceived Jesus by the Holy Spirit and gave birth to Him, the Virgin Birth. Indeed, since the second century CE, Mary has become the focus of worship for many Christians, especially Roman Catholic women. Several feast days are devoted to her. Most predominately Roman Catholic countries venerate a national Mary who manifested herself to devout Christians at a local site. The places of the Virgin's appearance have become important pilgrimage destinations. Perhaps the most famous is Lourdes in France. Other sites include Guadalupe in Mexico, Fatima in Portugal, Czestochowa in Poland, and Loreto in Italy (Warner 1976).

Sandro Botticelli, "Madonna della Loggia," tempera on panel, 72 cm x 50 cm, c. 1467. Uffizi, Florence.

In addition, Christians usually believe in the universality of God and the Church, the existence of saints, the concepts of sin and forgiveness of sin, and the reality of both Heaven with eternal life and happiness and Hell with eternal punishment. Almost all accept the Bible, Old and New Testaments, as the Christian sacred book. Most think that attending church and praying regularly are necessary to a good Christian life. A large number also insist that Christian faith demands that Christians put their ethics into action (Wiles 1993: 571-586).

Rituals

For most Christians, the main ritual day of the week is Sunday. We could classify Sunday as a festival, since, for the devout, it is a day of rest spent in prayer and meditation, at least in part in church, and it often culminates in a festive and ritualised family meal. However, many Christians attend church on Sunday mainly to take part in the most important ritual of their religion, the Eucharist.

"Eucharist" comes from Greek *eucharistos*, "grateful." Also called the Breaking of the Bread, the Lord's Supper, and Holy Communion, the Eucharist commemorates or renews the Last Supper of Jesus and His twelve disciples and Jesus's sacrifice on the Cross. In Roman Catholicism, the ritual of the Eucharist takes place at "mass." There are a number of different kinds of masses, including the wedding mass and the mass for the dead.

The Sacrament of the Eucharist begins when the priest consecrates bread and wine, which become, at least symbolically, the body of Jesus and the blood of Jesus. This rite of consecration is sometimes called Transubstantiation. In some Christian traditions, worshippers believe that the consecrated bread and wine *are* the body and blood of Christ. After Transubstantiation, the priest then ritually serves the bread and wine to the congregation (Ware 1997: 283; Wiles 1993: 581-582).

The Eucharist is one of the seven Christian Sacraments. The word comes from Latin *sacrare*, "to consecrate." One of the Fathers of the Church, St. Augustine of Hippo, described a sacrament as "a visible form of an invisible grace." The seven sacraments are: the Eucharist, Baptism, Confirmation, Penance for Sins, Marriage, Ordination of Clergy, and Extreme Unction, the anointing of the sick and dying. For most Christians, the Eucharist is pre-eminent, with Baptism next in importance (Ware 1997: 275; Wiles 1993: 580-581).

In the majority of traditions, before believers can partake in the Eucharist, they must receive the Sacrament of Baptism by immersion in or sprinkling with water. The ritual symbolically cleanses a person of sin and allows rebirth into a Christian life. The Rite of Confirmation makes a person a full member of the community by calling down the Holy Spirit again on those who have already been baptised. By restoring innocence to those who have committed serious sins after baptism, the Sacrament of Penance welcomes them back into the community. In the early Church, penance was both public and onerous, but in the Middle Ages the Church introduced private confession and allowed the priest to grant absolution and penance (Bowker 1997: 230-231; Ware 1997: 277-279, 288-290; Wiles 1993: 581).

In Christianity, the Sacrament of Matrimony confers grace on a union, which is often understood to exemplify the union of Jesus and the Church. At least in earlier times, it was considered permanent, as it still is in some Christian traditions. Another permanent sacrament is that of Ordination. A bishop confers on a priest the power to perform the Rite of Transubstantiation during the Eucharist. Extreme Unction, the anointing of the sick and dying by a priest, comforts and heals the sick and absolves the dying of sin (Ware 1997: 290-297).

Festivals

Christian festivals occur all through the year, mainly in association with the birth of Jesus, His life on earth, and his death and resurrection. There are also festivals dedicated to saints and martyrs. Festivals fall into two categories: movable feasts and immovable feasts. Some add a third festival, Sunday, which I have discussed above. The dates of immovable feasts, often commemorating saints and martyrs, are fixed, whereas those of movable feasts, which originated in Judaism, change according to the Lunar Calendar. For Roman Catholics, the most important festivals, including Sunday, are "feasts of obligation," when they are obliged to attend mass (Bowker 1997: 342).

The major Christian festivals are Christmas and Easter, the latter being pre-eminent in the Eastern Orthodox Churches. Western Churches celebrate Christmas on 25 December, but it can occur over a week later in some of the Eastern Churches. The festival commemorates the birth of Jesus. For most Christians, Christmas is both a communal and a family festival, during which the devout attend midnight mass and services on Christmas morning (Ware 1997: 298, 302; Morris 1993: 233-234).

Easter commemorates the Crucifixion and Resurrection of Jesus. It is a moveable feast; however, usually, but not always, it occurs around the same time as the Jewish Passover. As with Christmas, the date often differs for the Orthodox Churches. The Eastern Churches, however, celebrate Easter for a whole week, "Holy Week." Roman Catholics and Protestants usually celebrate Easter on a long weekend, beginning with Good Friday, the day Jesus died on the Cross, a day of mourning. Devout Christians attend contemplative church services and spend the day in prayer. Easter Sunday is a day of rejoicing, because it commemorates Jesus's Resurrection (Bowker 1997: 440; Ware 1997: 302; Chadwick, H. 1993: 39-40).

Though it is a time of fasting, not of feasting, Lent is also an important period for devout Christians. It is a forty-day fast that occurs before Easter, so that it is a movable holiday, depending for its date on the date of Easter. The Eastern churches still observe Lent, while the Western churches have varying practices associated with it (Bowker 1997: 342, 573-574).

Women's Ritual Roles

Particularly in Eastern Orthodoxy and Roman Catholicism, it is often women, who perform individual rituals at shrines of saints. A focus of their veneration is the Virgin Mary, foremost among the saints (Rubin 2009; Warner 1983). Women light candles or oil lamps in front of statues of the Virgin in churches and niches in house walls or roadsides and pray to her, as if to a goddess, for her compassion and intercession on behalf of their families or, sometimes, themselves. They celebrate Mary's feast days and make pilgrimages to places where the Virgin Mary has manifested herself to devout persons, for example, Lourdes (Bowker 1997: 624; Christ 1997: 25; Kinsley 1989: Chap. 10; Matter 1983: Chap. 7; Campbell 1982: 5-24).

Although the focal ritual of Christianity is a sacred meal, women are not normally responsible for providing the ritual foods for it. Most Christian traditions have no food taboos; consequently, there are few opportunities for women to become ritual experts as food preparers (Bowker 1997: 352).

TYPES OF CHRISTIANITY

Christianity consists of four main blocks: the Orthodox Church, Oriental Orthodox Churches, Roman Catholicism, and Protestantism; the latter divides roughly into two kinds: liberal Protestantism and conservative Protestantism. Protestantism includes numerous branches and sub-branches, including denominations that do not fit into either liberal or conservative category.

The Orthodox Churches

The Orthodox Churches are mainly found in Russia and Eastern Europe and along the eastern Mediterranean. The grouping is sometimes called Eastern Orthodoxy. In addition, there are Orthodox communities in Africa, Western Europe, North and South America, and Australia. Orthodox Churches conceive of their relationship to each other as that of a community of self-governing churches, decentralised in structure, with no single ruler (Bowker 1997: 719-721; Ware 1997: 5-7).

The Orthodox Churches consider themselves to be the *only* direct descendent of the early Church of the Greco-Roman world. They emphasise Tradition, which includes the Old and New Testaments, liturgy, canon law, Church Fathers, Ecumenical Councils, and Icons, paintings which reveal the Divine (Ware 1997: 8, 206). The Orthodox avail themselves of all seven sacraments. For them, the consecrated bread and wine of the Eucharist *are* the body and blood of Jesus. Baptism is always administered in infancy, along with Confirmation and First Communion. Confession is private, with the priest giving absolution and penance (Ware 1997: 277-78).

Further, the Orthodox Churches lay particular emphasis on the Holy Spirit. Indeed, during Chrismation, the Orthodox equivalent of Confirmation, children are anointed to confer on them the gift of the Spirit, so that they become prophets. Thus there is a strong tendency to ecstatic experiences and mysticism in the tradition (Ware 1997: 242, 278-279, 314).

Married men can be Orthodox priests, but not bishops. The tradition permits divorce. It disapproves of contraception, but is slowly changing its view. It condemns abortion and sexuality outside of marriage, and it opposes homosexuality (Karkala-Zorba 2006: 36-45; Ware 1997: 291, 295-296).

Oriental Orthodox Churches

Included under this category are the Syrian, Coptic, Ethiopian, and Armenian Orthodox Churches. They separated from the rest of Christianity after the Council of Chalcedon, which was convened in the Asia Minor town in 451 CE. The Council declared Jesus to be "in two natures," divine and human. The Oriental Orthodox Churches rejected this view of Christ. Since the 1960s, these churches have held conferences with the Orthodox and Roman Catholic Churches with the intention of "theological reconciliation" (Bowker 1997: 718).

Roman Catholicism

Roman Catholicism, the largest of all the Christian churches, is the main religion in Mediterranean parts of Europe, much of Eastern Europe, Ireland, and Latin America. It claims direct descent from the Church established at Rome by the Apostle Peter, the first Bishop of Rome. Peter's heir, the Pope, is the supreme head of the Roman Catholic Church. When he makes pronouncements on matters of faith and morals, the Pope is infallible; that is, he is prevented by God from making a mistake (Bowker 1997: 821-823; Ware 1997: 26-27; Chadwick, O. 1993: 381).

The organisation of the Church is hierarchical; the Pope rules from Rome, with bishops below him and priests at the bottom. In principle, the Pope manages all the Church's affairs. In practice, however, national Churches have varying degrees of autonomy. Further, in different national situations, Roman Catholicism can be very adaptive. The result is sometimes disagreement between national Churches and Rome.

Roman Catholics accept as dogma the Virgin Birth of Jesus and his Resurrection. The Church administers all the sacraments, but puts particular emphasis on the Eucharist, which priests celebrate at the Mass, the regular worship service. Catholics believe in Transubstantiation. Priests generally baptise infants by marking their forehead with water in the sign of the Cross. Children are confirmed by a bishop and take First Communion at around six or seven years of age. Roman Catholics confess their sins in private to a priest who gives absolution and sets penance (Ware 1997: 279). No Roman Catholic priest is allowed to be married. The Church does not permit divorce; it condemns artificial means of birth control, abortion, and sexuality outside of marriage; and it opposes homosexuality (Swidler 1993: Chaps. 5, 6). Like members of the Orthodox Churches, Roman Catholics venerate the Saints, especially the Virgin Mary, and Catholics pray to them to intercede with God (Chadwick, O. 1993: 387-391).

A number of Latin American, Caribbean, and North American groups have melded Roman Catholicism and African religions to produce enormously popular hybrid Churches. Examples include Vodou from Haiti, Shango from Puerto Rico, Santería from Cuba, and Candomblé from Brazil (Paper 1997: 219; Sered 1994: 32-34).

Protestantism

Protestant Churches agree in rejecting the authority of the Pope, and most reject all but two of the seven sacraments of Roman Catholicism: Baptism and the Lord's Supper, the Eucharist. Further, all Protestant priests can marry. Otherwise Protestants hold a wide variety of beliefs. The liberal or mainline Protestant stream is very varied. Many mainline Churches emphasise the individual, but are still hierarchically structured. Others are more liberal: they now accept female-male equality and are increasingly communal in structure. In addition, there are two kinds of Conservative Protestantism: one focuses on the nature of Jesus, the other on possession by the Holy Spirit (Bowker 1997: 771-772).

In North America, Europe, and elsewhere, there are a number of other Protestant groups, including Seventh Day Adventist, Amish, Christian Scientist, Mennonite, Mormon, Quaker, Reformed, and Unitarian. In addition, a variety of African-American and African-Caribbean Protestant Churches flourish (Collier-Thomas 2010;

Duncan 2008), as well as local versions of Protestantism in other parts of the world, especially Africa.

Liberal Protestantism

All liberal or mainline Protestant Churches practise infant baptism and celebrate the Lord's Supper, though their forms of worship vary. Included in this category are the following:

(1) the Anglican Church (Church of England), called Protestant Episcopal Church in the United States, established in 1534 when Henry VIII declared himself head of the Church in England (Bowker 1997: 67-70);

(2) the Lutheran Church, the direct result of the Reformation and based in the writings of Martin Luther (Bowker 1997: 591);

(3) the Methodist Church, originating in the ministry of John and Charles Wesley in the second half of the eighteenth century in England (Bowker 1997: 639);

(4) the Presbyterian Church, founded in Scotland in 1592 by John Knox on the teachings of his Swiss master, John Calvin (Bowker 1997: 766-767);

(5) United or Uniting Churches, formed in Australia, Canada, England, and the United States when two or more Churches merged. For instance, the United Church of Canada was established in 1925, when Methodists, Presbyterians, and Congregationalists, a group very like the Methodists, merged. Over the years, the United Church of Canada has been very progressive women's issues (Bowker 1997: 1005; Prentice et al. 1996: 315, 451).

Conservative Protestantism

Conservative Protestants seek the salvation of the soul through their faith in the atoning sacrifice of Jesus and through personal conversion to that faith. In addition, they emphasise the authority of the Scriptures and consider preaching more important than ritual (Wilson 1993: 612-613). They fall into basically two categories:

(1) Evangelical Churches emphasise Jesus and his (male) nature. They are usually quite restrictive of women, for they see males and females as essentially different, with distinct roles to play. Organization is hierarchical, and women are subordinate to men.

Baptist Churches are generally examples of this category: in 1998 the Convention of the Southern Baptist Church, the largest Protestant denomination in the U.S., adopted a declaration that women should "submit graciously" to the leadership of their husbands (*The Toronto Star* 20 June 1998: L18; Bowker 1997: 126, 326).

(2) Pentecostalists expect members to become possessed by the Holy Spirit. They worship with "speaking in tongues," as the Apostles did at the first Pentecost. Normally, they allow women to take spiritual leadership roles (Bowker 1997: 774; Wilson 1993: 601).

Other Protestant Churches

Some contemporary Protestant Churches that do not fit into either of the above categories have had special significance for feminism and women's spirituality.

(1) Quakers, the Protestant or Religious Society of Friends, have always been concerned with peace, education and social welfare; for instance, many nineteenth-century Quakers took active roles in the Anti-Slavery Movement and the Woman Movement. Among Quakers, women and men are equal, and women often serve as prayer leaders. A significant number of early feminists were Quakers (Bowker 1997: 159).

(2) Members of the Church of Christ (Scientist), founded by American Mary Baker Eddy in 1879, reject medical treatments and consult "practitioners" of either sex, who heal by prayer (Bowker 1997: 218).

(3) An example of the many African-Caribbean Protestant Churches is the Spiritual Baptist Church, which Carol Duncan studies in Toronto (2008). Duncan explains that the head of a Spiritual Baptist Church is called a "Queen Mother"; the Queen Mother may ask a man to serve as "a Bishop or Leader" with her (1997a, 1997b: 33). Bowker points out that there are a myriad African-American Protestant Churches, the first one founded being the African Methodist Episcopal Church (1997: 24, 918).

WOMEN AND RELIGIOUS LEADERSHIP

The majority of Eastern Orthodox Christians still oppose the ordination of women as priests, but Eastern Orthodoxy has never abolished the ordination of women as deacons; many Orthodox want to see that possibility revived (Ware 1997: 292-293). Despite considerable pressure, the Roman Catholic Church still refuses ordination to women (Bowker 1997: 1043).

Most Protestant denominations early experienced pressure to ordain women, and in general the smaller denominations have historically been more flexible than the larger ones. The first woman to become a Christian minister Antoinette L. Brown Blackwell (1825-1921) was eventually ordained in New York in 1853 by the Congregational Church. By 1921, when the Reverend Blackwell died, there were about three thousand female ministers in the United States. However, the liberal Harvard Divinity School did not admit women until the 1950s. The first Canadian woman to serve as a minister, Lydia Gruchy (1873-1989), was ordained by the United Church of Canada in 1936, not long after its formation in 1925. Contemporary Anglicanism ordains women not only as deacons and priests, but as bishops (Bowker 1997: 233-234; Prentice et al. 1996: 316; Finson 1995: 58-59; King 1989: 42).

CHRISTIAN FEMINISM AND FEMINIST THEOLOGY

In Christianity, with a few exceptions, such as the Shakers with their female Messiah, theology has been the preserve of men and based on the experiences of men, which theologians have then claimed as universal. However, in the last thirty years, Christian theologians have begun developing feminist theology first by exposing the male nature of "universal" experience and then by insisting on making women's experiences central to their theologising. Feminist theologians concern themselves with a wide variety of issues, such as the hierarchical dualism of the Christian world view, the sexism in the Bible and the Christian Churches, the problems that women have with the maleness of God language and images in sacred book and liturgy, and the paucity of female leadership in the Churches. The work of feminist theologians has affected all streams of Christianity, though change has come very slowly (Carmody 1995; Finson 1991; Carmody 1989: 178; Setta 1989: 221ff.).

Most Christian feminist theologians regularly use one another's work and adapt it to their own purposes. Thus, they often produce theological writing that falls into more than one of the categories that I outlined above: (1) Revisionist, (2) Renovationist, and (3) Revolutionary. Nonetheless, it is still possible loosely to apply these categories to the body of Christian feminist theological work. Normally, work fitting into category (4), Rejectionist, is no longer Christian theology.

The Dominant Stream in Christian Feminist Theology

In the work of some Christian feminist theologians of the dominant stream, we can trace a progression through the various categories. For instance, the publications of Mary Daly fit into at least two, and possibly three, of the above four categories.

Daly's book *The Church and the Second Sex*, which first appeared in 1968, attacked the Roman Catholic Church for its sexism, but now it seems primarily Renovationist in its overall conclusions. Describing herself as "a liberal Christian," Daly maintained that the "seeds" of transformation were already present in the tradition. This position is clearly Revisionist. However, in 1978, thinking back on the 1968 book, Daly commented that she considered its author (herself) to be "a reformist foresister" (Daly 1985 (1968): 220-221; Daly 1978: xi).

In *Beyond God the Father*, published in 1973, Daly went much further than she did in the 1968 book, though it pursued the same themes. It reached beyond Renovationist to Revolutionary, as Daly examined what religion would be like after the death of God the Father and when Eve was no longer associated with evil. By asking the question: "Jesus Was a Feminist, but So What?" she undermined one of the Revisionist defences of the Son. She concluded by exploring sisterhood as "Antichurch" and as "Cosmic Covenant." In discussing the death of God the Father, Daly argued that, when women leave "patriarchal time and space," they participate in "God the Verb," a "form-destroying, form-creating, transforming power" that renews everything. In 1978, looking back on *Beyond God the Father*, Daly said that she still considered herself its author, since she was not in basic disagreement with the argument of the book (Daly 1978: xi; Daly 1974: 43, 73).

Sculpture of Julian of Norwich by David Holgate. The sculpture flanks the left side of the Great West Door, West Front, Norwich Cathedral. Photo: David Holgate. Used with permission.

With *Gyn/Ecology* (1978), Daly repudiated Christianity all together and demonstrated that she was now Rejectionist. She concluded that God is irremediably male and masculine in imagery, and she stated that "Goddess affirms the life-loving be-ing of women and nature" (xi).

Like that of Mary Daly, the work of Rosemary Radford Reuther has moved through some of the above categories. Her very early work was probably Revisionist, but already tending toward the Renovationist stance of most of her articles and books since the mid-1970s. Even in the Preface to the early work *Religion and Sexism*, Reuther's ideas sound Renovationist: the essays suggest, she says, the ways in which believers have to reshape their patriarchal religions if they are to overcome their "unjust and debilitating effects on women" (1974: 10). By 1983, in *Sexism and God-Talk*, Reuther's thinking was beginning to move toward the Revolutionary position, with her concept of "God/ess" (46). In 1992, Reuther published *Gaia and God: An Ecofeminist Theology of Earth Healing*, which falls

Dante Gabriel Rossetti, "Joan of Arc," oil on canvas, 1882. Fitzwilliam Museum at the University of Cambridge.

somewhere between Renovationist and Revolutionary. However, Ursula King states that, compared to the extremist Daly, Rosemary Reuther is moderate and balanced, a "radical reformist" (1989: 172). Her recent book, *Goddesses and the Divine Feminine*, is a history of goddess worship in the West, which ends with a discussion of the modern "return" of the Goddess. She outlines the various "paths" that feminists have taken in their quest to "overcome patriarchy" in religions and comments that she is "more inspired" by "the reclaiming of prophetic, liberative themes" in Christianity and Judaism and the re-interpretation of them for women (2005: 306-307).

Revisionist Views

The earliest pieces of research that Christian feminist theologians undertook concerned the sexism of the various Christian denominations. Soon after, a number of women's accounts of their own involvement in various churches provided detailed evidence that Christianity did not speak of, or to, women's experiences. An example of such testimony is Canadian Sheila Conway's (1987) moving narrative of her life as a Roman Catholic, her attempts to reconcile herself to the Church, and her reasons for leaving the tradition.

Recovery of religious and Church history has also been a very productive area of Christian feminist-theological research. Especially influential have been the works of Elaine Pagels. Her first carefully researched book, *The Gnostic Gospels*, is a study of writings of egalitarian Gnostic Christians (early second century CE on), whom eventually the hierarchical, male-dominated Roman church declared heretics (1979: xv). As a result of their efforts, feminist historian-theologians of Christianity have now demonstrated that women were instrumental in the establishing of Christianity, as well as in its early spread (Kraemer and D'Angelo 1999; Kraemer 1993; Torjesen 1993; Fiorenza 1992).

Feminist historian-theologians are also recovering the names and lives of Christian women from the past: for example, earliest known Christian woman writer and martyr Perpetua, fourteenth-century English mystic and hermit Julian of Norwich, and fourteenth-century French mystic and heretic Marguerite Porete (Bova 1997; Garay 1997). They have also published feminist studies of women important in the Bible and to Christianity, such as the Virgin Mary (Berger 1985; Warner 1983) and Mary Magdalene (Haskins 1993), and saints such as Joan of Arc (Warner 1981) The Maid of Orleans, Jeanne d'Arc (c.1412-1431), was a peasant girl who said she heard voices from God urging her to arm herself and free France from English domination. She was burned at the stake on May 30, 1431, and became a saint in 1920.

Related to recovery work by Christian feminist historian-theologians is the task of feminist re-interpretation of texts, particularly Biblical ones. Much of the work of such theologians is Revisionist, in that usually their intention is to develop a feminist interpretive method that will uncover the Bible's liberating core, its revelatory message for women (Newsom and Ringe 1992).

One of the first feminists to venture into the formerly male preserve of Biblical exegesis was Phyllis Trible. In the early 1970s, she began publishing significant interpretive articles on the Hebrew Bible. In 1978 she published *God and the Rhetoric of Sexuality*, in which, using feminist methods of interpretation, she dissects texts from the Hebrew Bible. Her interpretation of the "Adam and Eve" story in Genesis 2-3 is fascinating to read, and it runs counter to the usually accepted explanation of the story as misogynist (1979: 73-83). Trible's *Texts of Terror* (1984) examines and re-interprets the horrifying Biblical stories of Hagar, Sarah's abused and cast-out Egyptian slave (Genesis 16: 1-16 and 21: 9-21); Tamar, King David's daughter, whom her brother rapes (2 Samuel 13: 1-22); the concubine whom her priestly master turns over to a mob of men who rape, torture, and kill her, and whom, in the end, her master dismembers (Judges 19: 1-30); and, finally, the virgin daughter whom her father Jephthah sacrifices (Judges 11: 29-40).

Another enormously influential scholar of Biblical interpretation, Elizabeth Schüssler Fiorenza, works on the New Testament. She too published important interpretive articles in the 1970s, and in one of them, she said that, in her opinion, the Goddess of feminist spirituality was "not so very different" from Jesus's God! However that may be, her difficult book, *In Memory of Her* (1983), represents a major breakthrough in feminist-theological methodology. Fiorenza demonstrates how the careful feminist interpretation of Bible passages can illuminate how early Christianity developed from inside Judaism. She discusses the widely used phrase "the hermeneutics of suspicion" (56). Finally, Fiorenza calls for Christian women to gather in what she terms an "*ekklesia* of women." She defines the Greek word *ekklesia* as an "assembly of free citizens" meeting to decide for themselves about matters of spirit and politics; she sees such a body as already in existence whenever women join together to assert their powers as religious beings, to get involved in making church decisions, and to support one another as female Christians. Fiorenza later called this gathering "women-church," and now the Women-Church movement is a significant world-wide phenomenon (King 1989: 179, 202-204; Fiorenza 2001; Fiorenza 1992: 344; Reuther 1985; Fiorenza 1979: 138).

Renovationist Views

Christian feminists have also been doing a great deal of work in the important areas of language, liturgy, and ritual. The language of religion, especially that referring to God, continues to be a central focus for many feminist theologians. Mary Daly was one of the first to call attention to the problems that the presentation of God as male causes for many Christian women. Later she also addressed both the issue of Jesus's maleness and the male-centred God symbolism of Christianity (1985 [1968]: 180-183; Daly 1974). Further, Rosemary Reuther devotes a whole section of one of her books to the problem of sexism and "God-Language," and she states that, whenever anyone concludes from the word *Father* that God is male and therefore His representatives have also to be male, then *Father* is "idolatrous." It is at this point that she suggests the use of the word God/ess (1983: 66-67).

The solutions that feminist theologians suggest for these and similar problems also fall into categories: a Revisionist approach advocates interpretation of language and symbols about deity in ways that are not oppressive or referring to deity in language that is sex neutral; a Renovationist position suggests that making deity language sex neutral is inadequate, because the "neutral" almost always translates as "male," and it insists on using some female symbols for deity and seeing deity in female roles; a Revolutionary answer is routinely to use female language and symbols for deity and even to import goddesses from other traditions. Rejectionists are already worshipping goddesses or following other spiritual traditions.

Since the mid-1970s, women (and men) have been publishing widely on topics relating to liturgy and ritual. They have been rewriting hymns, prayers, and liturgies; they have been collecting women's poetry for use in ritual; and they have even been writing new hymns, complete with music. They have also been developing rituals to celebrate girls' coming of age and lesbians' coming-out, rites of passage for divorce, and rituals of healing, especially for victims of violence and sexual abuse (Northup 1997; Northup 1993; Procter-Smith and Walton 1993; Reuther 1985).

Revolutionary Views

Ritual is the topic of one of the most stimulating feminist-theological publications to appear in the 1990s. In *To Make and Make Again*, Canadian Charlotte Caron starts from a series of questions like: "What if women's experience of the holy can never be validated?" She explores how religious rituals "challenge and nurture feminists" as they strive to promote "justice and well-being in the world." Caron based her study on participation in, and interviews with members of, two feminist groups: One is American and the other Canadian, and both are Christian, at least in origin. Many of the members are active in other spiritual groups and pursuits, and both groups often refer to "the Goddess" in rituals and discussions. Caron says in her introduction that she wants to find "a God/ess that is life-giving and sustaining." The result of Caron's research is the development of a "feminist ritual *thealogy*," which she defines as a ritual description of women's experience of deity. Caron's book clearly pushes Christianity to its limits, and her ideas certainly fit the Revolutionary category (1993: 1, 2, 10, 220).

Another Christian Revolutionary is Daphne Hamson (1996) who declares feminism and Christianity to be "incompatible" (2). She calls for "jettisoning" the Christian myth and doctrine, since they justifies patriarchy: "Women can have no stake in the previous order" (283). In her first book *Theology and Feminism,* she spoke of having had to "discard Christianity" (1990: 1), but she was unable to become an atheist. So she sought "new ways to conceive the presence of God in our world" (1990: 173). Her 1996 book is her attempt to do so.

Other Topics in Christian Feminist Theology

(1) *Christology,* the meaning of Jesus: Rosemary Reuther has contributed to this heated debate. In one place she even envisions Jesus as "*our sister*" (1983: 138). Many other feminist theologians have also been involved in the debate (Barger 2003). A visual image, "Crucified Woman," which stood outside of Emmanuel

College, University of Toronto, is *à propos*. It provoked a storm of controversy; Doris Dyke's published account (1991) discusses both the image and the controversy (Finson 1995: 21-22; Brock 30-53, McLaughlin 118-149, and Reuther 1993: 7-29).

(2) *Education,* particularly theological: A report of the Association of Theological Schools stated that, in 2005, women made up 36 percent of enrolment in all their schools (Lindner 2007: 395). Indeed, in many theological schools, women constitute about 50 percent of the students, and sometimes as many as 80 percent are female. Needless to say, this increase of women over a thirty-year period has had an enormous effect (Finson 1995: 26-27).

(3) *The ministry and ordination of women:* Since the 1980s, and especially since the 1990s, when women began to enter into ministry in considerable numbers, many studies, both experiential and scholarly, have appeared. Canadian women have made significant contributions on the subjects: essays on women's roles in Canadian churches (Muir and Whiteley 1995; Anderson 1990); views of women in ministry, including those of lesbians and of Native and Japanese Canadians (Lebans 1994); and women's ministerial experiences in four Canadian church traditions (Brouwer 2002, 1990; Rutherdale 2002). Canadian historians have written on the ordination movement in the Anglican church (Fletcher-Marsh 1995), Canadian Presbyterian women in missions to India, and Methodist women preachers in Upper Canada (Muir 1991).

(4) *Spiritual care and guidance of women and by women,* which includes handling such matters as violence and sexual abuse, poverty, and aging: Contributions in this area are many, but perhaps the most controversial publication on Christianity and abuse, edited by Brown and Bohn (1989), addressed among other topics, the possibility that ritual images of the suffering and violent death of Jesus might call up in survivors of abuse painful memories of the past (Finson 1995: 48-53).

(5) *Ethics:* Since the latter half of the 1980s, feminist theologians have been exploring issues such as abortion, homophobia, the function of power in pastoral counselling, power and sexuality, and suffering and evil. In 1992, Marilyn Legge published an im-

portant book on feminist theological ethics; in it she pursues issues that concern Canadian women in their daily lives (see also Finson 1995: 22-25). Another important book explores the relationship between women and suffering (Rankka 1998).

Dominant-stream Christian feminist theology has not gone unchallenged. Finson calls the backlash "the Rise of Neo-Sexism within the Church" (1995: 9). The negative reactions vary from attacks on any and all feminist criticism of traditional Christianity to Steele's attempt to demonstrate that, in the last twenty years, feminists have taken control of religion (1987). Steichen even asserts that most Roman Catholic nuns are now witches and Goddess worshippers (1991).

WOMANIST THEOLOGY

A little more than ten years after Daly's pioneering work appeared, African-American writer Audre Lorde wrote "An Open Letter to Mary Daly" criticising Daly's *Gyn/Ecology* in one of the first publications for and about women of colour, *This Bridge Called My Back* (Moraga and Anzaldua 1983: 94-96). The gist of Lorde's criticism is that Daly was generalising about women's experience from white women's experience, which was not the same as African-American women's experience. African-American feminist theorist bell hooks had been making similar criticisms since 1981. African-American feminist theologians called their approach "Womanist" (Coleman 2006; Townes 1995; Collins 1990), borrowing Alice Walker's term for a feminist who is also a woman of colour (1983: xi-xii).

Womanist theologians base their theology not just on some generic form of women's experience, but specifically on the experiences of African-American women, which is not the same as white women's experience (Grant 1989b: 213). Of course "black women's experience" is no more monolithic than white woman's experience, even in the United States; a more nearly appropriate description would be "black women's experiences." Womanist theologians also criticise African-American male theologians for not including African-American women in their theology. Though it began with English-speaking African-American women, Womanist theology has already influenced other women of African origins in North America and also women in other countries, including Africa itself

(Masenya 1995; Grant 1989a: 193; Grant 1982: 148).

Womanist theologians put African-American women's experiences at the centre of their endeavour and validate those experiences. For instance, Womanist theologians discuss the views that many African-American women have of Jesus. Womanist theologians point out that most African-American women have experienced Jesus differently from the way white people have, for they usually see him as co-sufferer, symbol of freedom, equalizer, and liberator (Grant 1993: 66-69; Williams 1993: xiv). In the perception of African-american women, Christ is "a Black woman" (Grant 1989b: 222).

Womanist theologians see all systems of oppression as interrelated in a single all-encompassing "structure of domination" (Eugene 1992: 140). Thus, their concept of liberation is not one that applies just to themselves, but has to work for all their people and also for all other oppressed people. Further, they maintain that "Afrocentric" ideas about the family and views of the community, which are quite different from those of the dominant culture, are an important focus of inquiry. Indeed, Womanists point out that many African-American women perceive white feminism, with its attack on family, as a threat to African-American family life and survival (Eugene 1992: 140-143; Grant 1989a: 201; Williams 1985: 103).

In a roundtable discussion on feminist theology and religious diversity published in 2000, Amina Wadud, who is African-American and Muslim, criticised Womanist (Christian) theologians for having "no place for" African-American Muslim women (see Gross 2000: 95). Her criticism was echoed by another African-American, Yvonne Chireau, who charged Womanist theologians with ignoring "religious diversity" and privileging "the study of Christianity" (see Gross 2000: 102). In her bibliographical essay, Shelley Finson does not report any Womanist theology in Canada, but she does discuss briefly the reactions of white Christian feminists to criticisms by Womanist theologians (1995: 19-20).

CHRISTIAN-FEMINIST THEOLOGIES WORLDWIDE

More and more women from all parts of the world are entering the Christian-feminist theological debate (Kim 2005). As do Womanist theologians, they point out to Western and particularly North-

American women the lack of universality in the words "women's experience"; they also emphasise the race and class privilege that most Western and especially North-American women enjoy. In addition, Christian-feminist theologians all over the world are developing feminist theologies appropriate to their own experiences. For instance, a feminist theologian from Indonesia used the Bible and Asian-women's experiences to construct a theology for Asian women. Since then, a number of works have appeared that construct feminist theologies in African, Asian, and Latin-American contexts (Katoppo 1996: 244-250; King 1996; Finson 1995: 17-19; Katoppo 1980).

Foremost African feminist theologian, Mercy Oduyoye (2004, 2001), argues that the church must emphasise "participation and inclusiveness" (2001: 77). It must "get out onto the streets" in an effort to heal the sick and oppose injustice (2001: 88). She reports the founding, in 1989) of the Circle of Concerned African Women Theologians (2004: xiii; Pemberton 2003).

Speaking directly to the issue of experience, a Chinese Christian feminist from Hong Kong discusses the effect of context on her spiritual life. Brought up in the Chinese religious tradition, she is now, as a Christian, "an *outsider-within.*" She also feels herself in the same position with respect to the Christian tradition in general. Further, despite her "wish to identify with Afro-American sisters' work," her experience of Christianity is, she says, "radically different" from theirs (Kwok 1996: 63-75, 236-242; Kwok 1992: 103-105). Since these early publications, Kwok Pui-lan has published extensively. In 2000 she issued an introduction to Asian feminist theology, and in 2002 she co-edited a collection of essays on post-colonialism and feminism: "gender, religion, and colonialism are inticately linked" in the domination of others (28).

Latin-American feminist theology has close relations with Latin-American Liberation Theology, as Linda Moody points out (1996: 46ff.). Latin-American feminist theologians recognise the attempts of male liberation theologians to come to grips with women's oppression, but they are clearer than their male colleagues about women's problems that result from male dominance not only in society but also in the Church (King 1996; see also Finson 1995: 18-19).

Hispanic women in the United States have also developed their own form of feminist theology that many call *Mujerista* theology

(Olazagasti-Segovia 1992: 110). They chose the Spanish word because most Hispanic women associated the term "feminist" with middle-class English speaking women and the translation of *Mujerista*, "womanist," was already in use. Others use the term "Latina" (Aquino, Machado, and Rodriguez 2002). In 1996, one of the leading *Mujerista* theologians, Ada María Isasi-Díaz, published in English her interpretation of *Mujerista* theology (1996, see also, Isasi-Díaz 1996a: 88-102; 1993).

Both Latina feminist and *Mujerista* theologians have much in common with Womanist theologians. They too emphasise the need to base theology on the experiences of poor and oppressed women and to acknowledge that, in large parts of the world, women are *the* poor, the poorest of the poor. They advocate struggle against the societal and religious oppression of Latina and Hispanic women. Like Womanist theologians, Latina-feminist and *Mujerista* theologians argue that community and the extended family are sources of strength for most Latina and Hispanic women. In addition, they point out that Latina and Hispanic women often understand divinity as immanent; for them, Jesus is "Emmanuel, 'God Within Us'" (Vargas 2007; Moody 1996: 46-47; Herrera 1993: 88-89; Berriozábal 1992: 117-118).

LESBIAN VOICES

Most Christian traditions, especially the conservative ones, consider homosexuality a sin. As recently as 1986, the Roman Catholic Church declared homosexuality "an objective disorder" and branded non-marital and non-procreative sex as "aberrant" (Carmody and Carmody 1993: 143). Many liberal Churches are sympathetic to those who know themselves to be homosexuals, but are not sexually active. Some Protestant churches fully accept and even ordain them. However, the difficulty normally arises on the matter of ordination (Ellison 1993: 150-151). The Roman Catholic Church established an organization called Dignity "to channel the aspirations of gay Roman Catholics" (Carmody and Carmody 1993: 135). Nonetheless, it is unlikely that most lesbians would feel comfortable openly expressing their spirituality as lesbians in most Christian Churches.

Sometimes lesbians are lucky enough to discover a sympathetic minister who will perform bonding or commitment (marriage) rites and other rituals for them. If they live in a large city, they can attend a gay and lesbian church, such as the Metropolitan Community Church in Toronto, Canada. Otherwise, lesbians sometimes form their own private worship groups. Often, however, lesbian feminists leave the church to involve themselves in other forms of spirituality.

In the last twenty-five years, feminist theologians who are openly lesbian have added their experiences to discussions of feminist theology. Carter Heywood, ordained as an Episcopal (Anglican) priest, is a leading American feminist theologian who now publishes from a specifically lesbian point of view. She writes about ethics and has explored what theology can say about the erotic. She is also interested in ritual; her account of a lesbian Thanksgiving ritual can be found in an anthology of rites for and by lesbians and male homosexuals (Kittredge and Sherwood 1995; Heywood 1989a, 1989b, 1984).

Lesbian Christians are also examining their relationships to the traditions of their upbringing, recounting their experiences and analyzing them from a lesbian point of view. For instance, lesbians who were raised as Roman Catholics have contributed their varied stories and reflections on them (Curb and Monahan 1985). Another important anthology presents the personal stories of a group of fifty lesbian nuns, who consider their motivations and the meaning of their experiences (Zanotti 1986). Further, a special issue of the American lesbian journal *Sinister Wisdom* was dedicated to discussing religion ("Lesbians and Religion" 1994-1995).

DISCUSSION

"Christianity, Feminism, and Feminist Theology" is a vast subject. This survey has managed to touch on only some of its most important aspects. Two of the most significant are, first, the fact that early Christianity, with its small, decentralised communities, allowed women not only considerable freedom in spirituality, but also leadership roles. The Women-Church movement today appears to following a similar pattern, with similar achievements. Second is the way in which, in both early Christianity and the Pentecostal Churches, women's ecstatic powers resulted in spiritual leadership.

Feminist theology has stimulated great changes in some Christian traditions, very little in others. The Eastern Orthodox tradition is just beginning to feel pressure from women. As most of the conservative Protestant Churches are doing, it may opt to respond very little or not at all. In the liberal Protestant Churches, the ordination of women is building a critical mass of potentially subversive insiders, and feminist theologians in those traditions continue to give them ammunition and support. Though the Roman Catholic Church still has a conservative Pope, a number of national Churches, urged on by women members, will continue to adapt locally and try centrally to have an influence.

In the past Christianity did not treat women well, and the changes that are occurring today are coming about slowly as a result of pressure. From the suppression of women's leadership as the Church became institutionalised to the witch craze of the sixteenth and seventeenth centuries and the recent reluctance of modern Churches to restore to women the right to become priests, the record has not been good. However, in the past women remained within the Churches despite Christianity's treating them as second-class citizens, and no doubt large numbers of women will continue to support their traditions. Just as certainly Christian feminist theologians will insist on change.

For me, one of the really exciting developments in the Christian tradition in recent years is what I have called the Revolutionary stream and what one of my students called "Pagan Christianity." A ritual example was reported from a Women-Church group: the ritual begins with a calling down of the spirits of the four directions, a borrowing from Wicca and other traditions; continues with the reading of Bible selections that praise Earth; and ends with worshippers weaving a communal web (Carson 1992: 154). Such a ritual certainly pushes Christianity to its limits.

It is a moot question whether such rituals and the positions Revolutionaries take in their work will, in time, bring about what many feminist theologians state that they want: complete transformation of the tradition (Johnson 1997: 32). We might ask ourselves, however, as with the drastically altered Judaism that many Jewish feminist theologians envision, whether the religion so transformed would still be recognisably Christian.

A hajj pilgrimage certificate, Mecca, 15th century. This illustrated scroll attests that Maymunah, daughter of Muhammad ibn 'Abd Allah al-Zardali, made the pilgrimage to Mecca and visited the tomb of the Prophet Muhammad in the year 836 AH (AD 1432-1433).

5.
ISLAM, FEMINISM AND FEMINIST THEOLOGY

ISLAM BEGAN IN the early seventh century CE in the Arabian peninsula in the Middle East. Today the peninsula encompasses Saudi Arabia and a number of smaller kingdoms, such as Kuwait, Bahrain, and Oman. That Islam is in the same tradition as Judaism and Christianity is obvious from a reading of Islam's sacred book, the Qur'an (Koran). Indeed, the Prophet Muhammad, to whom God revealed the Qu'ran, understood himself to be the last in a long line of prophets that included Abraham, Moses, and Jesus (Ruthven 1997: 28).[1] Like Judaism and Christianity, Islam is a patriarchal religion (Hassan 2003: 225).[2]

Today Islam is the religion of somewhat over one billion people worldwide (Crandall 2006: xiii). Despite the fact that it is not always safe for Muslim women to take feminist stances, feminists are active in most Muslim countries and communities. However, as a number of Muslim feminists point out, a Western model of feminism is not acceptable to most Muslim women, because they see it as ignoring motherhood and, at least in part, contributing to the destruction of the family (Mernissi 1987: 7-9). Thus, the majority of Muslim feminists have been engaged in developing what Mai Yamani describes as a brand of feminism "'Islamic' in its form and content." She calls it "Islamic feminism" (1996: 1, 13). Indeed, even in countries that have conservative Islamic governments or are experiencing powerful pressure from Islamic conservatives to base government in Islamic law, Islamic feminists are trying to use Islamic law to effect change (Ruthven 1997: 1, 114-117).

How successful Islamic feminists may be usually depends on whether their society is "fundamentalist." In the Islamic context, people use the term "fundamentalism" in a number of ways: It can mean supporting a return to following the teaching and ways of the Prophet. It can mean acceptance of the Qur'an, the Muslim sacred book, as the only guide for living. To some it just means "conservative." Ruthven adds that Islam as a religion is different from Islam as a "political ideology." He says that one should not describe political Islam by the term "fundamentalist," for, in so doing, one implies that "the defence of Islam's 'fundamentals' demands political action" and thus grants support to Islamic activists (Ruthven 1997: 4-7; Hourani 1991: 457).

In some Muslim countries, Islamic feminists seem able, more or less freely, to make known their views. In others, it can be dangerous for feminists to express their views, as a feminist writer from Bangladesh, Taslima Nasrin, found out. Accused of blaspheming and conspiring against Islam in her writings, she escaped Bangladesh with a price on her head (Alam 1998: 429). It is significant that many feminists writing about Islam live and work in Western societies (Yamani 1996: ix-xii).

BACKGROUND

Islam is one of the three monotheistic "Abrahamic religions," the other two being Judaism and Christianity. Islam continues the first two, but it has original elements. The Qur'an collects God's revelations to the Prophet Muhammad. For Muslims, the Qur'an contains the direct and everlasting Words of God. Thus, Islam reveres the Prophet as the instrument through whom God gave His revelations to the world. Later elaboration of Muhammad's image made him the role model for innumerable Muslims from early times to today (Ruthven 1997: 5, 45).

The Prophet Muhammad

The biography of Muhammad, at first orally transmitted, did not enter written record until more than a century after he died. Thus, absolutely reliable historical facts are almost impossible to uncover. Muslim tradition, however, has much to say about Muhammad (Ruthven 1997: 30-31; Hourani 1991: 15).

Born in Mecca in about 570 CE, when Christianity was still in the process of establishing itself in Europe, Muhammad was a member of a minor branch of a noble and powerful tribe that specialised in trading and also had "a connection" with the important Meccan shrine, the Kaaba (*Ka'ba*). Since ancient times, the shrine with its revered Black Stone had made Mecca a regional centre of pagan ritual and pilgrimage (Ruthven 1997: 32; Hourani 1991: 15).

At about twenty-five years of age, Muhammad married an older widow, his employer Khadija; it was she who proposed to Muhammad, a process quite normal for those times. Khadija and Muhammad had seven children, but only four daughters survived. The youngest, Fatima, gave Muhammad two grandsons, Hasan and Hussein. Until Khadija died in 620 CE at sixty-five, Muhammad took no other wives. After her death, however, he married at least nine women and possibly as many as twelve or thirteen. The most important of these later wives was Aisha (A'isha), young daughter of an early follower (Ruthven 1997: 33, 103; Jones 1996: xiv; Walther 1995: 103-105, 108; Mernissi 1987: 51).

Khadija supplied the wealth and personal support that Muhammad needed to pursue a spiritual life. He made regular retreats to a cave outside Mecca, where, around 610 CE, when he was about forty, Muhammad received the first of God's revelations. On the "Evening of Power or Destiny," in the month of Ramadan, during an awesome ecstatic experience, Muhammad received God's first communication through the Angel Gabriel, who instructed him: "Recite." He then began reciting what became the Qur'an, meaning "Recitation" (Ruthven 1997: 23, 33-34; Hourani 1991: 16).

Khadija persuaded him that he had received a calling as a prophet, and she became the first Muslim. The other members of his household and some friends soon followed. In 613 CE he began preaching to the mostly hostile Meccans that there was One God, who would, at the end of time, sit in judgment on all human beings. He also insisted that all were equal before the One God. Muhammad made very few converts in Mecca, where there was profit to be made from the city's polytheistic shrines (Ruthven 1997: 35; Jones 1996: xii-xiv; Walther 1995: 34, 104; Hourani 1991: 16-17).

In 622 CE, with about two hundred followers, the Prophet left Mecca for Yathrib. The *hijra*, as the journey is called, marks the

Goddess Al-Uzza, from the Manatu temple at Petra. Used with permission

beginning of the Muslim era and of the lunar Muslim calendar. In Medina al-Nabi, "City of the Prophet," formerly Yathrib, Islam became the dominant religion. Muhammad's first goal was to create a new way of life and community, *umma*, the Islamic community. During this period, Muhammad's continuing revelations had much to do with the details of the organization of the newly formed community. Much later, these became the basis of Sharia, Islamic law. In addition the Prophet's teachings began to be aimed at not only pagan Arabia, but the whole world (Jones 1996: xiv-xv; Walther 1995: 34; Cleary 1993: xii; Hourani 1991: 17-18).

Eventually, in 630 Ce, Muhammad and his followers returned triumphantly to Mecca. Taking over the pagan shrines, they destroyed cult objects, including those dedicated to the goddesses al-Uzza, Manat, and al-Lat. The Prophet circumambulated the Kaaba, blessed the Black Stone, and had it installed in the wall of the Kaaba (Ruthven 1997: 40; Hourani 1991: 19).

Two years later, after a short illness, Muhammad died in Medina. As legacies, Muhammad left, first, "his personality as seen through the eyes of his close companions"; second, the community of Islam; and, third, and most important, the Qur'an (Hourani 1991: 19-20).

THE HOLY QUR'AN

Muslims understand the Qur'an as containing God's words exactly as Muhammad heard them. Thus it is not just a sacred book like the Bible. Because Muslims came to think of it as "'uncreated', hence coextensive with God," it has for Muslims the same sort of place in Islam as Jesus Christ has in Christianity. Therefore, discussion of the sources of the text and the way it arrived at its present state, so important to scholars, are irrelevant for most Muslims. For them the Holy Qur'an contains the Word of God. Furthermore, many Muslims think that it should not be translated (Ruthven 1997: 23-24; Jones 1996: xxv; Walther 1995: 33).

Most non-Muslim scholars accept that the Qur'an is a record of God's words as Muhammad received them over a period of about twenty years (c.610-632 CE). Some evidence suggests that revelations were being written down before Muhammad left Mecca. Jones states that, by about twenty years after Muhammad's death, one version had been declared "authoritative" (1996: xix-xx). The only changes since that time occurred in conjunction with the improvement of Arabic script in the eighth century (Ruthven 1997: 24; Hourani 1991: 20-21).

The revelations in the Qur'an are arranged in 114 *sura*s, "rows"; these "chapters" appear according to length, longest first and shortest at the end. An exception is the ritually important "Opening" (*Sura* 1: 1-7); Muslims repeat this invocation of seven verses at each of the five obligatory daily prayers (Ruthven 1997: 24-25; Jones 1996: xxi). The Qur'an was essentially an oral composition and so was always intended to be read aloud. Recitation of sections of the Qur'an is today the most usual delivery of the text, and, for Muslims, hearing and silent reading of the Qur'an is a devotional act (Ruthven 1997: 29; Jones 1996: xviii).

The Qur'an's main theme is belief in the single deity Allah, literally "God," the merciful and omnipotent creator of the universe. Human disobedience to God's wishes will result in an apocalypse and then the Day of Judgment, the righteous going to Heaven, the unrighteous to Hell. The Qur'an contains stories of peoples and prophets, a large number known from the Bible. Abraham, a particularly revered prophet, rejected idolatry and, helped by his first son Ishmael, constructed the Kaaba as a shrine to God (Ruthven 1997: 26; Jones 1996: xxii-xxiii).

Despite its dealing with a number of figures and stories that occur the Hebrew and Christian Bibles, the Qur'an often develops a different theological perspective on them. A good example is its treatment of the "Adam and Eve Story" and the Fall, found in Genesis 2-3 of the Hebrew Bible. In the Qur'an, God punishes Satan for refusing to bow down to Adam. As in the Christian interpretation of the Genesis story, Adam commits sin when he eats the fruit of the forbidden tree, but in the Qur'an he repents. Then God appoints Adam as his deputy (*khalifa*). Thus, for Islam, there is no original sin and therefore no need of a redeemer (Ruthven 1997: 28).

The Qur'an and Women

According to Amila Buturovic, the Qur'an, more directly than other monotheistic sacred texts, concerns itself with women (*Sura* 4). The Qur'an specifies the social and religious obligations of each sex and specifies equality between women and men in matters of faith. The Qur'an's statements on women should, of course, be understood in the light of the period when the Qur'an was revealed and the pre-Islamic situation in Arabia to which it was responding (1997: 53).

In its pronouncement on the creation of human beings, the Qur'an states that God made men and women from "one soul" (*Sura* 4: 1). Thus, women have souls and can also claim a place in Paradise. In principle, the Qur'an expects women to fulfil all the religious obligations of Muslims (Ruthven 1997: 96; Rodwell 1996: 49, 280; Walther 1995: 51; Stowasser 1994).

Although the Qur'an considers human beings as equal spiritually, when it discusses specific issues of social ethics, it divides humans into male and female. *Sura* 4, chapter four, of the Qur'an is, for obvious reasons, traditionally called "Women." Since the Qur'an is for Muslims the revealed word of God, what it says about women has been central to Islam's attitude to women, and it proclaims that women and men are equal *in the faith*. *Sura* 4: 124-126 reads: "Anyone, male or female,/ who does what is good/ and is faithful/ will enter the Garden/ and will not be oppressed at all."

On the other hand, *Sura* 4: 34 states that men are superior to women because of "the qualities with which God [has] gifted [men] above [women]," and because of "the outlay [men] make from their substance for [women]." The passage continues: "Virtuous women are obedient" and chaste. If women are disobedient, then men should "remove them into beds apart, and scourge them" (Cleary 1993: 390; Rodwell 1996: 52, 62).

Sura 4: 3 permits a man to marry up to four women, provided he can support them economically and treat them all equally. However, the preference of both the Qur'an and Muslim custom is monogamy, and the ideal is the relationship of Muhammad and Khadija. The sacred book discusses divorce and men's right to initiate it, but it is silent on whether women also have the right so to do. The Qur'an forbids incest, as well as adultery. Four witnesses have to corroborate an accusation of "whoredom" against a woman. If she is found guilty, incarceration in the house until death is her sentence (*Sura* 4: 19, 24: 3). The law should punish both partners in fornication (*Sura* 4: 19-30) (Hamadeh 1996: 346; Rodwell 1996: 49-52, 230; Carmody 1989: 191).

The Qur'an states that women can inherit, but men inherit the equivalent of two women's portions (*Sura* 4: 12). *Sura* 4, indeed, specifies in detail various rights of inheritance, and it does not omit women. The Qur'an prescribes modesty for both men and women (*Sura* 24: 30-31). Above all, the sacred book makes clear throughout that a woman's primary role is to be a good wife and mother. These pronouncements on women in the Qur'an form one of the bases for the status of women in Islamic law (Rodwell 1996: 50-51, 232).

PRE-ISLAMIC ARABIA

According to Islamic historians, the time before the *Hijra* in 622 CE was a period of barbarism and ignorance. Islamic sources call it the "Period of Ignorance," when "People of Ignorance" did not know the One God. Traditionalists insist that the advent of Islam gave women far more rights than they had enjoyed in the "Period of Ignorance," and, indeed, they fear the return of pre-Islamic times with their inherent *fitna*, "chaos or disorder." Traditionalists especially fear women's power to create *fitna* through their sexuality as they did in those promiscuous days. Moroccan feminist theologian Fatima Mernissi argues that fear of a mythical, pre-civilised Arabic society underpins much of Islam's stance on women (Ruthven 1997: 95; Mernissi 1987: 31, 46, 65, 84-85, 166).

So what do we actually know about life in the Arabian peninsula in pre-Islamic times? Early society was nomadic, and people did not begin to settle down until the fifth century. Three towns gradually developed, Mecca, Yathrib (later, Medina), and Taif, and the populace slowly became semi-sedentary, though it continued to adhere to nomadic values (Jones 1996: xi-xii).

As to the organisation of pre-Islamic society, the evidence is not very abundant, but some scholars suggest that it was primarily matrilineal, with paternity of no great importance. Ghada Karmi adds that, well before Islam, there probably were religions dominated by women, and from this theory she concludes that the original structure of society was matrilineal or even matriarchal (1996: 77). Matriliny does not, of course, necessarily mean that women had high status. Indeed, the prohibition in the Qur'an against female infanticide may suggest that girl babies were not highly valued in pre-Islamic society (*Sura*s 16: 60, 81: 8-9) (Rodwell 1996: 175, 409; Watt cited in Ahmed 1992: 43; Mernissi 1987: 73-78).

Nevertheless, most Muslims believe that Islam ameliorated women's lives considerably. In support of this view, they point out that many of the Qur'an's revelations deal with improving the status of women, who were, they argue, subject previously to being bought, sold, and inherited. Men arranged women's marriages to suit their own plans, multiple marriages were common, and widowed and unmarried women were neglected. Further, since the honour of pre-Islamic tribe was closely connected to female chastity, men controlled female behaviour very strictly. Men could practise unrestricted polygyny, but women had no access to divorce, nor could they inherit (Karmi 1996: 76; Carmody 1989:

190). If all this is true, it is not surprising that as Mernissi tells us, in the seventh century, thousands of women left "aristocratic tribal Mecca" for the Prophet's city, Medina (1991: viii).

Unfortunately, the sparse evidence we have available to us about pre-Islamic Arabia derives mainly from sources hostile to pre-Islamic society (Ahmed 1992: 42). Nonetheless, Ghada Karmi argues that careful analysis of that evidence points to a pre-Islamic society in which women enjoyed "some prominence" (1996: 77). However, maybe it was the nature of pre-Islamic society that allowed Khadija not only to maintain a monogamous marriage, but to run a business (Buturovic, personal communication, January 1998).

In *Beyond the Veil*, Fatima Mernissi undertakes an analysis of the evidence on sex and marriage in pre-Islamic Arabia. She makes a case that, until the Prophet's time, society traced descent both matrilineally and patrilineally. She further states that women had many "sexual rights" in the pre-Islamic period (1987: 73-74, 78). Ghada Karmi, following Mernissi's lead, theorises that the advent of Islam completed a transition from matriliny to patriliny that had already begun in pre-Islamic times (1996: 79).

Pre-Islamic Religion in Arabia

Understanding pre-Islamic society in Arabia, let alone religion, is difficult, partly because Saudi Arabia does not permit archaeological digs and partly because most information about pre-Islamic spirituality comes, with some exceptions,[3] from later Islamic and Christian writings. The Islamic sources are usually accounts of the destruction of pagan shrines when Islam took control of them (Patai 1990: 157).

From these writings, we can deduce that the spirituality of the nomads of the area focused on a form of ancestor worship. Yearly there was a cessation of blood feuds, so that the tribes could make a pilgrimage to Mecca to visit its shrine, the Kaaba. The tribe into which Muhammad was born controlled Mecca, guarded the Kaaba, and formed a religious oligarchy that profited well from the Meccan shrine (Bowker 1997: 519; Ruthven 1997: 32-33; Jones 1996: xiii).

In pre-Islamic Arabia, the chief deity of the Kaaba appears to have been a creator and sustainer, and his name seems to have

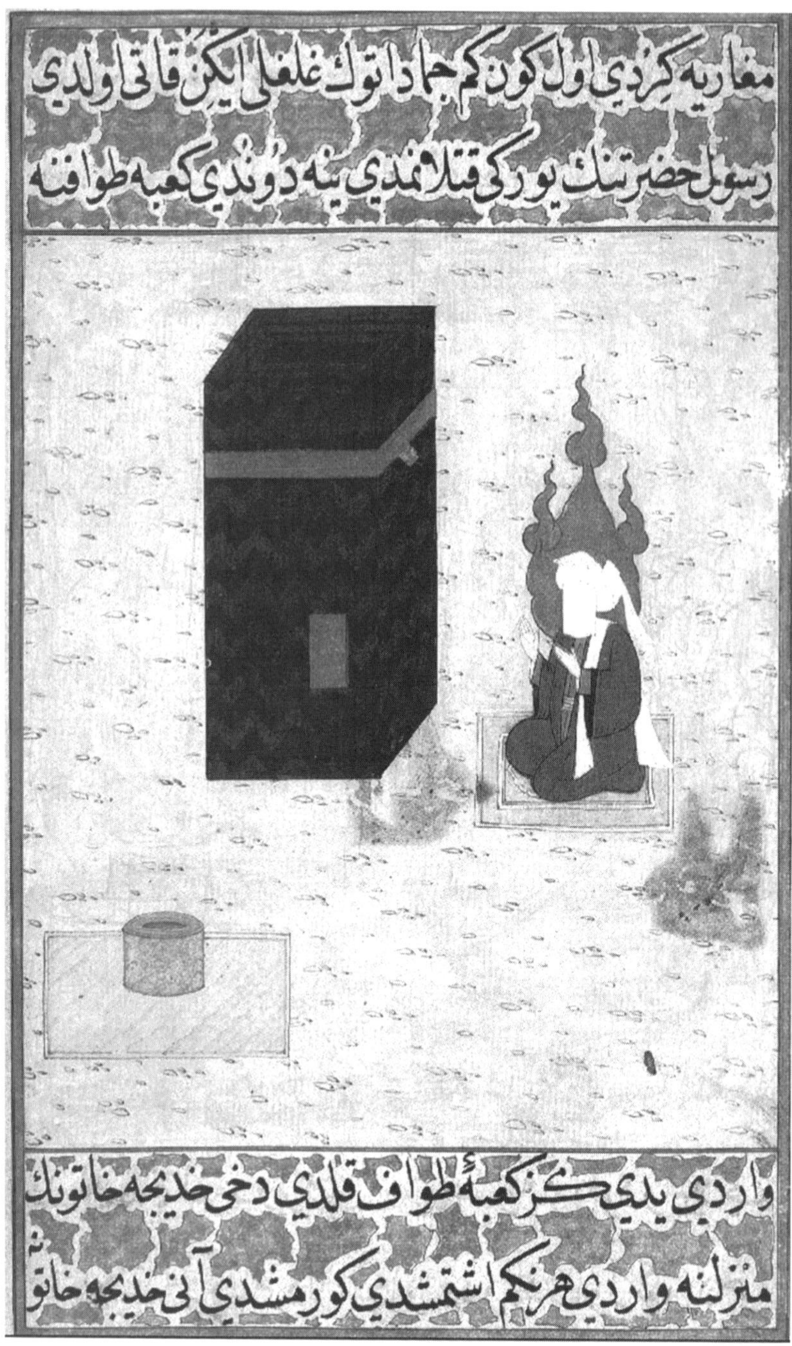

Muhammad at the Ka'ba. Istanbul, 1595.
From Siyer-i-Nebi: The Life of the Prophet. *Author unknown.*

been Allah. There is some evidence that goddesses also were worshipped by the pre-Islamic Arabians, and the best known, to whom many shrines were dedicated, were al-Uzza, Allat, and Manat (Ruthven 1997: 35, 40; Yamani 1996: 77; Walther 1995: 33; Hourani 1991: 16).

Allat, al-Uzza, and Manat were apparently closely associated with Mecca, and Robert Briffault thought that they were aspects of one goddess (1927: III, 79-81). Al-Uzza, "the Powerful One," was identified either with the planet Venus or with the moon. The name "Allat" is the Arabic equivalent of the West Semitic name "Elat," meaning "Goddess," an epithet of the goddess Asherah in Syro-Palestine.[4] Allat may have been a deity like Aphrodite, though some scholars think that she was a moon goddess. Manat probably represented fate or destiny (Ruthven 1997: 35; Ann and Imel 1993: 316-317, 320; Ahmed 1992: 48).

One of the most sacred objects at Mecca today is the Black Stone, framed in silver and fixed in the wall of the Kaaba, the oldest element in the structure. Briffault suggests that, before Muhammad blessed it, the stone may have been a goddess or a goddess symbol (1927: iii, 80). The Black Stone is probably a meteorite, and ancient peoples often venerated meteorites as tokens of the Queen of Heaven (al-Uzza?) fallen to earth. For instance, Roman historian Livy tells us that the Romans and before them the people of Anatolia in Turkey worshipped the goddess Cybele as a meteorite (Bowker 1997: 152; Meyer 1987: 122; Godwin 1981: 110).

Mecca, the town Muhammad grew up in, must have been a melting pot of ideas, but there is little doubt that its power elite was staunchly pagan and held out against Muhammad and his followers for over a decade. Eventually, early in 630 CE, the Muslims took possession of Mecca. Before Muhammad died in 632 CE, he had fulfilled his aim of seeing the populace of the Arabian peninsula converted to Islam (Jones 1996: xviii-xiv).

SUNNIS AND SHIITES

When the Prophet died in 632 CE, he had not named a successor or established rules of succession. Consequently, a crisis developed over who was to inherit the Prophet's authority, and, as Hourani says, it was a crisis that was never to be resolved. According to tribal custom, Abu Bakr, one of Muhammad's earliest followers and father of his favourite wife, Aisha, was acclaimed in Medina as caliph. The next three caliphs were chosen in the same way. However, this process slighted the claim of Ali, Muhammad's cousin and husband of his youngest daughter, Fatima. The result was the exacerbation of "personal and factional" disagreements that came to a head during the rule of the third caliph (644-656 CE) (Ruthven 1997: 15, 53; Hourani 1991: 22, 24-25). In 656 CE, when the third caliph was assassinated, Ali claimed the caliphate, but could not gain authority over the whole community. In 661, Ali was himself assassinated. Although Ali's elder son Hasan agreed that his father's rival should become caliph, Ali's younger son Hussein did not. When Ali's rival died in 680 CE, Hussein challenged the heir for the caliphate, but, in the same year, died himself at the battle of Karbala in what is now Iraq (Ruthven 1997: 53-54; Hourani 1991: 25).

These differences about how to establish Islam's leadership and about what constituted authority in the community of Islam eventually produced a permanent split in the religion. One group, now called Sunni, insisted that only a virtuous Muslim could become *imam*, meaning "guide," and, if he went astray, the community should withdraw its support from him. The other group, now known as Shiites, saw authority as derived from relationship, or close proximity, to the Prophet and his family. Eventually, Islam divided into these two main branches (Ruthven 1997: 8; Hourani 1991: 30-37).

WOMEN IN ISLAMIC HISTORY

Women were prominent in the rise of Islam, starting with Khadija, whose strength and influence cannot be overestimated. The women of the Prophet's family were, for the most part, clearly individual and by no means subordinate. After Muhammad's death, Aisha, his favourite wife, was often consulted on religious and socio-ethical matters. Aisha even led forces that opposed Muhammad's son-in-law Ali in his bid for the Caliphate, and so she is a heroine

Detail, Women of the Ottaman empire. German Federal Archive, Bild. 137-012802. Photo: Klinghardt, 1917. Used with permssion CC-BY.

for Sunni Islam. Aisha died in 678 CE, a venerated "Mother of the Faithful" (Walther 1995: 105-107, 111-112; Hermansen 1992: 115-116).

Another important female member of the Prophet's family was his youngest daughter Fatima, wife of Ali and mother of Hasan and Hussein. Ali did not withdraw his claim to the leadership of Islam until after Fatima's death. In Shiite Islam, Fatima is deeply revered as "the only female among the 'fourteen pure ones,'" who include, in addition to Fatima, Ali and the twelve Imams. For Islam, Fatima occupies a place in many ways similar to that of the Virgin Mary in Christianity (Walther 1995: 107-108; Hermansen 1992: 117, 137, n. 13).

In early Islamic times, it was not unusual for women to be present on the battlefield, to use tricks to help the men, and even to take part in battles. Warrior women also figure among the heroines of Islam. On one early battlefield, Umm Umara stood alone defending the Prophet and was wounded twelve times. Safiyya, Muhammad's paternal aunt, was also a strong warrior, and other Muslim women followed their example (Hermansen 1992: 118-124).

Some women religious scholars achieved fame as a result of both their learning and their piety. Born in Mecca in 762-3 CE, Nafisa, great-granddaughter of Hasan, Muhammad's grandson, was famous for her theological learning, her devoutness, and her devotion to justice, and, after she died in Cairo in 823-4 CE, people visited her mausoleum to say prayers that they knew would be answered. Shuhda Bint al-Ibari, who died in Baghdad in 1178, and Zaynab bint ash-Shari of Nishapur, who died in 1218, were

A Turbah or Mohr from Qum, Iraq, showing a prayer beseeching help from Fatima, daughter of the Muslim Prophet Mohammad, which reads: "Ya Fatima-ta Azzahra" ("Oh, Fatima!"). Photo: Bill Garrison, 2007. Used with permission GNU Free Documentation License, and CC-BY.

respected teachers, and some of their students followed in their footsteps (Walther 1995: 110).[5]

THE SPREAD OF ISLAM

Only twenty-five years after the death of Muhammad (632 CE), Islam was in control of the eastern part of the southern Mediterranean coast. Within two centuries of his death, the faith had spread by conquest to the Atlantic (Spain and France) and to India. Islam was basically a proselytising religion, and its military advance was fuelled by the urge to spread the faith. However, the march of the religion also promoted outstanding cultural developments in literature, science, philosophy, arts, and law (Walther 1995: 37-39; Cleary 1993: vii; Carmody 1989: 186).

Islam was also tolerant of the religious traditions of the conquered, but only if they were monotheistic. Jews and Christians had to accept the rule of Islam and pay tax, but then they were granted "a limited form of [religiously organised] self-government." Polytheists, however, were normally forced to convert under threat of death (Ruthven 1997: 119; Hourani 1991: 46-48; Carmody 1989: 186).

Throughout the Islamic world, cities based in trade slowly emerged. By ninth and tenth centuries CE, Muslim lands boasted the most extensive cities in the Western hemisphere. In these cities, Islamic Law was the generally accepted, and specially trained male judges (*qadi*s) administered it. Upper-class women were secluded and veiled and had little role in the city's economic life, though poor women were active at the bottom levels of society. By the end of the tenth century, there existed what amounted to a Muslim world, its parts connected by a common culture, based in religion and in the language of the Qur'an, Arabic (Hourani 1991: 83-86, 109-129).

Beginning early in the eleventh century, Western Christianity mounted eight Crusades. These military expeditions, mainly against Muslim lands, were aimed at freeing the Holy Land from Muslim control. The first, which started in 1095, resulted in the conquest of Jerusalem in 1099 and the founding of Crusader states along the Syrian coast and in Palestine. In 1182, the great Muslim leader Salah ud-Din (Saladin) liberated Jerusalem, and no Crusade afterwards was able to re-take it. The last of the Crusader states, Acre, now Haifa in Israel, fell to Muslim forces in 1299 (Bowker 1997: 247; Ruthven 1997: 56; Hourani 1991: 84).

During the period from the eleventh to the fifteenth centuries CE, there developed a number of male-dominated Muslim dynasties and empires. Nevertheless, in the thirteenth and fourteenth centuries, Christian forces expelled Islamic armies from Sicily and Spain, except for Granada in the south, which did not fall until 1492. At the same time, Islam continued to spread south and east in Africa and further into north India and the rest of Asia. Eventually, in the fifteenth and sixteenth centuries, the Mughal dynasty

(1526-1858), with Delhi as its capital, was in control of northern India, and small Muslim states were established in Africa (Hourani 1991: 85-86, 130-1, 489-490).

ISLAMIC LAW

For Sunni Islam, Islamic law, the Sharia, literally "the way to a watering place," embodies the laws of God, and so human beings must obey it. The Sharia is the practical aspect of Muhammad's religious and social doctrine (Ruthven 1997: 59, 75; Hourani 1991: 161).

The Sharia relies on four main sources, in order of importance: First, the Qur'an; second, the Sunna, which enshrines the sayings and deeds of the Prophet; third, *ijma*, consensus, usually local, about a specific issue reached by religious jurists-scholars, the *ulama*, "learned men"; and, fourth, *qiyas*, reasoning by analogy. What the Qur'an prescribes is final, binding, infallible, and not questionable, and the Prophet's sayings and actions, derived from divine revelation, are also binding. The other two, consensus and analogic reasoning, are not so unchallengeable. Over the centuries, the Sharia was developed gradually as the result of the complex interaction between, on the one hand, the prescriptions of Qur'an and the Sunna and, on the other, the local laws and customs of each community that converted to Islam (Ruthven 1997: 77-83; Connors 1996: 364; Hourani 1991: 161).

The Sunna, "practice or custom," contains the *hadith* collections, detailed records of the Prophet's utterances and actions. A *hadith* can address almost anything: for example, the Prophet once said, "People who do not like animals should not be trusted." Also included in the Sunna are Muhammad's "silent approvals and disapprovals." A long, interconnected line of authorities, authenticated by religious scholars as reliable, passed down these sayings and deeds, and the chain always went back to a member of the Prophet's family or one of his early followers. Together with the Qur'an, the Sunna represents the origin of law and the yardstick for telling what is true and what false, for separating what is allowed from what is forbidden. However, before invoking a *hadith*, religious scholars had to authenticate it, and then they had to interpret it (Ruthven 1997: 78-79; Walther 1995: 49; Mernissi 1991: 1; Hourani 1991: 67).

The validity of the consensus, *ijma*, reached by religious jurist-scholars, the *ulama*, was rooted in a *hadith*: "My community will never agree upon an error." It was soon understood that the consensus of the *ulama*, the religious scholar-jurists, expressed the consensus of the community (Ruthven 1997: 79, 81).

In Islamic law, *qiyas* is the systematic pursuit of logic. When a point of law occurred that no clear statement in the Qur'an or the Sunna covered, scholar-jurists interpreted it *by analogy* with the principles of another point of law or legal decision. In these ways, then, scholar-jurists elaborated the Sharia (Ruthven 1997).

Over time, in interpreting the sources, Shiite scholar-jurists developed a Shiite law system somewhat different from that of the Sunni Muslims. Most of their principles of jurisprudence the Shiites borrowed from the Sunnis. However, the only *hadith*s that were acceptable to them were those passed down by members of the Prophet's family and their descendants. In addition, community consensus was not as important for Shiites as for Sunnis (Hourani 1991: 183).

Islamic Law and Women

As a result of interpretation of the Qur'an, the Sunna, the Sharia, and other sources of community authority, Muslim women often become subject to demands concerning obedience and family honour that are very restrictive. In addition, selections from the *hadith* collections, as well as writings by prominent men, have disparaged women; for instance, Muhammad is reported to have said, "Consult [women] and do the opposite." However, the *hadith*s referring to women represent a very broad spectrum of opinions, with some contradictions (Ruthven 1997: 94; Abu-Odeh 1996; Walther 1995: 48; Carmody 1989: 195).

Although the Qur'an encourages women to fulfil all the duties of Muslims, the few exemptions that come from their biology, such as their being ritually impure during menstruation and after childbirth, have led to the development by scholar-jurists of legal arguments that women are inferior to men in religious matters. One result was an effort to prevent women from praying in mosques

"Femmes musulmanes Syriennes - Costume de ville (Syriam muslim women in town dress)," c.1880. Photo: Félix Bonfils (1831-1885).

(Bowker 1997: 1043; Walther 1995: 51-52).

Historically, Islamic societies have adhered closely to the male-dominated family and the extended kinship system. Certainly, the Sharia favours the family over other institutions, and so, in theory, women have rights as mothers and wives. Nonetheless, discrimination against women in various matters, such as inheritance and right to divorce, occurs in the Qur'an and so continues in Islamic law (Ruthven 1997: 93, 95).

The Qur'an and the Sunna both make clear that marriage is expected of Muslims, but it is understood as a contract entered into by the groom and the bride's closest male relative. These two men negotiate the dowry that the husband has to provide. Over time, other practices developed, varying from place to place, that often made marriage excessively restrictive, even punitive, for women (Walther 1995: 54-55).

In principle, a wife has legal rights. She can insist on the terms of the contract, and she retains her dowry; she also has the right to refuse a marriage. If her husband does not support her economically, she can seek redress from the law. She can also sue for divorce, though traditionally divorce has been easy for men and extremely difficult for women. For a man, divorce is a matter of unilateral repudiation according to a fixed formula, and he normally gets custody of children over a certain age. If a woman sues for divorce, she forfeits her dowry. Muslim men can marry Christian or Jewish women, but Muslim women do not have the same right (Bowker 1997: 1043; Ruthven 1995: 100-102).

Although the Qur'an requires neither veiling of the face, nor complete covering of the body, but only modesty of dress for both sexes, advocates of women's wearing the veil cite two passages as suggesting that women cover themselves when among males who are not of their close family (*Sura*s 24: 31, 33: 59). In addition, scholar-jurists who thought that women should stay out of the public sphere appealed to a Qur'anic passage, which stipulates that the Prophet's wives were to sit behind a curtain when conversing with men who were not close family members (*Sura* 33: 53, 55). The legal elaboration of ideas of female modesty based on interpretations of the Qur'an increasingly resulted in the seclusion of women in the home and the exclusion of women from public life, though in varying degrees depending on place and time (Bowker 1997: 1043; Walther 1995: 69, 71-72).

ISLAMIC MYSTICISM

Sufism, or Islamic mysticism, took its origin in an ascetic movement that promoted seeking personal salvation in an atmosphere free of the pleasures of the flesh and the urge to accrue "material gains." The name came from the "wool (*souf*) garment" these mystics wore against their skin. Gradually, Sufism became a popular spiritual choice and developed into the "Sufi order." Any Muslim, male or female, may become a Sufi; the only qualification is a desire to have personal experience of the Qur'an's "divine message" (Buturovic 1997: 53; Ruthven 1997: 64).

Not surprisingly, women found Sufism, which did not offer special privileges to men, very attractive, and many women joined the movement, some even becoming Sufi saints. Since Sufi teachings did not criticise involvement in family, many women managed to remain good wives and mothers while following Sufi practices. Others became ascetics. The most famous of them, Rabia al-Adawiya of Basra (c.714-801 CE), shocked her society by refusing to marry (Smith 1994; Helms 1992). According to Buturovic, she was "the first true saint of Islam" (1997: 54-55). Ursula King notes that women have been patrons of Sufi orders, directors of Sufi convents, Sufi saints, and Sufi "spiritual guides" (1989: 106).

LATER DEVELOPMENTS

By the fifteenth and sixteenth centuries, a large part of the Muslim world belonged to three empires. In Persia, now Iran, the Safavid dynasty (1501-1732) declared its empire officially Shiite in religion. The second of the Muslim empires was in north India, and its Sunni Muslim rulers were members of the Mughal dynasty (1526-1858). The third, the Ottoman Empire, eventually gained control of what are now Algeria, Tunisia, Cyprus, Egypt, Syria, Turkey, Iraq, and western Arabia. Its rulers, from the Ottoman dynasty (1281-1922), were Sunni Muslims. Although today there are often large Shiite minorities in predominantly Sunni areas and vica versa, the majority of Middle Eastern and Indian Muslims are Sunnis, while Shiism remains the official religion of Iran (Hourani 1991: 96, 207, 489).

In the nineteenth and early twentieth centuries, a powerful nationalism developed in most areas of the Muslim world as a reaction to European domination and European influences. With nationalism came an increase in support for various national movements to emancipate women. For example, when a nationalist revolt against European domination led to the founding of the Republic of Turkey in 1923, the new country abolished the Sharia to secularise its government and was the first Muslim country to ban the veil. In the period after World War I, many young, educated women in the large cities of the Muslim world began to abandon the veil or, at least, go out with only a light covering. Nonetheless, by 1939, despite the fact that education for women was increasingly available and they were getting involved in nationalist political activities, the status of women had not changed in most Muslim countries (Hourani 1991: 263-264, 303, 327, 344-345).

World War II (1939-1945) completely altered power relations throughout the world. Great Britain, France, and other European powers withdrew from their colonies in the Middle East, Africa, and Asia. For instance, the Dutch left the Dutch East Indies in 1949, at which point the islands became independent as Indonesia; today Indonesia has the largest Muslim population in the world. In 1955 Britain (and Egypt) relinquished control of the Sudan, one of several African countries with large Muslim populations (Hourani 1991: 362).

Nationalism, both Hindu and Muslim, led to the end of British control of India, when, in 1947, India was divided into India and Pakistan. Thousands upon thousands of Muslims and Hindus migrated from their original homes, but many chose to continue where they were. Muslim Pakistan originally consisted of East and West Pakistan, but East Pakistan became Bangladesh in 1971 after a revolt. Both Pakistan and Bangladesh now have fundamentalist Islamist governments (Alam 1998: 432-436, 444; Ahmed 1992: 242).

When the British left Palestine in 1948, the state of Israel came into being. The result was an enormous increase of nationalism in all Arabic-speaking lands. Indeed, the 1950s and 1960s were a time of nationalistic fervour in the Middle East and in other predominantly Muslim areas. During this period, many Muslim countries also experienced changes in the social role of women and the family, but even though some countries moved to revise or change some laws that affected women, there was little alteration in social customs and attitudes (Hourani 1991: 264, 351, 441).

By the late 1970s and 1980s, "Islamic feelings and loyalties," augmented by aversion to Western ideas and customs, were combining with nationalistic sentiment to produce fundamentalist or "revivalist" movements and extremely conservative governments in many predominantly Muslim countries. The revolution of 1979 in Iran seems to have been a major factor in this development (Afshar 1996: 199; Hourani 1991: 352).

The Iranian Revolution ousted the Shah of Iran and brought the Ayatollah Khomeini to power. Under the Shah, Iran had been highly secular, Westernised, and politically oppressive, though women had experienced considerable personal freedom. Since the revolution, however, Iran has been an extremely conservative theocratic state, governed by a group of religious scholar-jurists. Though women in large numbers supported and worked to bring about the Iranian Revolution, the Islamic Republic of Iran began, almost as soon as it came into being, to enact laws to restrict women socially, economically, and politically (Afshar 1996: 201-203; Hourani 1991: 352).

In the late 1970s and 1980s, many young Muslim women took to wearing the *hijab*, an Arabic word meaning "any partition which separates two things," usually referring to the veil. They covered their hair, but not necessarily their faces. Most presented this decision as deliberate, to demonstrate their opposition to Western imperialism, their nationalism, and, above all, their commitment to Islam (Marshall 2005; Bowker 1997: 428; Hourani 1991: 442;457; Mernissi 1987: ix).

In the past three decades, increased numbers of Muslim immigrants have brought such complex issues with them to the West, especially North America (Moghissi 2006). It is quite usual for women in the *hijab* to be seen in public areas in Canada, the United States, Australia, and other Western countries. In the summer of 1993, the Toronto newspaper *The Globe and Mail* published an article by a Canadian-born Muslim woman on her decision to wear the *hijab*, and the next week it printed another woman's negative response. The topic recurred in the same newspaper over a year later (*The Globe and Mail* 1993, June 29: A24; 1993, July 5: A10; 1995, January 31: A18).

ISLAM TODAY

"Islam" means "surrender" or "submission" to the will of God. Thus, "Muslim" refers to anyone who surrenders to God and keeps His Commandments. A secondary meaning of "Muslim" is, according to Ruthven, a person, male or female, whose father was Muslim and who accepts the "confessional identity" of the parent without necessarily practising the faith. Thus, a person may be able to be an agnostic or an atheist and still identify as a Muslim (1997: 2-3). In sum, Islam can be a religious commitment, an ideology, or a sign of individual or communal identity, or two or three at once (Cleary 1993: vii).

All Muslims revere the Qur'an, and most of them follow the laws that Islam derived from the Qur'an and from the Sunna, the next in importance and complementary to the Qur'an as a place to look for Muslim values.

Even more than Christianity, Islam is a proselytising religion. A Muslim has an obligation to tell others about God's will and plan for living as revealed in the Qur'an. Islam has always respected the other "People of the Book," Jews and Christians, and allowed them to maintain their own religions. In principle, Islam does not today convert pagans by force, as in the past it did (Bowker 1997: 236).

In his book on Muslims in Indonesia, Iran, Pakistan, and Malaysia, V. S. Naipaul explores the issue of conversion. Islam is in origin Arab, and all non-Arab Muslims are converts. Their holy sites are no longer in their own countries, but in Arab lands; their own language is no longer sacred, for Arabic is the tongue of the sacred book of their new religion. They often suffer identity crises, personal, social, and political, that span generations, as a result of turning away from indigenous traditions. An example is an Indonesian woman who was reared both as a Muslim and as the proud and independent heir of a prominent matrilineal family (1998: xi, 54, 61).

Muslims total about 1.3 billion worldwide, approximately 21 percent of world population (Crandall 2006: xiii). In 1989, approximately 237 million lived in Africa, while South Asia was home to 535 million. The former Soviet Union's Muslims numbered 31.5 million, and East Asia's 24 million. Nine million Muslims resided in Europe. There were two million, 675 thousand in North America, while Latin America's total was 625,000. Finally, 95,000 of Oceania's population was Muslim (Carmody 1989: 188). Ruthven's 1997 estimate of the number of Muslims worldwide was around a billion (1).

Central Tenets

First and foremost, Islam is monotheistic. It is further characterised by lack of separation between secular and sacred. For practising Muslims, their religion *is* their way of life (Ruthven 1997: 51; Cleary 1993: vii). Muslims proclaim a number of articles of faith:

(1) *Tawhid*, "Oneness": The Oneness and Uniqueness of God is the most important. The concept of "Oneness" demands pure monotheism and prohibits idolatry, the greatest of all sins. God is the Creator, and He disposes of all lives and events in His creation (Bowker 1997: 479; Ruthven 1997: 51).

(2) *Nubuwah*, prophethood: Muhammad is God's messenger. The great prophets have been the means by which God has guided humans. The line of prophets began with Adam and ended with Muhammad. Although there is some dispute about some of the following names, the prophets that preceded Muhammad may include Noah, Abraham, Ishmael, Isaac, Lot, Moses, and Jesus (Ruthven 1997: 25).

(3) The *Qur'an*: The Qur'an is the last great book of guidance for living, and it came directly from God. More than a sacred book, it was "uncreated" and so is "coextensive with God." Thus, Muslims live under the authority of the Qur'an (Ruthven 1997: 23; Hourani 1991: 147).

(4) *Aakhirah*, life after death: On the Day of Judgment, God will assess all according to their faith, with the obedient, the faithful, going to an eternal and happy Garden, a Paradise, and the evil, the unbelievers, going to suffer in the Fire of Hell (Bowker 1997: 1055; Carmody 1989: 187).

(5) The *umma*, the community of Islam: Muslims constitute a world-wide community, which struggles to understand and fulfil the commandments of God. In so doing, members achieve a correct relationship not only with God, but also with one another, so

that all are kin one of the other (Ruthven 1997: 7-8).

(6) *Jihad*, "struggle": Muslims as a community have an obligation to perform *jihad*. The first meaning of the word is "struggle," so that the translation "holy war" can be misleading. Traditionally, Muslims undertake *jihad* using heart, tongue, hands, and sword, the heart being most important. In one of the *hadiths*, the Prophet distinguished between lesser and greater kinds of *jihad*, the lesser struggle against polytheists, the greater struggle against evil. The latter was one that a believer carried on throughout life. Since a ruler can undertake *jihad* for the community, it can, however, become a policy tool (Ruthven 1997: 118-122).

Rituals

Muslims ensure the continuity of the community of Islam by practising certain obligatory rituals, which link together not only worshippers in the present, but also establish a "chain of witness" that begins with Muhammad and ends when the world does. It passes on the "truth" from generation to generation (Hourani 1991: 147). These rituals make up the "Five Pillars of Islam."

The Five Pillars of Islam are five acts or duties of worship. They originated in Muhammad's lifetime, but the Qur'an does not mention them all; some come from the Sunna, "the Way of Life" of Muhammad (Ruthven 1997: 147-151; Bowker 1997: 348).

Shahadah, the first pillar, is the testimony of faith: "There is no god except God, and Muhammad is His Prophet." In order to convert to Islam, a person has formally to give this testimony. The minority Shiites add to it: "Ali is the Friend of God." Muslims repeat the *shahadah* every day in prayers (Ruthven 1997: 147; Hourani 1991: 147).

In *shahadah*, the central pillar around which the others cluster, Muslims assert pure monotheism and proclaim Muhammad as "The Seal of the Prophets," the last in a long line of prophets and the especially chosen one. In this profession of faith, Muslims depart from Christianity in that they do not recognise either the Trinity or the divinity of Jesus. However, the God of Islam is the same God as the Jewish and Christian God, and, in Islam also, He has no proper name (Carmody 1989: 187).

Salat, the second pillar, is compulsory prayer five times a day. After doing ritual ablutions, worshippers perform a series of bodily motions, including prostration, with exact movements being as important as spoken prayers and thoughts. The obligatory prayers are fixed; after them, worshippers may utter personal petitions. Obligatory prayers can occur almost anywhere, in private, in public, or in a mosque, provided worshippers are facing Mecca and the Kaaba. The Friday noon-time prayer, however, has to be performed in public as a meeting of a community's adult males. A mosque is the normal venue for this ritual, and after it the imam, "prayer leader," or a preacher gives a sermon. Women pray in a special area of the mosque, to the side or behind the men (Ruthven 1997: 147; Hourani 1991: 148).

Zakat, the third pillar, is the giving of alms, a donation of a portion of income to the poor; it is an extension of worship. This practice Muhammad introduced to promote social justice and, through sharing, to reduce injustice (Ruthven 1997: 147-148; Hourani 1991: 148).

Sawm, the fourth pillar, is fasting or, more appropriately, obligatory abstinence, once a year from sunrise to sunset during the month of Ramadan. Fasting means strict abstinence: no eating, no drinking, no smoking, and no sexual activity. Muslims over the age of ten are expected to fast. Muslims understand the ritual of *sawm* as self-denial for the sake of God and a way of repenting for sins. Ramadan, the ninth lunar month, in which Muhammad experienced "the Evening of Power," is traditionally a period for reflection and family gatherings. To recite the complete Qur'an during the month is a very worthy act (Ruthven 1997: 149-150; Hourani 1991: 149).

Hajj, the fifth pillar, is pilgrimage to Mecca. This demanding ritual duty is required of all adult Muslims at least once in a lifetime. The annual pilgrimage to Mecca occurs in the final ten days of the twelfth lunar month of the Muslim calendar. It is a communal event involving the *umma*, the whole of Islam. As well as being the directional focus for prayer, the Kaaba is now the principal destination of pilgrimage.

Thousands of pilgrims walk seven times around the Kaaba, an imposing square building in the great mosque at Mecca, and it is the aim of all pilgrims to touch or kiss the Black Stone. The completion of other arduous rituals is also expected. The pilgrimage demonstrates a Muslim's faith in God and is a manifestation of the solidarity of the *umma*. When a pilgrim returns home from Mecca, he or she receives honour as *Hajji*, a person who has fulfilled the obligation of *hajj* (Ruthven 1997: 150-151; Hourani 1991: 149-151).

Since there are no priests in Islam, it is the responsibility of all Muslims to follow God's laws, but women, at least for most of their lives, may have trouble performing all five of the duties. In principle, women should have no problem observing the first, for, though God is presented as grammatically masculine, He is not Father, as is the God of Christianity and Judaism, nor does He have sex or gender characteristics. Thus, the sex of God cannot, therefore, be an issue for women. The giving of alms should, in principle, cause no problem either (Marcus 1992: 66).

The remaining duties are, on the other hand, public and demand ritual purity. If a woman is pregnant or menstruating, she is exempt from fasting and pilgrimage. However, both menstruation and having recently given birth render women ritually impure. Further, women of child-bearing years usually cannot fast for the full thirty days of Ramadan, because they are bound to menstruate for some part of the month and so become ritually impure. The same is true for the time it normally takes pilgrims to get to Mecca. Thus, they have little chance, until they are middle aged or old, to garner the great respect accruing to persons who have made the *hajj*. In fact, few women can, at least while young, fulfil the main duties of Islam. However, women can still remain good Muslims, for, just as God excuses from duties the sick and the poor who cannot afford to make the *hajj*, God excuses women (Bowker 1997: 1043; Ruthven 1997: 150; Buturovic, personal communication, January 1998; Walther 1995: 51).

Prayer at a mosque on Friday and at dawn on feast days also demands total purification. For women of child-bearing years, this would be impossible for a week or so each month. So women usually have to pray in private, though Muslims value communal prayer more highly. Islam does not forbid women to study the Qur'an or to read prayers in mosques. In fact, it encourages them to do both. However, there are no women's mosques (Bowker 1997: 8-9; Marcus 1992: 65-69; Hourani 1991: 148).

Circumcision is not mentioned in the Qur'an. However, ritual circumcision, *khitan*, is obligatory for a Muslim boy, though the details of the rite and the age of the recipient vary from society to society. To celebrate the event, his family may hold a festival. As far as I can ascertain, there is as yet no parallel obligatory Islamic ritual or festival for a girl (Bowker 1997: 224; Rodwell 1996: 504).

Female circumcision, *khafd*, often called "genital mutilation," is not compulsory in Islam, although many Muslims think that it accords with the Sunna. Female circumcision occurs as a normal practice only in Saudi Arabia, Iraq, Yemen, Egypt, and the Sudan. However, because of appeal to the Sunna, it may be becoming more common than before in sub-Saharan Africa, Ethiopia, Somalia, Jordan, North America, and the United Kingdom. Opposition to the practice comes from both non-Muslims and Muslims, the latter arguing that the process causes both physical and psychological pain and, against the Qur'an's prescriptions, perpetuates male dominance (Bowker 1997: 224).

In male-female relationships, as in every other sphere of life, the first duty of Muslims is always to enter into them only with God in mind, for God sees and knows everything. Further, Islamic restrictions on women are deeply imbued with ideas of sacredness. The Arabic word for "sacred" is *haram*; the word for the women's section of the house is *harim*; they both come from the same root, as does *mahram*, the kin with whom a woman can associate, but not marry (Ruthven 1997: 94; Carmody 1989: 191-192). In Islam, as in Judaism, marriage is a contract, not a sacrament, as it is in Christianity. Hence, it does not have to entail a religious ritual, though the contract is supported by divine law. In most Muslim societies, however, weddings are ceremonies with religious content and much festivity (Bowker 1997: 621; Ruthven 1997: 101-102; Walther 1995: 54-57).

Festivals

The two great festivals in the Muslim liturgical year are *Eid al-fitr* and *Eid-al-adha*. The first, the "small feast," *Eid-al-Fitr*, occurs at the end of Ramadan and consists of two or three feast days when people pay visits and give presents. In most Muslim communities, this festival is, however, primarily a religious occasion, at which communal prayers express gratitude to God for the opportunity to experience Ramadan. Muslims eat specially prepared dishes, visit relatives and friends, and give gifts to children (Bowker 1997: 464; Hourani 1991: 149).

The "great feast," *Eid-al-Adha*, the "Feast of the Sacrifice," coincides with the end of the pilgrimage to Mecca. It is a day-long festival to commemorate Abraham's sacrifice of Ishmael; again, the community offers prayers and, where possible, animal sacrifices (Hourani 1991: 151).

Among Shiites, the most important festival is the *ashura*, which commemorates the battle of Karbala, in what is now Iraq. Imam Hussein was killed at Karbala. At this festival on the anniversary of the battle, the devout wear mourning and attend mosques to listen to sermons on the meaning of Hussein's sacrifice. In many Shiite towns and villages, mourners flagellate themselves in punishment for their betrayal of Hussein. Hussein's martyrdom at the "massacre" of Karbala in 680 CE is the "defining myth" of Shiite Islam (Ruthven 1997: 57-58; Hourani 1991: 184).

Women's Ritual Roles

In 1989, Anne Betteridge described religious practices of urban Muslim women in predominantly Shiite Iran in the 1970s before the revolution. Women were then deeply involved in religious life, in the ceremonies surrounding marriage contracts, funerals, pilgrimages to local shrines, and making vows and fulfilling them, as well as preparing religiously significant foods.

Muslim women are to some extent ritual experts in that, like Jewish women, they usually prepare meat after slaughter and other foods as well. Seeing that the food consumed daily be *halal*, "lawful," is usually their responsibility, as is the preparation of special foods for festive and ceremonial occasions. Through ritualising and sacralising food preparation, like Jewish women, Muslim women can achieve considerable "devotional autonomy" (Betteridge 1989: 103; Jamzadeh and Mills 1986: 51).

The Qur'an distinguishes two categories of foods: the lawful, *halal*, and the unlawful, *haram*. The unlawful foods were initially pig meat, carrion, blood, and any meat from sacrificial animals. Later, the list was expanded to include human and dog flesh and other "unclean" foods such as impure parts, "faecal and sexual areas," and food prepared by unbelievers or women who are ritually impure, for instance, who are menstruating. Normally, however, *halal* refers to the proper Islamic way of killing animals. Wine and other alcoholic drinks are also forbidden. As in Judaism, since food preparation usually falls to women, they have to be acutely aware of these ritual strictures. For many of them, the handling and cooking of *halal* food often becomes a ritual (Bowker 1997: 45, 352, 544; Ruthven 1997: 49, 81; Betteridge in Falk and Gross 1989: 103; Sered 1992: Chap. 5).

Tradition indicates that, in early Islam, women regularly prayed in mosques, indeed were expected to do so, but, even in early times, they may have been separated from the men. Nonetheless, there is also very early evidence that some men thought women should not be allowed in mosques, and, as time passed, increasingly women were excluded from them. Erika Friedl pointed out that very few Iranian village women attended rituals in the mosque; those that did were hidden and "never directly addressed" (1989: 127; see also Walther 1995: 52; Ahmed 1992: 72).

Women in the Iranian village Friedl studied did, however, get involved in other ritual activities. They attended dramatisations about saints' lives performed by itinerant preachers and snake handlers; they served as mourners at funerals, though they had to leave when the prayers started; they used private rituals to deal with illnesses and other domestic problems; and they made vows to saints and went on pilgrimages to saints' shrines (Betteridge 1989: 127-129).

In her book on women in Turkey, Julie Marcus discussed women's involvement in rituals mainly to do with women's life cycle, especially birth and death. She concluded that the female world view was egalitarian. Furthermore, Marcus, like other scholars, demonstrated that, even in Islam, as in other extremely male-dominated religions, women did manage to find ways to express their spirituality (1992: 121ff.; see also Wadud 2006: 255; Betteridge 1989; Friedl 1989; Mernissi 1989).

TYPES OF ISLAM

Today, Islam is a very complex and varied religion (Haddad, Smith, and Moore 2006: 4-8), but it divides broadly into Sunni and Shiite Muslims, with Sunni being the tradition that the vast majority of Muslims follow. However, most Muslim societies contain both Sunnis and Shiites.

Sunni Muslims subscribe to a concept of community which allows for differences of opinion in legal matters. They believe that God's will was revealed "finally and completely" by the Qur'an and the Sunna. For Sunnis, the interpretation of both is the business of the *ulama*, a body of learned men steeped in the Qur'an, the Sunna of the Prophet, and Islamic law. The *ulama*, the guardian of the community's "moral conscience," has a role is closer to that of Jewish rabbis than to Christian priests.

The *ulama*, a respected class of scholar-jurists, has traditionally been overwhelmingly male. Members of each local *ulama* reach consensus according to rules developed in academies in various parts of the Muslim world. As a result, Islamic law is not uniform across Sunni Muslim societies. The members of the *ulama* do not themselves have political power, but they have enormous influence. For Sunni Muslims, there is no divinely inspired interpreter (Ruthven 1997: 10, 53; Hourani 1991: 158).

Sunni Islam has no "Church" and no equivalent to the Papacy, no formally recognised institution or person that sets the religious agenda. Prayer is led by the head of a congregation, often called imam, meaning "pattern, leader"; hired by a mosque, the imam is usually someone who has had theological training (Bowker 1997: 469; Ruthven 1997: 9-10; Yamani 1996: 2).

For Shiites, on the other hand, religious authority rests with the Imams and their descendants, who are divinely inspired and thus infallible in their interpretation of the Qur'an. Shiite religious leaders are understood to be deputising for "the absent Imam" and wielding authority for him. The result has been the development of a religious hierarchy very like the Christian priesthood, but without "formal sacerdotal powers." A senior member of the Shiite *ulama* receives the title Ayatollah, "sign of God," and all Ayatollahs are *mujtahid*s, scholar-jurists capable independently of interpreting the Law. All

Shiites are expected to be guided by a *mujtahid*, who becomes a role model (Bowker 1997: 116; Ruthven 1997: 55, 85).

Shia means "partisan," in this case, partisan of Ali. Shiite Muslims are committed to the line of Ali, Muhammad's son-in-law and father of Hussein, the martyr of the battle of Karbala. The Shiite Imams were all secretly murdered, and the twelfth Imam disappeared. Thus, most Shiites are called Imamis or "Twelvers," followers of the twelfth Imam, "the Awaited One." When the world ends, the lost Imam will come back as *al-Mahdi*, the Messiah. Today, divinely inspired *mujtahid*s guide Shiite communities; the most revered *mujtahid*s sometimes are titled Imam, for example, Imam (Ayatollah) Khomeini of Iran (Bowker 1997: 889; Ruthven 1997: 55-56; Walther 1995;37).

Strict allegiance to specific Imams has caused the Shiites to splinter into a variety of sects (Bowker 1997: 889; Ruthven 1997: 8, 35, 54, 56-58; Hourani 1991: 31, 37). Among the most important of them are the following:

(1) The "Seveners" or Ismailis, followers of Ismail, the seventh Imam, who either died before his father or "was passed over" as Imam. They espouse Seven, not Five Pllars of Islam, the additional two being purification and spiritual struggle (Bowker 480-481);

(2) the Nizaris or "Aga Khanids," a branch of the Ismailis originally from India, who venerate the Aga Khan as the forty-ninth Imam in the direct line of Ali (Bowker 1997: 28, 481);

(3) the Druzes of Lebanon, Syria, and Israel, followers of a religion derived from Ismaili Shiism, the details of which were secret until recently (Bowker 1997: 295-296);

(4) Baha'i, now a separate religion, resulted from a nineteenth-century Iranian messianic movement (Bowker 1997: 120-121).

Islamic Fundamentalism

The Muslim world has also undergone a few significant, usually fundamentalist reform movements. One of them, Wahhabiya, began in the eighteenth century in what is now Saudi Arabia. Founded by Muhammad 'Abd al-Wahhab, it is an extremely conservative group which adheres to the Qur'an and "the authentic Sunna" only and left its influence especially on Saudi Arabia, which still holds to its tenets (Bowker 1997: 1031). The Muslim Brotherhood, which began in Egypt in the 1920s, is another example. It was and is religious and political organisation, and its original intent was to throw out the British and then establish a strict Islamic state (Bowker 1997: 47). Reformist associations such as these are normally "Islamist"; that is, they use their religion as a support for and source of political activism (Marshall 2005: 104; see also Winter 2001: 9; Cooke 2002: 145). In many ways, Islamic fundamentalism constitutes another type of Islam.

Fundamentalists adhere to what they believe to be the original truths, values, and practices of their religion and try to "purify Islam." They want to alter society "along `Islamic' lines" (Maumoon 1999: 269). Central to their value system is usually the conviction that women belong in a "women's place," the domestic realm. Muslim fundamentalists in the twentieth century think of themselves as "revivalists" returning to the origins of Islam to recover what Haleh Afshar calls "a purified vision" (1996: 198). Fatima Mernissi argues that Islamic fundamentalism is about the search for identity, and she sees the fundamentalist demand that women be veiled as "painful but necessary" to the search (1987: ix; see also Bowker 1997: 360).

When Islamist "revivalist" groups have taken over governments, as the Taliban Islamic movement did in Afghanistan in 1996, they have imposed a strict interpretation of Islamic law on the society. For example, the Taliban barred women from working outside the home, except in medicine, and denied them access to education. Members of the Taliban use threats and force to make people to abide by their reading of Islamic law, for instance, that men grow beards and women be covered head to toe in public. In June 1998, the Taliban closed all foreign-run private girls's schools and vocational centres as "un-Islamic" (*The Globe and Mail* 1998 June 17: A15, March 8: A8, April 9: A16; see also Afshar 1996: 201). In sum, most Islamist governments and movements are "highly intolerant and oppressive" (Barlow and Akbarzadeh 2008: 21).

WOMEN AND RELIGIOUS LEADERSHIP

Pious women abound in the history of Islam, especially in Islamic mysticism, and Islam boasts many female saints. However, historians refer to only one woman who ever functioned as a prayer leader. The Prophet himself is said to have instructed her, and she was also one of the very few women involved in handing down the Qur'an before it reached the final written version (Walther 1995: 108-111).

Today Muslim women do not serve as prayer leaders, except in special circumstances. In 1989, Anne Betteridge reported that, in Iran in the 1970s before the Islamic Revolution, older women functioned as ritual leaders at women-only rituals, and they were well known for reading Arabic well and usually for religious learning. Such women often conducted Qur'an reading and religious-knowledge classes in their homes. She mentions one woman who was a *mujtahid*, a person recognised by the Shiite *ulama* as learned and having the right to make independent interpretations of Islamic law (1989: 102-103, 110 n.20).

Perhaps the most important point about Muslim women is that, as with women of other traditions, there is enormous variation in their social, political, economic, and religious experiences (Mohagheghi 2006: 63). There can be vast differences between Muslim women even in basically the same religious context; thus, the social, economic, and political context is extremely important. Indeed, many Muslim feminists insist on distinguishing between the religious, "spiritual Islam," and the social, "political Islam," in dealing with women's status and religious role in Islamic situations (Mernissi 1993: 5).

ISLAMIC FEMINISM AND FEMINIST THEOLOGY

Today most Islamic countries are home to a variety of feminisms. In her introduction to *Feminism and Islam*, editor Mai Yamani agrees and comments that the book introduces an "Islamic" feminism different in "form and content" from other feminisms. Islamic feminism deals with issues that challenge the religious and political establishment of Islam, and particularly its scholars. However, it is not "a coherent identity," but a "contextually determined, strategic self-positioning" (Cooke 2001: 59). Although Islamic feminism is thus very diverse, yet all Islamic feminists have as their goal female empowerment from inside "a rethought Islam" (Yamani 1996:

1-2). Islamic feminists plan to achieve their goal mainly through appeal to the rights that Islam grants women.

In many predominantly Muslim countries, however, male-dominated "[religio-]political Islam" will make sure that they encounter many difficulties pursuing their goal, and in some Muslim societies, such as extremist-controlled areas of Afghanistan, Islamist governments will almost certainly threaten them with danger not only to limb, but also to life (Yamani 1996: 1-2; see also Jamali 2007; Moghissi 1999). It should come as no surprise that many Muslim feminists live and write about Islam in Western societies (Webb 2000; Yamani 1996: ix-xii)

Another term "Islamist" is sometimes used to describe a Muslim feminist who sees herself as adhering to orthodox Islam. Well-known Egyptian feminist Margot Badran prefers the term "Islamist woman" to "Islamist feminist," according to Buturovic (personal communication, January 1998). However, the description "Islamist" is usually applied to movements, normally fundamentalist, that advocate total adherence to Islamic law and practices derived from the central texts of Islam. So, perhaps, Yamani's term "Islamic feminist" would be preferable, for they seem to mean the same. For instance, Buturovic defines an "Islamist feminist" as one who engages in dialogue with the tradition and tries to bring out the best in it. Islamist feminists, she adds, think that, in Islam, there is space for female empowerment without the need to reject certain Islamic values (personal communication, May 1997). This definition would also serve for "Islamic feminist" (El-Nimr 1996; Ahmed 1992: 2).

Whether Islamist or Islamic, this kind of feminism does not go far enough for Yasmin Ali, who considers it a "highly unsatisfactory" way for a small number of women to gain a slight increase in opportunity; in other words, Ali sees Islamist feminism as both elitist and limited in what it is likely to achieve (1992: 121). Leila Ahmed also has reservations about the "Islamist" route as a way of improving the status of women (1992: 236; see also Anwar 2006: 1-2: Osman 2003, Moghadam 2002: 1150).

Since it is difficult for an outsider to detect the nuances in the various proposed terms, for purposes of this discussion, I shall use Yamani's term "Islamic feminist" (for a debate on feminism in Islamic countries, see *Signs* 23/2 (1998) 321-389).

MUSLIM WOMEN AND WESTERN FEMINISM

On the subject of the feminism developed in Western countries, many articulate Muslim feminists, including Islamic feminists, join Womanists, Latina and Hispanic feminists, and other Third World feminists in judging it to be an inappropriate model for them. Not only do they consider Western feminism as one of the tools of colonialism and imperialism, but they also deplore many of the freedoms that women in the West have sought and been offered. In their view, Western feminism has freed women only to act as sex-objects and to sell their sexuality to capitalist advertising, and these Muslim women point especially to what they see as Western feminism's failure to include in their agendas a discussion of marriage and motherhood that accords them a suitable, respected, and valued role (Maumoon 1999: 275, 279). Further, Western feminism has tried and has failed to make women into "quasi men" and thus has rendered them permanently second class. Finally, Western feminists, they contend, have presented as universal the minority experience of well-off, middle-class white women. Thus, Western feminist analysis is almost irrelevant to the majority of women worldwide (Afshar 1996: 200).

Some Islamic feminists consider as basically Western the thinking of such well-known Muslim feminists as Nawal El-Saadawi, Egyptian physician and writer, who has been a prominent women's rights activist for many years. Islamic feminist Leila Ahmed concedes that El-Saadawi criticises the West. However, Ahmed accuses her of having as her base Western intellectual and political assumptions, among them a commitment to individual rights, a concept "formulated by Western bourgeois capitalism" (1992: 235-236; *Human Edge* 1990; El-Saadawi 1980).

Over thirty years ago, El-Saadawi was condemning the way in which reactionary scholar-jurists used Islamic law to maintain women's inferior status, attacking the polygamy and genital mutilation rife in her society, and exploring the veil's implications for women. In his recent overview of Muslim feminism, Anouar Majid praises El-Saadawi for her thorough feminist critique of the system of male dominance the runs Arab society (1998: 322-323a).

In elucidating the attitude of women of Muslim societies to Western feminism, Leila Ahmed argues that, in the colonial past, the male colonisers appropriated the language of Western feminism, although, in their own countries, they regarded feminism as an enemy. They then used that language to attack Muslim men's "degradation" of women and justify Western subversion of the cultures of the colonised. In Ahmed's opinion, Western feminists have done the same. Although they denounce as sexist the attitudes to women of men of their own societies, Western feminists have supported European male presentations of "Other men" and their cultures and united with Western men in attacking the practices of Muslim societies, in particular the veil. Ahmed maintains that today these attacks are "transparently obvious," and the invoking by Western media and scholarship, even Western feminist scholarship, of "Muslim 'oppression' of women" in order to validate negativity towards Muslims is, to say the least, disheartening to Muslims (1992: 243-246).

It is no wonder, then, that, for many women in Muslim countries, identifying oneself as a feminist or a women's liberationist is, in Mernissi's words, the equivalent of "surrender to foreign influences" (1987: 8). There is one way, perhaps only one way, for a Muslim woman to criticise Islam without having to face the charge of being "a Western-inspired lackey." That is to call herself an "indigenous feminist," an Islamic feminist (Ruthven 1997: 115).[6]

"POLITICAL ISLAM": WOMEN'S RIGHTS AND ISLAMIC LAW

For Fatima Mernissi and many other Islamic feminists, "sound religious values" begin with the Prophet's message, that is, the Qur'an, which, they argue, is egalitarian. Amila Buturovic, among others, qualifies that position by identifying the message's egalitarianism as applying to the practice of religion (1997: 53). In support of this idea, Leila Ahmed reports that, usually "to the astonishment of non-Muslims," Muslim women often insist that Islam is not sexist. She attributes this sincere belief to the fact that these Muslim women are referring to egalitarian and ethical Islam, rather than legalistic, technical Islam of the established male elite, the version that is powerful politically (1992: 239). By making the distinction between "political Islam" and "spiritual Islam," as Mernissi calls them, Islamic feminists can begin to expose the sexism in their societies and gain improvements in women's rights (1993: 5, 1991: ix).

In *Beyond the Veil*, Moroccan feminist Fatima Mernissi situates her arguments firmly in "political Islam," not "spiritual Islam." She says that male Muslims usually react negatively to any attempt to alter the status of women and the situations they endure; Muslim men immediately appeal to "spiritual Islam" and interpret any such attempt as an assault on God's order and His rule of the world. In response, Mernissi argues that making changes to benefit women in any society is actually mainly a matter not of religion, but of economics. Further, as she sees it, a main problem is that the Muslim world knows only two patterns for women's liberation, women's autonomy in pre-Islamic society and the Western one. They both terrify Muslim men. Mernissi's considered conclusion is that what is needed is radical restructuring of "political Islam" beginning with economics and ending with grammar (1993: 5, 166, 1987: 165, 176).

A case in point is the so-called "crime of honour," which is enshrined in a number of the penal codes of Muslim countries, especially those in the eastern Mediterranean area and northern Africa. Lama Abu-Odeh (1996) discusses crimes of honour and their relationship to the construction of sex-gender roles in Muslim countries. She gives as a typical example of such a crime the killing of a daughter or sister by her father or brother because they suspect or have found out that she has been sexually active before or outside of marriage. Abu-Odeh tells the story of a sixteen-year-old girl killed by her father, with her mother's help, because she walked home with a boy who was close kin. Killers and courts justify such killing as defending or restoring the family honour. Abu-Odeh explores the concept of honour, prepares "sexual" typologies of Arab women and men, and presents a number of feminists' responses.

On September 3, 1981, the United Nations' Convention on the Elimination of All Forms of Discrimination Against Women (CEDAW) came into force. It was produced during the United Nations Decade for Women (1975-1985), and it was quickly ratified by many countries, among them a number whose population is predominantly Muslim. However, by January 1995, forty-two countries declared reservations about "ratification, accession or signature." Among the forty-two were twelve countries whose population is predominantly Muslim; most of their reservations had to do with maintaining the Sharia, Islamic law, in their countries; in particular, they were concerned about "personal law, including the law of succession" (Connors 1996: 351-352, 354).

In an article on CEDAW and its reception in the Muslim world, Jane Connors tries to evaluate the motivations of predominantly Muslim countries that made reservations on the Convention. She wants to know whether Islamic law required those countries who follow the Sharia to enter reservations or whether ideological positions prompted them to do so. She concludes that countries that adhere to Islamic law cannot agree to some provisions in the Convention, but that they could still ratify most of them.

She further remarks that, if the requirements of the Women's Convention actually do contravene the tenets of Islamic law, then she strongly supports the efforts of scholars who are uncovering egalitarian themes in the Qur'an, the Sunna and other early works. She encourages their challenging of the opinion of traditionalists that no evolution in Islamic law is possible (Connors 1996: 352, 365-366). Islamic feminist theologians are attempting, with some success, to do just that.

The fourth world conference on women in September of 1995, sponsored by the United Nations Development Programme, attracted representatives from all the countries with predominantly Muslim population, except Saudi Arabia. Though a number of women attendees made statements that were very traditionalist, the delegates were united in supporting women's "demand for rights in an Islamic context." Pakistan's representative, then Premier Benazir Bhutto, emphasised that an Islamic society had the potential to offer women "economic freedom and independence" (Yamani 1996: 26-27). It seems clear that Islamic feminists are right. To improve the status of Muslim women, feminists have to use the full strength of Islamic tradition and do so in the Islamic context. In this way, they will, against great odds, make changes in "political Islam."

Feminists are also beginnings to get together to discuss feminist issues. In October 2005, in Barcelona, Muslim and non-Muslim feminists, including activists and scholars, attended the First International Conference on Islamic Feminism; there was a follow-up in 2006. In addition, in New York City in 2006, around a hundred female Muslim leaders gathered at the Women's Islamic Initiative in Spirituality and Equity. This meeting set up the International *Shura* (Advisory) Council of Muslim Women to make recommendations to Muslim leaders and establish scholarships to aid in producing ten female *muftias,* women qualified to deliver judgments (*fatwas*) in Islamic legal situations (McGinty 2007: 481).[7]

"SPIRITUAL ISLAM" AND ISLAMIC FEMINIST THEOLOGY

In the work of Islamic feminist theologians, there does not seem to be even as clear a distinction between feminist-theological positions as we encountered in the work of Christian and Jewish feminist theologians. The positions of most Islamic feminist theologians probably fit most easily into the Revisionist category and that of a few, like Mernissi, at least occasionally, into the Renovationist one.

There is enormous variety, economic, political, social, and religious, in women's conditions in Muslim countries in the Mediterranean area alone, not to mention the Indian subcontinent and other areas of south Asia, East Asia, Oceania, Europe, the Muslim countries that emerged from the former Soviet Union, Africa, South and North America. Because of this diversity in the world of Islam, it seems unlikely that, as Julie Marcus says, the Qur'an and the law "said to be based upon it" is as controlling as it is often purported to be (1992: 64). Nonetheless, the sacred texts are often used to justify not only the politics of power, but also sexual politics.

Most Islamic feminist theologians agree that, although one cannot charge Islam's sacred texts with being an origin of the privileging men over women, one cannot exonerate "religious practices" (Marcus 1992: 64). Thus, they scrutinise the widely varied religious practices of Islamic communities.

Religious Practices

Fatima Mernissi argues that Muslim society has two universes: that of men, the *umma*, "the world [of] religion and power," and that of women, the domestic sphere concerned with "sexuality and the family" (1987: 138). Following Mernissi, Marcus describes the *umma* as traditionally exclusively male where there is no room for the female (1992: 65;). Islam has, then, two domains, "the moral community" and the domestic community, "the world of daily life." The connection between them is the five obligations (Pillars) of Islam.

Further, as feminist critics point out, jurist-scholars (*ulama*) are Sunni Islam's closest approximation to "a teaching authority." In Shiite Islam, the members of the *ulama* have more the status of Christian clergy. In both cases, they form an elite minority of highly educated officials, and they are almost to a person male. Indeed, it is exceedingly difficult, though not completely impossible, for a woman to join this group. The official education necessary to enable one to engage in the complicated process of Islamic theological-legal reasoning is offered only in public areas "not accessible to women"; thus, as Buturovic says, only men have access to it (1997: 53; see also Ruthven 1997: 85; Hourani 1991: 163; Betteridge 1989: 103, 110 n.20).

Since there are no priests in Islam, it is the responsibility of Muslims, including women, to follow God's laws and to appeal to their community's body of all-male, religious jurist-scholars, the *ulama*, if they have difficulty understanding, or existing within, the law. Thus, a woman seeking a divorce or support payments from an unwilling husband can, in principle, appeal to the local religious court, the *ulama*, for redress; in practice, depending on the country, it has been very difficult for a Muslim woman to initiate divorce proceedings and to get a divorce (El-Nimr 1996: 98-99; Hamadeh 1996: 334-338).

Islamic feminist theologians also explore and criticise later customs and traditions that may, or may not, get their validity from sacred texts. They deal with many topics and issues, but first and foremost, they tackle family law and its abuses. For example, in a recent edited book, *Feminism and Islam*, several Islamic feminists address these matters. Najla Hamadeh examines Islamic family law from a Revisionist position and indicts Islamic jurists for preserving for men privileges greater than "God has already bestowed on them" (1996: 345). Also taking a Revisionist-Renovationist stance, Munira Fakhro discusses the need for family-law reform in Arabian Gulf countries and envisions a time when Islam will come to terms with "modernity," what is perceived as "the modern, the new, the innovative, and the powerful" (1996: 261). Sharia-based discourses in post-Khomeini Iran interest Ziba Mir-Hosseini, who argues for a Revisionist position, the possibility of a "feminist re-reading" of Islamic law (1996: 285).

In the same publication, Islamic feminist theologians investigate the way in which the construction of gender interrelates with religion in Muslim countries. Maha Azzam's article explores gender and "the politics of religion" in the Middle East and recommends that Muslim women should "unapologetically" use religion to manage their lives and seek empowerment in a context of deepening "Islamisation" (1996: 228).

Discussion of the Islamic requirement of modesty and the controversy over the veil reveals among Islamic feminist theologians both Revisionist positions and stances verging on Renovationist. Among those who have published views on the issue are Faegheh Shirazi (2009), Sajida Alvi, Homa Hoodfar, and Sheila McDonough (2003), Haleh Afshar (1996), Maha Azzam (1996), Afaf el-Sayyid Marsot (1996), Saeeda Khanum (1992), and Fatima Mernissi (1987). This debate continues. Anouar Majid discussed the meaning of the veil in various Islamic countries, and he suggested that, since around the late 1970s, the veil acquired a new symbolic meaning, a statement against secularism and about "class struggle" in the world of Islam (1998a: 334-338). In her response to his article, feminist scholar Ann Mayer accused him of trying to "explain away" such things as discriminatory dress codes (1998: 370).

Some Islamic feminist scholarship is Revisionist recovery work in women's history. For instance, B.F. Musalla has done a history of birth control in Islam (1989). Scholars such as Margot Badran (1995), Huda Sharawi (1986), Elizabeth Fernea and Basima Bezirgan (1977), and Lila Abu-Lughod (1993) are also making available women's stories and recording their voices. Others have studied women and women's movements both in the Muslim world in general and in various Muslim countries and probed their relationship to religion (Barlow and Akbarsadeh 2008 (Iran); Osman 2003 (Egypt); Al-Ali 2000 (Egypt); Sabbagh 1998 (Palestine); Yamani 1996: Part 1 (history); Makdisi 1996 (Lebanon); Badran 1995 (Egypt); Afshar 1993 (Middle East); Mernissi 1993 (history); Sansarian 1992 (Iran); Wikan 1991 (Oman); Lateef 1990 (India); Mumtaz and Shaheed 1987 (Pakistan); Tucker 1985 (Egypt); Minces 1982 (Arab); Tabari and Yeganeh 1982 (Iran); Beck and Keddie 1978 (history).

It is not surprising that a number of the Islamic feminist theologians who write in *Feminism and Islam* recommend or conclude that Muslim women should work within Islam to improve their religious and social status. They include scholars originally from, among other places, Iran, Egypt, the Gulf States, Lebanon, and Saudi Arabia. Many of these authors point out that role models for Muslim women should be Islamic and that women have to become increasingly involved in interpreting the core sources of Islam (Yamani 1996: 10, 24).

Interpretation of Core Texts

Becoming involved in interpretation of core sources such as the Qur'an and the Sunna is extremely difficult for Muslim women. For Muslims, not only is the Qur'an sacred, but it is the Word of God. No true Muslim, therefore, would question its statements, and it is the very centre of Islam. On it, finally, rests women's role in Islamic societies. The Sunna is almost as sacrosanct. Further, for the vast majority of Muslim women, getting the religious education they would need to do such theological interpretation is well nigh impossible. Nonetheless, a few Muslim women have succeeded in acquiring a university education, sometimes at a Western university, and some of these, as Muslim feminist theologians, do not shy away from interpretation of the Qur'an and other sacred texts of Islam (Wadud 1999; Hassan 1997; Hamideh 1996; Yamani 1996: ix-xii; Betteridge 1989: 103, 110 n.2; Buturovic 1997: 53).

As we might expect, some Islamic feminist theologians, such as Raga El-Nimr (1996), take a conservative or orthodox stance and argue from a traditional Islamic position. They maintain that, since the Qur'an enshrines the actual Word of God, interpretation is unnecessary as long as Muslims act upon "the correct meaning," surely a circular argument.

In her article, "Women in Islamic Law," Raga El-Nimr puts her basic position clearly: Islam supports female-male equality and grants rights equally to women and men "in all matters of vital concern." Nevertheless, she continues, the Qur'an recognises that the sexes are entirely different in nature, a result of divine will, but are complementary to each other. Hence, women should not demand to be equal to men except in spiritual matters. El-Nimr says that Islamic law is "evolutionary" and has taken into account these natural differences in prescribing the rights and privileges of women and men. She scathingly concludes of feminists that only their ignorance of these facts would lead them to "believe" that women and men should have the same responsibilities. A few of El-Nimr's arguments in her article fall into the Revisionist category of feminist theology, while others are completely orthodox (1996: 88-89, 93; see also Yamani 1996: 7).

Recently, a few Islamic feminist theologians have appealed to Islamic tradition and not only urged the re-interpretation of the Qur'an, but have also begun the process. For example, Najla Hamideh criticises Islamic family law in the light of the interpretation of its sources, the Qur'an and the Sunna, and even conservative feminist Raga El-Nimr does not hesitate to interpret the Holy Book (1996). Indeed, as Mai Yamani points out, they are only following Islamic tradition. There is in Islam a long history of interpretation of the Qur'an by the all-male jurist-theologians of the *ulama*. Furthermore, these authorities, all male, have often manipulated sacred texts to their own advantage, while repressing dissent. Now, however, women are engaging in "Islamic discourses" and are starting to produce their own interpretations (Wadud 2000: 3-21; Wadud 1999; Hamideh 1996: 332; Yamani 1996: 2).

When dealing with the Qur'an, however, most Islamic feminist theologians explore and explicate its message and ignore, or try to explain, its sexism, but they do not question the authority of the text. For instance, an Islamic feminist cannot reject polygamy outright because the Qur'an expressly permits it (*Sura* 4: 1-10); she can, however, situate the statement in its historical background, explain the limitations it places on men who wish to practise polygamy, and point out that monogamy is the Muslim norm (El-Nimr 1996: 100-101; Rodwell 1996: 49-50).

Some Islamic feminist theologians have directly addressed the issue of sexism in *Sura* 4 and other places in the Qur'an. For instance, Ghada Karmi acknowledges the sexism, notes the contradictions in the text, and recommends regarding the Qur'an as two documents. The first is responding to the political and social situation in seventh-century Arabia, while the second contains the "eternal message of Islam." The first document, she argues, can be adapted to later times. In effect, Karmi is also advocating the separation of "political Islam" from "spiritual Islam" (1996: 80-81).

Sura 4: 34, which states that men are "managers" in their relations with women and may punish them for disobedience by beating them, has not only had enormous impact on Muslim thinking on women's status, but has also caused Islamic feminists great distress. An example is Fatima Mernissi, who is, in Ann Mayer's words, one of "the bravest and most outspoken feminists in the Arab world" (1998: 371). In her comments on *Sura* 4, Mernissi points out that the *Sura* makes it clear that women can inherit wealth and property, and she maintains that this provision constitutes an improvement over the situation in pre-Islamic times. However, when she comes to *Sura* 4: 34, which states that men have charge of women and may beat them for disobedience, she resigns herself to accepting contradiction, for Muhammad, she notes, was opposed to violence (1991: 120, 154-155).

Riffat Hassan, on the other hand, analyses the actual text of the difficult passage (*Sura* 4: 34) in considerable detail and proposes a novel, if not entirely convincing, interpretation, quite different from the accepted one. She begins by arguing that the statement is not directed to a husband or even a wife, but to the whole community, that is, the *umma*. She goes on to deconstruct the language of the passage word by word. Finally, she enunciates a "radically different" conclusion about the significance of the passage from the traditional interpretation. *Sura* 4: 34, she explains, instructs men as a group to take responsibility for women as a group whenever women are bearing and rearing children. As to the passage's advice about handling women's disobedience, Hassan understands this to refer to "rebellious women" who refuse to bear children for the *umma* (2003: 236-239, 1997: 54-57).

If the text of the Qur'an is, to all intents and purposes, been inviolable, the Sunna is another matter; it is, of course, almost as inviolable as the Qur'an, but Islam has had a long tradition of *hadith* study and validation. One of the criteria for validation of a *hadith* "conformity to the Qur'an" (Hassan 2003: 220). Thus, some Islamic feminist scholars examine key *hadith*s and sometimes question their authenticity. Fatima Mernissi discusses one such *hadith*: "Those who entrust their affairs to a woman will never know prosperity." She states that this *hadith* is "omnipresent" in Muslim societies and thus extremely important for attitudes to women. The consensus of Muslim scholars is that it is authentic. Nonetheless, many scholars challenged its authenticity, and there was a fierce debate about it. Mernissi researched this *hadith* to ascertain its provenance, what companion of the Prophet it originated with, what were the situation and the objectives of its pronouncement, and what was the chain of transmission (1991: 1, 61).

Mernissi is now of the opinion that more traditions are false than are authentic. Those who can have always manipulated sacred texts, she warns, and such manipulation is "a structural characteristic of the practice of power in Muslim societies." A false *hadith* would have been one method of exercising power, since only religion could legitimate power. She concludes by advising "redoubled vigilance" whenever one Muslim argues from the sanctity of the text and attacks another with a so-called fundamental truth, which is, in reality, only a political tool, but as "terrible" and having "such grave historical consequences" as the one she discusses has had (1991: 3, 8-9, 61). Incidentally, Mernissi's research started when two men in her local store hurled this anti-woman *hadith* against her!

LESBIAN VOICES

Since early times, Muslim debates on sexuality have been various and varied. They have focused mainly on heterosexuality and relations between the sexes. However, they have not entirely neglected homosexuality (Duran 1993; Dunne 1990; Mernissi 1987: 27-64).

Historically, there has been no unanimous agreement in Islamic law regarding homosexuality. Even though a section in the Qur'an about Lot and Sodom is interpreted as condemning male homosexuality, the passage does not name a specific punishment (*Sura* 27: 54). The result has been some room for discussion of the issue among Islamic scholars. On the other hand, as Ayesha Imam remarks, Islam seems always to have maintained "a loud silence" on lesbian relations (1997: 19; see also Rodwell 1996: 252).

Commonly, today's Islamic communities regard heterosexuality as the only acceptable form of sexuality. They generally agree in condemning homosexuality as unnatural, although Shahnaz Khan, a lesbian scholar, points out that there is nothing in the Qur'an that explicitly condemnds homosexuality (2002: 329). It is not surprising, therefore, that, when I first researched this topic (1998), I was able to discover very little material, whether in Muslim societies or in the Diaspora, on Muslims who were, may have been, or are lesbians. However, some Muslim feminists even then were prepared to discuss the subject (Imam 1997; Ahmed 1992: 184-187; Mernissi 1987: 27-64).

Indeed, Leila Ahmed notes that the issue of "affectional, erotic, and sexual love between women" is one on which there is very little material from Muslim societies, but she looks forward to the exploration of these and other matters as women's diaries, autobiographies, and such like become available (1992: 184-187). Possibilities for such exploration, however, may be limited, for, as Ayesha Imam tells us, modern Muslim governments support right-wing religious groups in their condemnation of "unnatural deviations," for instance, female and male homosexuality, transsexuality, transvestism, and other such. Strident condemnations of such "deviations" have recently specifically included lesbian relationships. Not only are they "unnatural," but also "anti-Islam," the result of the West's negative influence or of the evils of feminism, "a solely Western construct," or both (1997: 10, 19).

Today, for Muslim lesbians (and Gays) living in North America, Europe, and elsewhere, usually in the Diaspora, the situation appears to be improved. In 2003 a conference took place in Toronto under the auspices of the Muslim homosexual group Salaam Canada and the American Al-Fatihah Foundation; both have web sites (Giese 2003). Also in 2003, Canadian feminist lesbian broadcaster and writer, Irshad Manji, published a book in which she named Islam as, among other things, homophobic. In May 2007 a group of lesbian Arabs gathered in Haifa, Israel, for a well-protected conference. In addition, lesbians and Gays have formed several other groups, among them, Queer Jihad, al-Fatihah, and South Asian Gay and Lesbian Association. The Gay and Lesbian Arab society now has an Internet address, as does the lesbian magazine *Bint el Nas*. Further, the magazine *Azizah* is devoted to Muslim women's issues (Haddad, Smith, and Morris 2006: 97).

DISCUSSION

Islam began in a seventh-century pagan society that clearly allowed strong social roles for women; for example, Muhammad's first wife Khadija was an independent woman who made her own decisions about her successful business, her marriage, and her spiritual life. It may be that pre-Islamic women in Arabia filled religious roles as well. Women in early Islamic society, at least during the first century, also had considerable social and religious freedom. Nonetheless, there was, from quite early times, pressure to curtail women's public activity, and, by the tenth and eleventh centuries, after the development of Muslim empires and large cities, upper- and middle-class women were sequestered in special section of the house and had little or no public role; though lower-class women were seen in public, they too took no part in the politics of the cities.

By this time, Islamic law, the Sharia, was the law of the cities and the empires, and an all-male body of jurist-scholars, the *ulama*, had elaborated and was administering it. Their interpretations of the Qur'an and the Sunna both reflect and comment on their specific time and place, as had the revelations of the Qur'an themselves. As in Judaism and Christianity before it, Islam became very restrictive to women as a result of two main factors: institutionalisation and the male control of religious authority. One area that continued to afford women considerable religious freedom was ecstatic experience. The mystical tradition of Islam, which became Sufism, offered women religious roles different from those of the rest of society. Some female Islamic ecstatics were ascetics and marriage-avoiders, but, since the Qur'an recommends marriage to all believers, Islam does not value asceticism highly as a way of life. Thus, Islam did not, and does not, support monasticism, though some Sufis undertake it as a life choice (Bowker 1997: 651).

In Muslim societies, women's expression of their spirituality takes place mainly in the family and with other women. They usually pray at home, and, in some societies, they take part in all-women ceremonies. Further, they are the ones who prepare religiously significant foods, so that they are in that respect ritual specialists. They also have important roles in life-cycle rites such as weddings and funerals. Singly or in groups, women also make pilgrimages to the shrines of saints. Undoubtedly, despite restrictions, they carve out spiritual space for themselves.

In most primarily Muslim countries, there seems to be feminist activity, and usually it is what its adherents describe as Islamic feminism; that is, it is feminism that functions inside Islam and uses Islamic law to further the rights of women. It sees itself as an indigenous feminism, which eschews the aims and methods of Western feminism and recognises that feminism in an Islamic context has to deal with broad issues of oppression. In many predominantly Muslim countries, the rights that Islamic feminists seek for women are equally denied to men, including freedom of speech and association and tolerance of divergent opinions (Yamani 1996: 24).

Despite the fact that Islamic law is not the same, nor is its application the same, from country to country throughout the Muslim world, it is Islamic law that feminists have to address. Further, even Islamic feminists are faced with the fact that ultimately Islamic law is based on the sacred Qur'an and the only slightly less sacred Sunna. As a result, most Muslim feminists follow Fatima Mernissi in distinguishing between "political Islam" and "spiritual Islam." Thus, from country to country, they can challenge a society's customary law which, over time, the male members of its *ulama* have elaborated. Among their numbers in each Muslim country, they will have to continue to search out women to become properly trained Qur'an interpreters, experts in the Sharia, and scholars of the *hadith* collections.

Over the past decade or more, a few Muslim feminists have acquired the rigorous training necessary to question the sources and interpretations of the Sunna, and, following Muslim male tradition, they are even examining and producing interpretations of the Qur'an. As Islamic feminist theologians, they generally find the Revisionist position both possible and acceptable, and most of their arguments fall into that category. A few have even ventured an occasional Renovationist idea. However, Islam's uncompromising monotheism and repudiation of paganism preclude their ever taking a Revolutionary stance and hoping to remain Muslim.

It is ironic that, given the fact that, in spiritual terms, the Qur'an is an egalitarian document, Muslim societies have over the centuries appealed to its seventh-century social statements to justify their undoubted oppression of women. Islamic law in its various local versions took time to develop the anti-woman elements that are so oppressive in some countries. Like the patriarchy that it supports, it was man made, and, as with patriarchy, it will take time to effect changes in it. However, the plan of Islamic feminists to use Islamic law and follow "strict Islamic values" in their pursuit of women's empowerment seems appropriate (Yamani 1996: 13). Above all, it is very hopeful that one of the major projects of Islamic feminist theologians is the examination and re-interpretation of the textual sources that underpin Islam. The result will probably not, any time soon, lead to drastic changes, but, given the spiritual adaptability that Muslim women have already shown under undoubtedly difficult circumstances, there is little doubt that, one day, they will be ready and able, once again, to take their place as full members of the *umma*.

Notes

[1]Earlier in the twentieth-century, Muslims were often called "Muhammadans" and their religion "Muhammadanism." However, the correct name for the religion is "Islam," an Arabic word meaning "self-surrender to God," and the correct name for an adherent of Islam is "Muslim,"

an Arabic word meaning "one who surrenders him- or herself." To call Islam Muhammadanism is "highly offensive" to most Muslims, for the term suggests that Muslims worship the Prophet, as Christians worship Jesus Christ (Ruthven 1997: 3, 22).

[2]Not surprisingly, the rate of literacy among Muslim women is the world's lowest (Hassan 2003: 225).

[3]Among the exceptions, Mesopotamian sources suggest that southern Arabia in pre-Islamic times was ruled by queens (Anon. 1901: 120). Islam, of course, developed in the northern part of the peninsula.

[4]According to Raphael Patai, ancient peoples in Southern Arabia venerated Atharath (Asherah) (1990: 37).

[5]Keddie (2007: Book I) provides an overview history of women in the Middle East.

[6]In the Preface to her book Suzanne Gauch examines the influence of the Shahrazad (Sheherezade) stories on Western views of the Muslim world (2007). The work continues with discussion of women artists, writers, etc., in various Muslim countries.

[7]Kareema Altomare has compiled a list of organisations in the United States of America that focus on Muslim women's rights and advanced Islamic educstion for women. It begins with a short list of similar international organisations (2000: 249-257).

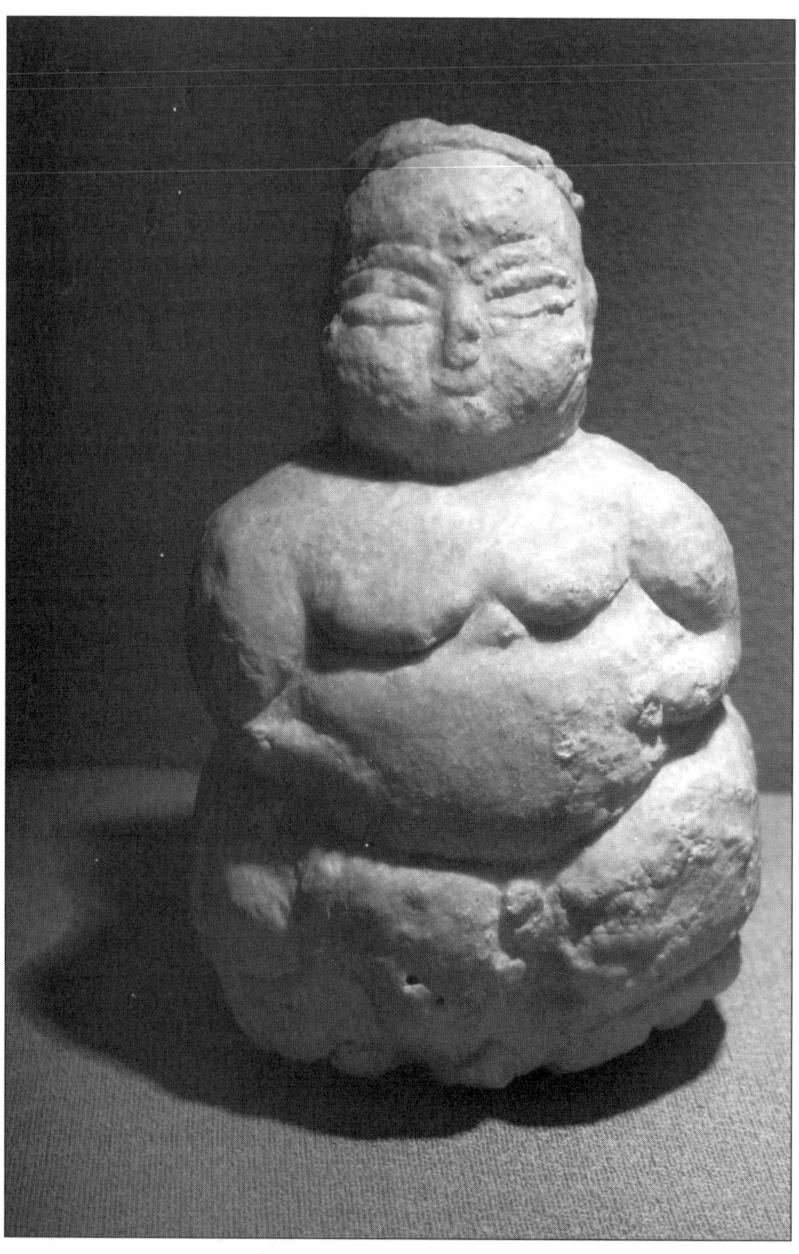

A mother goddess figurine from Canhasan, an archaeological site in Turkey. Museum of Anatolian Civilizations. Photo: Noumenon 2008. Used with permission

6.
FEMINIST GODDESS WORSHIP, FEMINISM AND FEMINIST THEALOGY[1]

OCCASIONALLY OVER THE twenty-five years or so that I taught courses on Goddess worship in the Ancient Eastern Mediterranean and Ancient Europe, students confronted me with annoyance, sometimes verging on anger, saying that I stated, for instance, that Marija Gimbutas's views are what, from a scholarly viewpoint, they are—hypotheses. Since I considered my courses to be scholarly explorations of the topic, I found myself at a loss to understand the problem these women were having with my statements. Then one day, about twenty years ago, after class, a group of us went for coffee and had a discussion that cleared up my difficulty. I realized that what I was, in effect, doing, all unknowingly, was challenging the beliefs of a new kind of feminist spirituality. A number of women believers were attending my classes to find out more about the origins and background of the religion that they were in the process of creating (Christ 1997; Eller 1993; Gimbutas 1991, 1989, 1974).

That Feminist Goddess Worship exists as a distinct variety of feminist spirituality seems clear from the enormous proliferation of books about *(The)* Goddess and the increasing number of feminists who belong to small Goddess worship circles (Gottschall 2000: 59). The burgeoning interest of scholars over the past fifteen years also supports the idea that it is a separate phenomenon (Gottschall 2000: 60). One such scholar is Cynthia Eller, whose sociological study, *Living in the Lap of the Goddess*, gives a good account of the religion in some of its forms. She is right when she singles it out among the religious phenomena of the last three decades as "one of the most fascinating" (Eller 1993: ix; Frymer-Kensky 1992;

McCance 165-178, Townsend 179-203, Wall 1990: 205-226).

However, I take issue with her use of the phrase "feminist spirituality" as a name for the developing tradition she describes in her book, even though other writers have called it that. What Eller is discussing is actually a feminist form of goddess worship.[2] "Feminist spirituality" is what I have been discussing for much of this book, but only occasionally before now have I mentioned goddess worship. I have tried to come up with an accurate phrase to describe the new feminist goddess-focussed spirituality, and I suggest "Feminist Goddess Worship"[3] (Christ 1997: title page; Gross 1996: 44).

Though Feminist Goddess Worship has affiliations with many other contemporary religious phenomena, nonetheless, over the past thirty years, it has become a separate and unique, if highly varied, spiritual entity, with followers who are committed to (*The*) Goddess and to supporting women and their issues, whether spiritual or political (Eller 1993: ix). They are searching for spiritual paths that empower women and assist them in changing their lives (Reuther 2005: 4). Feminist Goddess Worship attracts "a wide variety of people" resulting in "an exceedingly diverse body of practitioners" (Gottschall 2000: 59, 60; Glory and G'Zell 1996: 31). However, from my over thirty years of teaching about goddesses and listening to, by now, thousands of students, I can state, with no uncertainty, that, whatever form it takes, goddess worship is very empowering for women.

BACKGROUND

Why, in the mid-1970s, would second-wave feminists, most of whom originally repudiated religion as irremediably sexist, develop an interest in religion? For some women, Cynthia Eller suggests, finding feminism was an especially overwhelming and satisfying experience, and their need of a similar experience may have led them eventually to seek out compatible forms of spiritual expression. For many of us, indeed, discovering and being involved in feminism was definitely like a spiritual experience, and it might have been a factor in the development of Feminist Goddess Worship (Eller 1993: 41).

Eller's other reason seems less likely: Feminists felt a need for a new form of spirituality because, she thinks, some Jewish and Christian feminists practised a spirituality that overshot "the bounds of orthodoxy" (Eller 1993: 41). Eller is, of course, referring to Revolutionaries, like the Jewish and Christian women I discussed above, who still consider it crucially important to stay inside their traditions, no matter how far they push the tradition's limits. Further, many feminists who saw the monotheistic traditions as irretrievably sexist had already become Rejectionists before Revolutionaries began to practice inside their traditions. It seems to me much more likely that Feminist Goddess Worship took its beginnings in a combination of influences, not the least of which was Wicca.

In 1979 Carol Christ gave one convincing explanation for the burgeoning interest in spirituality among feminists in the mid-1970s; she commented that there was, among women, "a widespread sensing" that women had not told their stories, that women had not "experienced their own experience" (Christ 1979: 228, also in Spretnak 1982: 71-86). As a result, women realised that they had not shaped the language or the myths of our culture; its sacred stories were rarely women's own stories. Indeed, much of contemporary feminist spirituality and Feminist Goddess Worship has arisen from women's trying to rediscover or develop languages and myths that speak to their experiences. There is no question that, in the concept of (*The*) Goddess, feminists have discovered not only an extremely empowering symbol, but also a powerful and convincing sacred story.

THE HISTORY OF (*THE*) GODDESS AND HER WORSHIPPERS

Goddess Remembered, Donna Read's visually stunning, popular documentary which the National Film Board of Canada released in 1989, gives a beautiful and compelling statement of the sacred history or myth of Feminist Goddess Worship. Canadian actress Martha Henry, the narrator of the film, announces that, throughout the Western world, wave after wave of conquerors came down on "peaceful goddess-worshipping cultures." After thousands of years of prehistoric peace and harmony in woman-centred, goddess-worshipping cultures, violent and aggressive patriarchal conquerors erupted from desert or steppe, devastated the gentle matriarchal societies, and, by force, instituted male-dominance or patriarchy (Christ 1997; Gimbutas 1991; Gimbutas 1989; Eisler 1987). Such invaders sometimes explicitly include the Israelites who "conquered" Canaan (Stone 1977; Davis 1972).

In some places, according to the sacred history, the patriarchal invaders murdered queens and priestesses or, in other places, forced them into marriages that validated the right of the conquerors to rule. Many of the myths extant today about male deities killing monsters, especially serpents and dragons, are interpreted as accounts of the destruction of matriarchal or matrilineal cultures (Christ 1997: 62ff.).

The foundation or origin myth of Feminist Goddess Worship looks far back into prehistory to Stone Age societies that, it states, revered the Great Goddess and forward to the present day. As male dominance began in rape, forced marriage, torture, and murder, so it continued. The witch-hunts of the early modern period are a major example of the continuing persecution of Goddess worshippers. The National Film Board of Canada's 1990 release, Donna Read's *The Burning Times*, focuses on this aspect of the history (Christ 1997: 50ff., 66-69; Eller 1993: 170-176).

The sacred history of Feminist Goddess Worship does not constitute dogma or scripture, and, indeed, today many devotees do not insist that what the history recounts actually happened. Though it often gets written down, it is primarily an oral history, made new by every woman who interprets it and adds to it as she tells it. Storytellers pass on it, worshippers hear or refer to it during ritual, and women exchange it at parties and celebrations. Feminist Wiccans also share much of this sacred history (Gross 1996: 210-211; Eller 1993: 153; Starhawk 1989b: 15ff.).

As sacred history, the story is both extremely emotionally satisfying and deeply enriching for Feminist Goddess Worshippers. It tells women about ancient goddess worship, ancient matriarchies, the violent patriarchal take-over, women's creativity and wonderful bodily functions, women's natural power and strength, the return of (*The*) Goddess, and women's re-empowerment in a Goddess-centred spirituality. As Melissa Raphael says, the sacred history "underpins [the] whole political and religious self-understanding" of many Feminist Goddess Worshippers (2000: 75). No wonder Feminist Goddess Worshippers get annoyed at scholars like me who suggest that it may not have happened that way!

Many Goddess Worshipers had similar reactions to Cynthia Eller's latest book *The Myth of Matriarchal Prehistory: Why an Invented Past Won't Give Women a Future* (2000).[4] In her 1997 book, Carol Christ explores the reasons for this "resistance" among scholars to what she calls "the Goddess hypothesis" (Chap. 4). Ultimately, though, many Feminist Goddess Worshippers think that it does not matter whether "the theory of a prehistoric past" can be proven (Coleman 2005: 217).

SECOND-WAVE FEMINISM AND SPIRITUALITY

In the light of the fact that second-wave feminists at first wanted nothing to do with male-dominated religions or, indeed, spirituality of any kind, the feminist development of interest in spirituality, especially goddess worship, does seem to cry out for an explanation. However, I do not think that the interest was sudden, nor do I think it came primarily from feminists involved with Christianity and Judaism, though they were certainly influential in its growth. The strongest spiritual seeds lay dormant in second-wave feminism from close to its beginnings. A brief review of some of the writings of early second-wave feminists will, I think, support this contention.

In the late 1960s, when I was a member of Toronto New Feminists, a radical feminist group that was firmly opposed to any truck with religion, I remember the books we all read and discussed. Of course they included all the standard works: Betty Friedan (1963), Simone de Beauvoir (1949, 1970), Shulamith Firestone (1970), and Kate Millett (1970), but we were also reading and discussing Abraham Maslow's *Toward a Psychology of Being* (1968), with its heady and spiritual theories of self-actualization and "peak-experiences."

I also remember our intense and sometimes overwhelming consciousness-raising groups, at which we exchanged significant stories, personal myths, and private aspirations. In retrospect, I realize that they were a combination of therapy session, discussion

Painted image of the goddess Isis from a shroud made of linen and tempera, c. 2nd to 1st Century BC. Metropolitan Museum of Art. Photo: Keith Schengili-Roberts 2007. Used with permission CC-BY.

group, healing circle, and prayer meeting. One of the reasons why, I think, many feminists turned to spirituality in the mid-1970s was the immense success of consciousness-raising groups. Some women missed the elation that often accompanied a somewhat ritualised sharing of experience and the communal validation that usually followed; also they missed the comfort and safety, the release, and the support that those groups had provided. Feminist Goddess Worship circles function in a similar way (Driver 1998: 117; Christ 1997: 3; Eller 1993: 42ff.; Starhawk 1989b: 35).

Another reason for Second Wave feminists' interest in spirituality in the 1970s was an amazing little book, *The First Sex*. In 1971, Elizabeth Gould Davis published the first statement of what later was, in slightly altered form, to become the sacred history of Feminist Goddess Worship. Davis condemned received history as consisting of "two thousand years of propaganda" about female inferiority. She then examined myth, literature, the findings of archaeology, and patriarchal history in search of the "Lost Civilization" of the female-dominated past (1972: 18-19).

I vividly remember the first time that I heard of Davis's book: I was at a feminist celebration, a reunion of the Toronto group, New Feminists, about a year after our disbanding, when an excited New Feminist waved a small paperback at me and announced: "It's all here, proof that there was a matriarchy, proof that women once ruled." Doubting scholar that I was even then, I muttered something non-committal and thought no more of it, until a feminist friend gave me Davis's book for my birthday. Leafing through it, I became intrigued, and I read it at once, with increasing annoyance at what seemed to me to be Davis's cavalier treatment of evidence. Perhaps it is to Davis—and also to my two feminist sisters—that I owe my eventual interest in Goddess worship. I went through Davis's sources with enormous attention to detail, with the result that I dismissed her work as, in large part, fanciful. Nonetheless, without realising it, I had just started research into Goddess worship. What I did not then understand, of course, is that Davis was a kind of prophet for a brand of feminist spirituality that would be around twenty years in the making.

Davis's aim was not primarily spiritual, but political. She wanted to empower women by demonstrating that women not only had once been powerful, but had also ruled. The first part of her book addresses "The Gynocratic World," the lost women-dominated civilization of prehistory and early history; the other three parts are a litany of female loss, male domination, and increasing disaster. However, throughout the work, religion and spirituality are central. Further, Davis mentions a number of goddesses—Tiamat, Aphrodite, Potnia, Artemis, Isis, Mary, Astarte, Erinyes, Diana, Athena—and some of them I had never encountered before. It was not long afterwards that I found myself consciously doing

Astarte, terracotta statuette from Syria. Istanbul Archeological Musuem. Photo: QuartierLatin1968, 2007. Used with permission CC-BY.

research into goddesses of the Ancient Eastern Mediterranean. Davis certainly succeeded in empowering me, and, indeed, many other women, though perhaps not in the ways she had foreseen.

The Influence of Books About (the) *Goddess*

In 1976, five years after Davis's book appeared, Merlin Stone released her enormously influential *The Paradise Papers* (U.S. title: *When God Was a Woman*) (1977). The new religion had its scripture, or rather the first of its sacred books. Many writers about Feminist Goddess Worship credit Stone with being the one who started the movement in earnest (Christ 1997: 189, n.1). While quoting Davis and associating her with ideas of pre-historic matriarchy and patriarchal invasion, Eller, in effect, regards Stone's work as pivotal in inspiring women to seek out goddesses (1993: 58). Undoubtedly, Merlin Stone's work came at a critical time for the fledgling spiritual movement, and, after Davis's death, Stone became the doyenne of Feminist Goddess Worship in North America, if not the Western world.

After Stone's first incredibly successful and influential book, works on goddesses and the central myth of Feminist Goddess Worship began to proliferate. Carol Christ comments on the demand for them, which does not seem to have abated (1997: 3). In fact, the myriad of books and articles published each year contribute heavily to the spread of Feminist Goddess Worship (Eller 1993: 10). Some of the most popular include Riane Eisler's *The Chalice and the Blade* (1987), Elinor Gadon's *The Once and Future* Goddess (1989), *The Myth of the Goddess* by Anne Baring and Jules Cashford (1991), *The Great Cosmic Mother* by Monica Sjöö and Barbara Mor (1987), Lotte Motz's *The Faces of the Goddess* (1997), and Rachel Pollack's *The Body of the Goddess* (1997).

WICCA AND FEMINIST SPIRITUALITY

In the mid-1970s, feminists who had rejected Christianity and Judaism, as well as feminists who had not previously considered themselves to be spiritual, started looking around for some communal way to express their spirituality. They found a ready-made religion that they could connect to: Wicca or Witchcraft (see Griffin 2003: 243-281). Even today the "largest contingent of modern Goddess-worshipers" consider themselves Wiccans or Witches (Glory and G'Zell 1996: 31).

Some Wiccans or Witches or Pagans, as they variously call themselves, trace their religion back to Stone Age Europe, to over "35 thousand years ago" (Starhawk 1989a: 3). Others trace the origin of their tradition to the modern witchcraft revival under the impetus of the work of Gerald Gardner (1959). In any case, often, for many feminists, their introduction to the Alternative Religious stream was through Wicca, and many still consider themselves to be Wiccan. As a result, there is much overlap between Wicca and Feminist Goddess Worship, but there are also a number of differences (Eller 1993: 51; Starhawk 1989b: 10-11).

Wicca as a religion is very varied, and Wiccans agree on only a few points, one of which is to disagree and be tolerant of others' positions. They all practise worship of Nature, who is alive and sacred. Most think that human problems, especially psychological ones, result from alienation from Nature (Starhawk 1989b: 13, 189).

For Witches, deity is immanent, not transcendent. Most worship both a goddess, or goddesses, and a god, or gods, but they usually understand *(The)* Goddess to be more important than the God.

Many Wiccan rituals cannot function without at least one woman to embody (*The*) Goddess. However, Witches tend to be polytheists. They also think that balance is essential to the world and that the deities and humans contribute to that balance. Hence, Wiccan groups normally worship female and male deities and include as members both women and men. Wiccans tend to think that all sexuality is sacred, provided, of course, that it not harm another (Starhawk 1989b: 9-10, 12).

Witches usually meet in small groups, called "covens," and each is quite independent. Their worship centres on ritual. Often members gain status because of their learning and from having undergone stages of initiation. Wiccans also hold to the "Three Fold Rule," that whatever a person sends out comes back to her threefold. Some Wiccans led by Zsuzsanna Budapest were reasonably successful in creating a feminist form of Wicca. Usually called Dianic Wicca, it boasts Starhawk as its most prominent descendant. Margot Adler's *Drawing Down the Moon* provides a thorough overview of contemporary Paganism, including Wicca, in United States, while Kevin Marron concentrates on Wicca in Canada (Eller 1993: 55ff.; Marron 1989; Adler 1986; Starhawk 1989b: 10, 13, 264).

Why did the seemingly perfect match between Wicca and many spiritually inclined feminists not work out? First, there was, and is, the problem of deities; generally, feminists have not been pleased about worshipping a male deity, let alone sharing sacred space with men. Next, feminists often have problems with complementarity based in gender duality of the kind Wiccans practise; they do not always interpret it as egalitarian. Third, Wiccan groups often expect potential members to embark on training leading to initiation. Often initiates can undertake advanced training leading to priesthood. Often, when others proposed training, feminists left Wicca, being opposed to any kind of hierarchy, no matter how functional. Fourth, Wiccans, being rightly afraid of discrimination, often require secrecy; most feminists, on the other hand, insisted on being free to talk to other women about what was important to them. Feminists, it seems, are born proselytisers. Fifth, elaborate ceremonial is often very important to Wiccans, but many feminists distrusted such display. Sixth, and above all, feminists insist on revering a powerful goddess, a goddess, as Eller puts it, "bigger than the god of patriarchy" (1993: 58-59). Only *(The)* Great Goddess was large enough. Therefore, for many, Wicca would not suffice: they needed to create their own form of spirituality (Starhawk 1989b: 159-164).

Nonetheless, Wicca and Feminist Goddess Worship have influenced one another, mainly because of the extremely popular work of Starhawk, who, though she sees herself as Wiccan, is also feminist, having come into the orbit of Zsuzsanna Budapest in the seventies (Starhawk 1989b; Starhawk 1987a).

Other Significant Connections

Other contemporary spiritual practices with which Feminist Goddess Worship has connections include the New Age Movement and Jungian Therapy. The New Age Movement and Feminist Goddess Worship began around the same time, though they have different motivations. New Age seems to refer to a very amorphous set of leanings, for instance, toward exploring Eastern religions, the occult, and various kinds of divination and healing techniques, to name only a few. There is considerable overlap between the two movements; they often use the same venues for classes, talks, workshops, sale of ornaments and cultic tools, and so on. New Age interest in crystal, horoscopes, and tarot reading have also influenced Feminist Goddess Worshippers.

Jungians and Jungian therapists always had an interest in goddesses, and Jungian psychology has drawn feminist seekers for spiritual expression to its obvious goddess content. Jung's archetypal theory appears to be common knowledge among Feminist Goddess Worshippers (Jung 1959), probably the result of the work of Jungian mythographers like Joseph Campbell (1965, 1964) and feminist Jungian therapists like Jean Bolen (1984) and Sylvia Perrera (1981). However, it is unclear how Feminist Goddess Worshippers handle the sexism in Jungian theory (Christ 1997: 86).

In the theories of Jung and his followers, goddesses usually appear as temptresses or good and bad mothers, with whom heroes have to deal. As bad mothers, goddesses usually are monsters whom the hero defeats. Carol Christ's discussion of the writings of Erich Neumann (1971, 1970), as well as those of Joseph Campbell (1965, 1964: 109-126) and Robert Graves (1961), concludes that we must approach "with great caution" the work not only of Neumann, Campbell, and Graves, but also of the master Carl Gustav Jung (1997: 86-88). Canadian scholar Naomi Goldenberg does a thorough evaluation and critique of Jungian ideas as they affect women and religion (1979).

RELATIONS WITH JUDAISM AND CHRISTIANITY

Many Feminist Goddess Worshippers are refugees from Christianity and Judaism. As a result, we might expect the new spirituality to borrow from these traditions. In the main, such borrowing seems not to have not occurred on any large scale. Individual women do use elements of Judaism and Christianity in their own worship, but groups seem less likely to do so, unless the group is expressly trying to link traditional religions and the new spirituality. It is much more the case that Revolutionaries, especially in Christianity, experiment with borrowing from Wicca and Feminist Goddess Worship (Christ 1997: 29; Eller 1993: 73).

APPROPRIATION FROM OTHER TRADITIONS

In addition to what seem to have been quite amicable and fertile interrelationships, there are other connections fraught with difficulties, and the most contentious issue is appropriation. Perhaps the source of ritual and symbol that Feminist Goddess Worshippers most often use is Native Canadian/American. They also borrow from African religions. Since most of the borrowers are white and middle class, many Native and African Canadians, as well as Native and African Americans, object to these women's appropriating traditions not their own. White women who, despite protests, continue to "borrow" from these and other traditions often justify themselves by saying that borrowing always goes on or that they are very careful and respectful in their borrowing or that they always give something in exchange, for instance, make a donation or write a protest letter (Eller 1993: 77).

Some Native and African Canadians, as well as their American counterparts, do, however, run classes on their traditions, and some lead worship groups which white feminists can attend. There are also popular books which detail these traditions (Allen 1991; Allen 1986; Gleason 1987; Teish 1985).

One way in which some white, middle-class women have dealt with this problem of appropriation is by trying to adhere to traditions they think are already theirs: for instance, women of Celtic background attempt to recover what must have been a very powerful and beautiful spiritual tradition. The books of prolific writer Caitlin Matthews are popular storehouses of information about the Celtic tradition (Matthews 1991; Matthews 1989). Others insist on borrowing only from ancient cultures that, to all intents and purposes, have ceased to exist; I suspect that some of my students fell into this category.

FEMINIST GODDESS WORSHIP TODAY

Since Feminist Goddess Worship usually occurs in small, independent groups, it is difficult to be certain what principles and practices are normative for the whole of the growing spiritual practice. The myriad articles, books, and even films now available on the topic do, of course, give us a good deal of information (see Isherwood, ed. 2005; Christ 2003; Wendy Griffin, ed. 2000; Christ 1997). So do the few studies of particular groups, such as those of Jone Salmonsen (2002), Charlotte Caron (1993), and Cynthia Eller (1993). In addition, I have myself attended many Feminist Goddess Worship circles as a guest. From these sources, then, it is possible to make general observations about the tenets and practices of the new spirituality (Caron 1993; Eller 1993).

Central Tenets

The first principle of Feminist Goddess Worship is that the deity is a goddess, or goddesses, and does not just include the female in a pair or as an aspect of divinity (Christ 2003: 227). Feminist Goddess Worshippers insist that it is not enough to reject a male-dominated system and its symbols, for the symbols will continue to exert their influence. Such symbols need replacing, so that we will not fall back on "familiar structures" when there is a crisis, we are at a loss as to what to do, or we have suffered a defeat. Thus, Feminist Goddess Worshippers insist on making femaleness central to the beliefs, symbols, and practices of their religion (Eller 1993: 3). They also regard *(The)* Goddess as validating the female body and its functions, and they refuse to accept the body/mind-spirit dualism of Western culture (Christ 1997: Chap.1, 91-93; Christ 1982: 73).

Second, Feminist Goddess Worshippers, almost to a woman, agree that female empowerment—for many empowerment means healing—is the primary aim of their spirituality. With the proviso that it not harm another, whatever helps a woman to achieve that end is valid (Christ 1997: 167ff.).

Third, they are generally united in the view that Nature is alive and sacred, often personified as a goddess—Mother Earth, Mother Nature, Gaia (Raphael 2000: 103ff.). Many see human psychological problems as the result of alienation from Nature (Low and Tremayne 2001). Often they regard the concept of progress with a jaundiced eye, the "ascent of man" being the main reason for today's ecological disasters. Thus, ecological activism often attracts those members of the religion who define their spirituality as one of ecology (Christ 1997: 27, 44-45, 117, 134, 177; Eller 1993: 192-193).

Fourth, tolerance of other people's differing views, ways, and actions or non-actions is a given in Feminist Goddess Worship, as it is generally among Wiccans and other Pagans (Adler 1986: 101). This tolerance stems from the conviction that diversity constitutes "the great principle of the earth body" (Christ 1997: 152-153).

Fifth, many espouse the sacred history that I outlined above. Further, like many Wiccans and other Pagans, Feminist Goddess Worshippers are often serious students of ancient cultures and myths, and they read widely, attend classes, and pass on their knowledge to other women (Christ 1997: Chap. 3; Eller 1993: 9).

Sixth, decentralization and lack of hierarchy are absolute rules; there can be no central authority and no hierarchy in worship. Feminist Goddess Worship groups are, like most Wiccan groups, usually small and fiercely independent. In addition, there are no received and inviolate scriptures and no collective liturgy, though much sharing and borrowing goes on (Christ 1997: 29).

Detail, Mesopotamian "Ishtar [Inanna] Vase," terracotta with cut, moulded and painted decoration, 2nd millennium BC. Photo: Jastrow 2009. Used with permission CC-BY.

Other tenets about which there is some general agreement among Feminist Goddess Worshippers include the following: First, many regard their spirituality as forcing them into political action, while others see it as tending to separate them from politics (Christ 1997: 27). Second, for most devotees, the sacred is neither transcendent, "out there," nor immanent, that is, in all Nature including us, but both (Christ 1997: 104-105; Eller 1993: 130-131). Third, borrowing from Wicca, a number of worshippers think that sexuality is sacred, whatever its expression, with, of course, the proviso that it not harm another (Christ 1997: 146-148). Fourth, again borrowing in part from Wicca, a large number of Feminist Goddess Worshippers repudiate the concepts of evil, sin, and guilt that they see as central to the three Western monotheistic traditions (Christ 1997: Chap. 6). This list is by no means exhaustive. Carol Christ's book on the new religion gives a detailed account (Christ 1997).

Of course, there are some tensions and disagreements among Feminist Goddess Worshippers. One concerns the role and nature of men. There are differences about whether men belong in the religion, whether women and men are similar or different, and whether women are superior to men. Another disagreement is over what the ancient matriarchies were like, where patriarchy came from and what it is, and what a truly woman-centred culture would look like. There is, in addition, some dispute over the nature of *the* Goddess, though this is not a problem for most Feminist Goddess Worshippers. Some disagreement occurs over the ethics of appropriation from other traditions, and ethical issues also surface over ideas of good and evil, especially with respect to the practice of "magic" in ritual (Christ 1997: 41-41, 58-62, 148-150, 177; Eller 1993: 4, 115ff.).

Rituals

Like Wiccans, most Feminist Goddess Worshippers employ ritual as a tool. In fact, their spirituality manifests itself primarily in ritual (Christ 1997: 25-26, 42; Northup 1997; Gross 1996: 210; Eller 1993: 84). Ritual connects participants to (*the*) Goddess and aids them in getting into contact with the sacred whenever they wish to. Ritual also brings them into harmony with Nature. By keeping them so, rituals help effect the healing that all women whose experience is moulded by male dominance need (Raphael 2000: 120-121). In a real sense, then, Feminist Goddess Worship promotes healing, for the empowerment of women consists in their finding ways not only to counter, in Mariechild's words, their "oppression and pain," but also to develop their "wisdom and strength" (1988: xi).

Ritual circles meet monthly, or more often, to recognise the new or full moon, to mark other cosmic events, to celebrate life-cycle transitions, and to perform specific healing rituals. They usually meet in one or other member's home. There is, of course, a social element in the meetings, as well as a therapeutic one. As in early second-wave feminism's consciousness-raising groups, Goddess groups provide support for members, validation for changes they may be making in their lives, and, on occasion, group therapy and healing. Women come together in small Goddess groups to mark events in one another's life-cycle or the life-cycles of relatives and friends: menarche, middle age, menopause, marriage, divorce, conception, birth, abortion, and miscarriage. All merit special rituals (Christ 1997: 3, 25-30; Eller 1993: 85-89).

Feminist Goddess Worship rituals can occur anywhere that is quiet and safe from interruptions. Rituals do not have a specific pattern. Worshippers are extremely innovative and creative in constructing rituals. In addition, rituals are also very personal and flexible, changing with the situation. The rule is: Do whatever works. Devotees are also very eclectic in their rituals, and they often borrow freely from many cultural traditions. As do many aboriginal peoples and also Wiccans, Feminist Goddess Worshippers include, near the beginning of rituals, the addressing the spirits of the four directions, West, East, South, and North, a practice that now seems now to be obligatory. Some circles borrow a Native American tradition, "smudging," the burning of sage or some other aromatic plant and purifying the participants with the smoke (Christ 1997: 29; Eller 1993: 93, 95; Walker 1990: 4, 11, 31-32).

In principle, Feminist Goddess Worship circles are leaderless, with anyone who chooses to acting as leader at some point in the ritual: thus, all are priestesses. In larger gatherings, however, normally one or more women act as leaders, and they are usually women who have an aptitude for spiritual leadership (Eller 1993: 90-91).

In Feminist Goddess Worship, as in Wicca, a typical ritual starts with the setting up of an altar. After a silent period of "centring," devotees create a sacred space and time by the "casting of the circle." Participants do this by "calling the four directions." When the circle has been "closed" and newcomers introduced, the ritual can begin. Chanting almost always occurs. An example of a chant is: "We all come from the Goddess, and unto Her we shall return, like a drop of rain flowing to the ocean." Meditation, often guided, is another ritual technique. Another ritual activity is role playing; rhythmic dancing is yet another (Walker 1990: 11-12, 20-31, 51-56, 58-60, 61, 68, 78, 85, 90, 92, 130, 173).

Sometimes a woman will go into trance; sometimes she becomes possessed by a goddess or other spirit. Worshippers bless one another and themselves. They also listen to the telling of sacred and personal stories. Usually, participants share food and drink as part of the ritual. Many of these practices Feminist Goddess Worshippers have borrowed piecemeal from Wicca, often from the writings of Starhawk (Eller 1993: 12-13, 92; Walker 1990: 29-30, 125-130, 183-185; Mariechild 1988: 30-31; Starhawk 1989b: 139-158).

The aim or focus of most rituals is the creation of a "cone of power," as Wiccans call it. On most ritual occasions, through drumming, dancing, and chanting, the circle generates a state of ecstasy in its members and then focuses the collective energy on a task, such as healing a member or a member's friend or bolstering the resolve of a protest group or someone under pressure (Eller 1993: 93, 99-100). Then the circle "grounds" the energy through a precise ritual technique. As the members become calm again, they "open" the circle by releasing the spirits of the four directions and pronouncing the circle "open, but unbroken." The group then relaxes and enjoys the food and drink that almost always accompany such occasions (Christ 1997: 41; Gross 1996: 213; Starhawk 1989b: 134, 157-158).

The rituals of Feminist Goddess Worship circles give women an opportunity to talk about personal problems and sense the support of the other women. Usually a sick or distressed woman requests her circle to perform a healing rite. However, often during a ritual, after the group has raised and concentrated energy, a participant will ask that some of the power be directed to her for healing. Then the group will focus energy on her and her problem. Feminist Goddess Worshippers do not claim that their rituals cure the body, but rather that they work holistically by affecting the mind and strengthening the will. Thus, ritual healing contributes to the efficacy of medical treatment and stimulates the person's own "regenerative resources" (Caron 1993: 92-93; Walker 1990: 168-169).

A controversial topic for Feminist Goddess Worshippers is "magic." It properly belongs under the heading "Rituals," because, like scholars of Ritual Studies, many Feminist Goddess Worshippers define rituals as magical (Driver 1998: 183-185). Their magic lies in their ability to effect transformation. The understanding of magic current in the religion is that magic is the ability to achieve contact with the power of (*the*) Goddess and to focus and, as in Wicca, direct it through the will. A large number of Feminist Goddess Worshippers would agree with Starhawk's view that magic is the "art of changing consciousness at will" (Starhawk 1989b: 109). The consciousness is that of the practioner of magic, and so is the will. Further, this alteration of the practitioner's consciousness can, and does, change the world, for, like Wiccans, most Feminist Goddess Worshippers think that everything in the universe is interconnected. Not all Feminist Goddess Worshippers employ magic, but most believe that it is very potent (Christ 1997: 42; Eller 1993: 115).

Festivals

Following an ancient Celtic calendar, like Wiccans, Feminist Goddess Worshippers normally recognise eight major holidays evenly spaced throughout the year: Samhain or Halloween on the eve of November 1; Midwinter Solstice or Yule, December 20-23; Imbolc or Candlemas on the eve of February 1; Spring Equinox, March 20-23; Beltane or May Eve on the eve of May 1; Midsummer Solstice, June 20-23; Lughnasad or Lammas Eve on the eve of August 1; and Autumn Equinox, September 20-23. Even small groups normally hold special celebrations for these important festivals. In addition, there are usually large Pagan festivals at certain of these dates, and Feminist Goddess Worshippers often attend them. They also arrange their own festivals (Eller 1993: 88, n.; Walker 1990: 102).

One of the most popular times of year for large celebrations is Samhain, November Eve or Halloween. The Feast of the Dead, it is one of the points in the year when there is "an opening in the crack between the worlds," the ghosts of the dead can intermingle with the living, and it is possible to contact the ancestors. The "death-dealing Crone" presides over Samhain, which is the Wiccan New Year (Eller 1993: 88-89; Walker 1990: 102, 115-118; Starhawk 1989b: 193).

Almost as important are Beltane and the Midsummer Solstice. In the northern hemisphere, a number of large celebrations occur at these times; in the southern hemisphere, the months of festival differ, but the holidays are the same. Sometimes, Feminist Goddess Worshippers choose to celebrate life-cycle rituals, when numbers of women gather for a holiday festival; an example is the "Croning" ritual that Eller describes at the beginning of her book (1993:

Demeter (with sceptre) and Kore (with torch), fragment of a votive relief, marble. From Rhamnus in Attique (probably from Nemesis Temple), c. 420-410 BC. Glyptothek, Munich, Germany. Purchased in 1853 from Count Anton Prokesch-Osten.

1ff.; see also Christ 1997: 29; Walker 1990: 107-111; Adler 1986: 535-544). Another occasion for celebration is the pilgrimage. Increasingly, devotees organise their own travel or join specially structured "Goddess tours" to visit sites sacred to ancient goddesses, such as the temples of the islands of Crete and Malta. They also re-visit places in their own land where they have felt the sacred before or that are holy to the land's Aboriginal people. During the pilgrimage, they perform rituals, enjoy feasts, and exchange personal experiences and Goddess lore (Christ 1997: 27-28).

Women's Ritual Roles

For the most part, Feminist Goddess Worship is a women's religion, and, thought there are some exceptions, men are not involved in it. Women construct and perform the rituals, they act as ritual leaders, and they produce thealogy. Above all, they consider women's experience central to the religion (Sered 1994).

Types of Feminist Goddess Worship

Many Feminist Goddess Worshippers begin goddess worship as solitary devotees. Often the first ritual act a woman performs is the construction of an altar in an appropriate spot in her house. She then uses the altar as a focus for meditation, prayer, inspiration, and grounding. Some Feminist Goddess Worshippers choose to continue to worship (*the*) Goddess alone, perhaps occasionally joining group rituals at festivals; Wiccan call such practitioners "solitaires." Usually, after women discover (*the*) Goddess, they soon begin looking for a group to join (Christ 1997: 25-26; Walker 1990: 178-180; Starhawk 1989b: 215, p.28n.).

Most Feminist Goddess Worshippers belong to independent "circles," small gatherings of women who meet periodically to worship the Goddess by doing rituals. Starhawk points out that, in Witchcraft, a circle is a loose-knit group, often the stage prior to the formation of a "coven," a tightly bonded group of never more than thirteen members (1989b: 49, 220, p.49n.). Some Feminist Goddess Worshippers use the word "coven" for their circles, but, since "coven" has a recognised connection with Witchcraft, others choose not to use it. For much the same reason, many Feminist Goddess Worshippers avoid calling themselves Witches. Over time, a Feminist Goddess Worship circle becomes as tightly bonded as Starhawk's coven (Eller 1993: 5-6, 8, 61; Walker 1990: 2-3)

In the United States of America, Feminist Goddess worshippers have experimented with communes and formed umbrella organisations to help facilitate communication. For example, the Re-Formed Congregation of the Goddess provides, among other things, networking through its publications and its annual conference (Eller 1993: 8-11; Adler 1986: 531). Since 2001 a "Goddess Scholars" group has been functioning by email, and in 2009 its members met in person at a symposium in Madison, Wisconsin. At this meeting long-term plans for a new scholarly society were finalized; the Association for the Study of Women and Mythology was founded (www. womenandmyth.org). It will hold its first conference in April 2010.

Women and Religious Leadership

In principle, Feminist Goddess Worship has no leaders, no priests, for women in the religion are all priests. In practice, however, women who have an aptitude for spiritual leadership tend to take leadership roles, especially in large rituals. In circles, women often alternate in presiding over rituals. Furthermore, members of a circle are usually very active in devising their own liturgies, music, altars. Part of the appeal of Feminist Goddess Worship is the freedom it affords women to structure ritual and to lead it (Eller 1993: 90-91).

FEMINIST GODDESS WORSHIP AND *THEALOGY*

To a large extent, Feminist Goddess Worshippers are all theologians. For designating inquiry into the nature and meaning of goddesses, Feminist Goddess Worshippers prefer the term "*thealogy*," which is usually attributed to Canadian feminist theologian Naomi Goldenberg (1979: 96). In developing their new religion, devotees have had to address the question: "Who is (*the*) Goddess?" Despite this, the *thealogy* of Feminist Goddess Worship has attracted few systematic thealogians. It is clear that thealogy has not been a priority for a religion that is still very young, intentionally loosely organised, and primarily experiential (Christ 1997: 184, n.5; Eller 1993: 130-132; Walker 1990: 135-139; Adler 1986: 203-205). Nonetheless, one of the earliest Feminist goddess worshipers, Carol Christ, began publishing *thealogy* in the late 1990s. With *Rebirth of the Goddess* (1997), she produced the first systematic work on *thealogy*, and she followed it up in 2003 with *She Who Changes*, another important contribution.

Robert Burns, "Diana [Goddess of hunting and skies] and her Nymphs," 1926, National Gallery of Scotland.

(The) *Goddess—One or Many?*

Whether or not Feminist Goddess Worship is a monotheistic religion is a question that practitioners themselves do not seem very worried about. Sometimes the divinity is One, sometimes Many.[5] Cynthia Eller reports on the responses of Feminist Goddess Worshippers to her questions about the nature of the Goddess. When she asked them whether they believed in one goddess or many, they answered: "Both, both at the same time." On whether She is immanent or transcendent, their reply was : "Both, both at the same time." To the question of whether She exists "independently of human beings" or is an invention, their answer was the same: "Both, both at the same time." Eller concludes that this unwillingness to apply "theological labels" to their Goddess actually is what,

Richard B. Godfrey (1728- ?), "The Goddess Kali," 1770 print, coloured etching on paper.

for her worshippers, makes her a real goddess (1993: 130-131). In any case, the majority of Feminist Goddess Worshippers are, in my experience, too busy worshipping, too busy experiencing and experimenting, to be concerned even with *thealogy*

Nevertheless, most Feminist Goddess Worshippers would, if they could bring themselves to declare themselves on the matter, say that they think of (*the*) Goddess in terms of "The One and The

Many" (Griffin 2004: 190). This concept presents polytheism in a way that may not be too offensive for monotheists. It subsumes polytheism into an over-arching monotheism (Adler 1986: 205).

In the polytheistic religions that I have studied, religious functionaries and devotees seem to understand deities and other spirits to occupy separate niches in the universe, to supervise different realms. Though they may have diverse aspects or may even, over time, become identified with one another, they still oversee distinct realms as distinct deities.

The modern Goddess chant "Isis, Astarte, Diana, Hecate, Demeter, Kali—Inanna" names a number of deities from a variety of ancient cultures. I suspect that the chant would make little sense to an ancient Mesopotamian polytheist, even if she knew of the deities from other cultures. She would have had experience of the Great Goddess Inanna/Ishtar, Queen of Heaven, Goddess of Love/Sex and Warfare, a goddess who had some affinities with the much later Astarte. She would also have made offerings to Ninhursaga, the Great Goddess of Earth, but never would she have confused Inanna/Ishtar and Ninhursaga; they had distinct realms, distinct areas of expertise. Inanna/Ishtar definitely bequeathed some of Her traits to Astarte, and Inanna/Ishtar and Kali also had a few in common; Isis and Demeter were definitely identified with each other in some places in the Greco-Roman world, but Kali and Isis—not possible! The only way the chant would make sense to our ancient polytheist would be if it were saying that these goddesses were equivalent to each other, as she would know, and we now do also, that they patently were not.

However, that is the only way to interpret the chant today, that all those ancient goddesses from cultures as distinct as ancient Greece and India are aspects of the Great Goddess. Those chanting are invoking (*the*) Goddess by some of Her myriad names. One of the women Eller interviewed told her that there is only one Goddess who "'manifests in different forms'" (1993: 133).

Even a quick glance at the many feminist goddess books on my shelves indicates the primacy of *the* Goddess, and Eller reviewed thirty-two books, only seven of which mention deity in the plural (1993: 133). Clearly, *the* singular Goddess is a central concept for Feminist Goddess Worshippers.

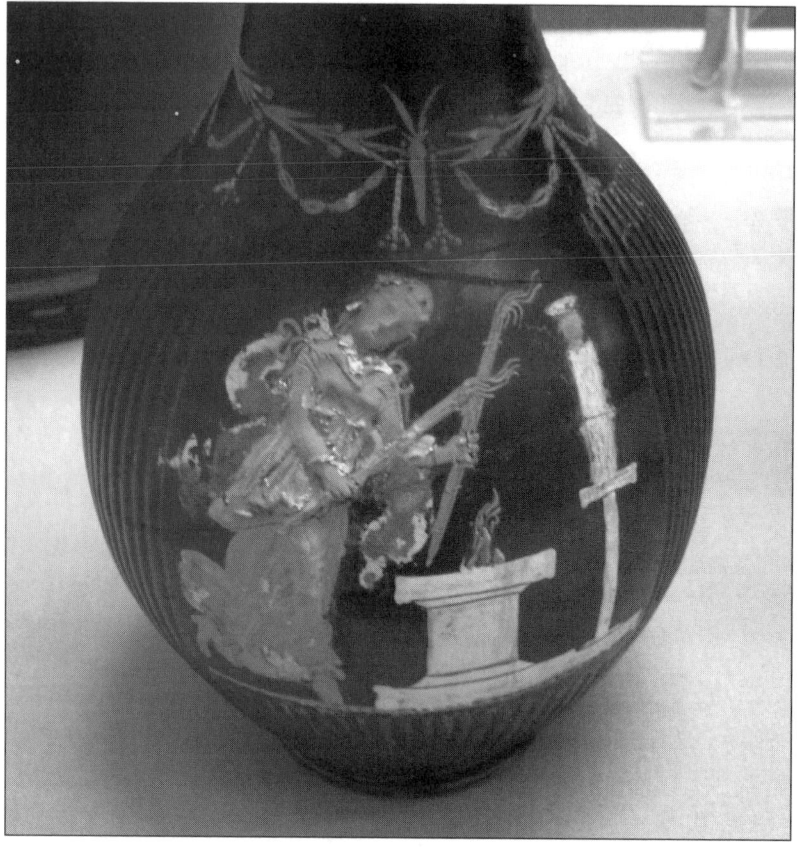

Hecate holding two torches and dancing in front of an altar, beyond which is a cult statue. Attic black-glazed oinochoe, h. 23.5 cm., c. 350-300 BC*, from Capua, Italy. Castellani collection, British Museum, London,* UK*. Photo: Bibi Saint-Pol. Used with permission by* CC-BY*.*

Yet Feminist Goddess Worshippers often have a special relationship with one particular goddess, who is obviously Herself and not just an aspect of (*the*) Goddess (Eller 1993: 134). Thus, we seem to be dealing with monotheism and polytheism together, a problem that becomes even more difficult when we consider the "Triple Goddess." In Feminist Goddess Worship, she is the epitome of the One and the Many—normally She is the Moon, whose three phases are three distinct goddesses: Feminist Goddess Worshippers give as an example the Greek goddesses Persephone, Demeter, and Hecate. The Triple Goddess also corresponds to the three phases of womanhood: maiden, mother, and crone. The Triple Goddess is, it seems, the Feminist Goddess Worship Holy Trinity, "The Many in The One" (Christ 1997: 109-112).

FEMINIST GODDESS *THEALOGY*

Unquestionably, one of the earliest feminists to attempt *thealogy* was the feminist Witch Starhawk. Her chapter on the Goddess in *The Spiral Dance*, first published in 1979, has had enormous influence on Feminist Goddess Worshippers. For Starhawk, the essential quality of the Goddess is immanence (Starhawk 1989b: 91-92, Chap. 5).Even before Feminist Goddess Worship had fully emerged as a separate spiritual entity, it did have at least one budding *thealogian*, Carol Christ (Christ 1997: 103).

Carol Christ's Goddess Thealogy

From the first time that she heard of (*the*) Goddess in one of Starhawk's workshops, well-known feminist scholar and Christian theologian Carol Christ has been moving inexorably towards writing a *thealogy* of the Goddess. First, she had to leave the Christian tradition in which she had been raised and in which she studied theology. Gradually, she made the difficult journey, and she recorded its landmarks for others to follow. By the late 1970s, however, she had begun to write Goddess *thealogy* (1997: 2-5, 1995, 1987, 1983, 1979).

In her very influential essay, "Why Women Need the Goddess," first published in 1979, Carol Christ discusses four reasons why women need the Goddess as symbol. First, the Goddess validates power in women as both independent and good. Second, She affirms women's bodies and the life cycle they represent. Third, She represents "the positive valuation of will" through rituals that are Goddess centred. Fourth, She gives women the opportunity to re-assess the ties they have to one another and to their heritage (Christ and Plaskow 1979).

In support of the first reason, Christ explores the necessity of replacing the symbol of the God of traditional religions with another symbol: (*the*) Goddess, but she does not address the issue of the Oneness of (*the*) Goddess, though it seems obvious that Her Oneness counterpoints the Oneness of traditional God. On the other hand, the Goddess's many aspects have to do, first and foremost, with women's experiences of their bodies, their cyclical and processual natures. This is obviously true of the Triple Goddess, and it is also true of the many goddesses of Feminist Goddess Worship.

A Systematic Feminist Goddess Worship Thealogy

After over twenty years of studying the Goddess and writing about Her, Carol Christ has produced a systematic *thealogy* of the Goddess. In her book, she examines the relationship between *thealogy* and women's experience, the sacred history of Feminist Goddess Worship and reactions to it, the meaning of the Goddess, the relationship of the Goddess and the universe, the relationship of humans to the Goddess and the universe, the connection between myth and way of life, and, finally, ethics (Christ 1997).

In *Rebirth of the Goddess*, Carol Christ pays tribute to the many Feminist Goddess *thealogians* who have preceded her. Although other Feminist Goddess Worshippers will undoubtedly produce their own systematic *thealogies* in the future, they will all have to take into account Christ's work. Her 1997 book has secured her place as the foremost *thealogian* of the new religion.

LESBIAN VOICES

According to Cynthia Eller, Feminist Goddess Worshippers in the United States was, in the early 1990s, "disproportionately lesbian," and she stated that Feminist Goddess Worship was now the religion of large numbers of the "lesbian feminist community." Lesbian feminists discovered Goddess Worship, Eller argued, as a "natural outgrowth" of their Radical Feminism, which attributes women's low status in Western society solely to patriarchy (1993: 18, 20-21, 35, 42). In 1996, Melissa Raphael agreed with her (13, 272). In the 1970s, a collective from Oregon began the magazine *WomanSpirit*, which appeared from 1974 to 1984. The magazine was extremely important for the development of Feminist Goddess Worship. Though not primarily a lesbian publication, the lesbian community provided many of its workers (Adler 1986: 185-186).

Although it did not at first attract only lesbians, Dianic Wicca was, and is, separatist. Its adherents prefer to do ritual only with women and to worship female, not male deities. Originally, the term "Dianic" was the one Zsuzsanna Budapest used for her feminist witchcraft. Today the term "Dianic Wicca" usually refers to lesbian Witches (Eller 1993:). It seems likely that Dianic Wicca was for many lesbians the way into Feminist Goddess Worship (Eller 1993: 60, 242, n.40; Starhawk 1989b: 121, n.5; Adler 1986: 184, 188, 226).

The new spirituality has benefitted greatly from the strength and energy of lesbian women. Further, lesbian feminist writers like Adrienne Rich (1976) and Audre Lorde (1989) have made important contributions to the literature of Feminist Goddess Worship (Adler 1993: 340).

DISCUSSION

Feminist Goddess Worship, which still manifests itself in various forms, has only in the past twenty-five or thirty years emerged from identification or confusion with related forms of spirituality, particularly Wicca. At present, its great strength lies in its deep commitment to ritual. Through personal involvement in creating the elements of ritual, worshippers themselves ensure that their ceremonies are spiritually satisfying. Essentially, most Feminist Goddess Worshippers are doers, not theorizers, and, as long as the religion can remain one of doers, feminists interested in spirituality will continue to be drawn to it. Not only does Feminist Goddess Worship offer women personal involvement in the creation of rituals, but it also invites all participants to take religious leadership roles. At the same time, it rejects hierarchy and usually considers leadership to be temporary or alternating among worshippers.

In the final chapter of her 1993 book, Cynthia Eller presents several sociological theories to explain the phenomenon of Feminist Goddess Worship. Sociologists have hypothesised that alternative religions become havens for society's "oddballs" (the "defective individual theory"), that such religions appear and recruit members when mainstream society does not satisfy their needs (the "social disorganization theory"), and that those lacking status, self-worth, health, or money flock to alternative religions (the "deprivation theory"). Eller thinks that all three theories can, to some extent, explain Feminist Goddess Worship, but she judges the latter to be the best fit (208-209).

Eller argues that an aspect of the deprivation theory, "power deprivation," elucidates the main reason for women's attraction to Feminist Goddess Worship. The disillusionment of many white middle-class women with "political feminism" in its failure to give them equality with men led them to opt for another kind of feminism, in which religion promises to fulfil "its dreams of social power" (210-211). This theory may be correct for certain Feminist Goddess Worshippers, but it tends to overlook the overwhelmingly spiritual motivations of most others

Eller follows her outline of the "power deprivation" theory with a re-interpretation of it that is quite convincing, for it could apply large numbers of Feminist Goddess Worshippers. In her re-interpretation, Eller notes that they are seeking empowerment as females, as women (1993: 213). That Feminist Goddess Worship is about power and especially women's empowerment is clear, and empowerment is certainly central to the concept of (*the*) Goddess. First and foremost, what (*the*) Goddess empowers is the body and femaleness. (*The*) Goddess, says Elinor Gadon, models "woman's nature in all its fullness"(1989: xiv). Thus, (*the*) Goddess provides an antidote to Western society's devaluation of body and the female body in particular.

Furthermore, (*the*) Goddess empowers women as persons and actors in the world. Eller argues that (*the*) Goddess does so by expanding the category "feminine" to include traits that our culture usually designates as masculine (1993: 213-214). I would rather put it another way: (*The*) Goddess undermines the societal application of the categories of femininity and masculinity to women and men, respectively. In that She as female also encompasses what our society deems masculine, (*the*) Goddess becomes a powerful role model for women.

Finally, Eller has reluctantly to admit that spiritual motives do play a part in many women's choice of Feminist Goddess Worship. Nevertheless, she immediately goes on to propound theories about the alienation and ambivalence of individual participants, as well as their sense of being persecuted. She also examines the negative attitudes of Feminist Goddess Worshippers to Christianity, and, in a long footnote, she discusses their reactions to Judaism (1993: 218-226).

The spiritual motivations for a woman's becoming a Feminist Goddess Worshipper seem obvious and overwhelming. However, a belief in (*the*) Goddess is not necessarily one of them, nor is such a faith essential for involvement. Participants in Goddess rituals often differ widely on who or what (*the*) Goddess is. Undoubtedly, the main attraction is ritual, about which scholars of the recently established field of Ritual Studies have a good deal to say (Christ 1997: 28).

For instance, in his book *Liberating Rites*, Tom Driver discusses four performance qualities essential to effective ritual: "space, time, word, and rhythm." Space must be flexible and non-hierarchical, in order to allow spontaneity and freedom; most Feminist Goddess Worship circles meet in the informality of women's homes. Time too must be flexible, so that a ritual "simply lasts until it is finished"; most participants in Feminist Goddess Worship rituals, myself included, have had the experience of forgetting time. One of Driver's maxims for planning rituals is: "Ritual loves not paper"; a fixed and printed "order of service" is, he maintains, alienating (1998: 212-215, maxim 11 p. 212). In Feminist Goddess Worship rites, women both re-member and reconstruct rituals and also invent them. An effective ritual has strong rhythm; drumming and chanting give Feminist Goddess Worship rituals a powerful beat. Feminist Goddess Worshippers not only focus on doing ritual, but they also do it extremely effectively (Gross 1996: 211; Eller 1993: 83).

Rituals bestow on Feminist Goddess Worshippers what Driver describes as the "three major gifts" of ritual: "order, community, and transformation" (Driver 1998: 131). First, through ritual, Feminist Goddess Worshippers re-iterate the supremacy of (*the*) Goddess, recognise Her existence both in the world and as the world, and proclaim Her spiritual and societal order. For Feminist Goddess Worshippers, She is all Nature, and, in adoring Her, devotees, especially city-dwellers, can find a way back to a forgotten understanding of the interrelatedness of humanity and nature, their place in the "Web of Life" (Christ 1997: 25-30, 113).

Second, Feminist Goddess Worshippers build community by means of the emotional bonding of ritual (Eller 1993: 83-84). Feminist love of other women gets affirmation and expresses itself primarily in rituals. Rituals also validate love of self, which is closely connected to love of other women and also to the sense of the deity's immanence. One of the characters in Ntosake Shange's play, *for colored girls who have considered suicide/ when the rainbow is enuf*, made the now-famous statement: "I found God in myself and I loved her fiercely" (cited in Christ 1982: 71).

Finally, through rituals, Feminist Goddess Worshippers use their *will* to bring about transformation in themselves and in their society. One of the main aims of all Feminist Goddess rituals is healing, as Caron broadly defines it, the promotion of personal well-being and "wholeness in community" (1993: 96). Above all, healing involves the kind of nurturing that will result in unity of "body, mind, and spirit." Ultimately, Feminist Goddess Worshippers seek through ritual not only profound changes in self and other, but also basic change in "the dominant culture" (Eller 1993: 117; Mariechild 1988: xii).

Through promoting order, community, and individual and societal transformation, Feminist Goddess Worship adds a dimension to feminism that it has lacked since consciousness-raising ceased to be popular. Further, women are creating, from day to day, an empowering, fulfilling alternative to the other religious traditions and one from which feminists in other traditions are already borrowing. Since Feminist Goddess Worship is so new, it is hard to foresee how it will develop. If women now involved in the religion have their way, it will stay decentralised and non-hierarchical, but its members will continue to innovate ritually. After all, that is what they do best.

Notes

[1]I italicise *thealogy* to distinguish it from "theology."

[2]One sort of "Radical Witchcraft," as Kevin Marron names it in his discussion of Canadian witchcraft, may be what I call "Feminist Goddess Worship" (Marron 1989: Chap.7). Carol Christ has called it variously

"the Goddess movement," "the religion of the Goddess," and "feminist spirituality" (Christ 1997: xv, xiii, title page). In her newest book she describes its various forms as "spiritual feminism" (2003: 23). Rita Gross names it "the feminist spirituality movement, or feminist Wicca" (Gross 1996: 44). Melissa Raphael calls it "Goddess feminism" (2000: 75).

[3]I considered staying with the name "Feminist Spirituality," but then I was faced with finding a term for the varieties of feminist spiritual expression inside Judaism, Christianity, and Islam. Since I consider many Jewish, Christian, and Muslim feminists to be practising feminist spirituality, I had to eliminate that term, even though some feminist writers do use it for the phenomenon (Eller 1993: 7). I then tried "Modern Goddess Worship," but this phrase faced me with the problem of what to call contemporary worshippers of Hindu deities like Durga, Lakshmi, Kali, and Sita, Chinese who venerate Guan-yin and Ma-tsu, and so on. "Feminist Goddess Worship" seemed to be the best alternative.

[4]For a critique of Eller's work, see Dashu 2005.

[5]Melissa Raphael says that the Oneness of (*the*) Goddess answers the Oneness of the traditional God of monotheism (2000: Chap. 2).

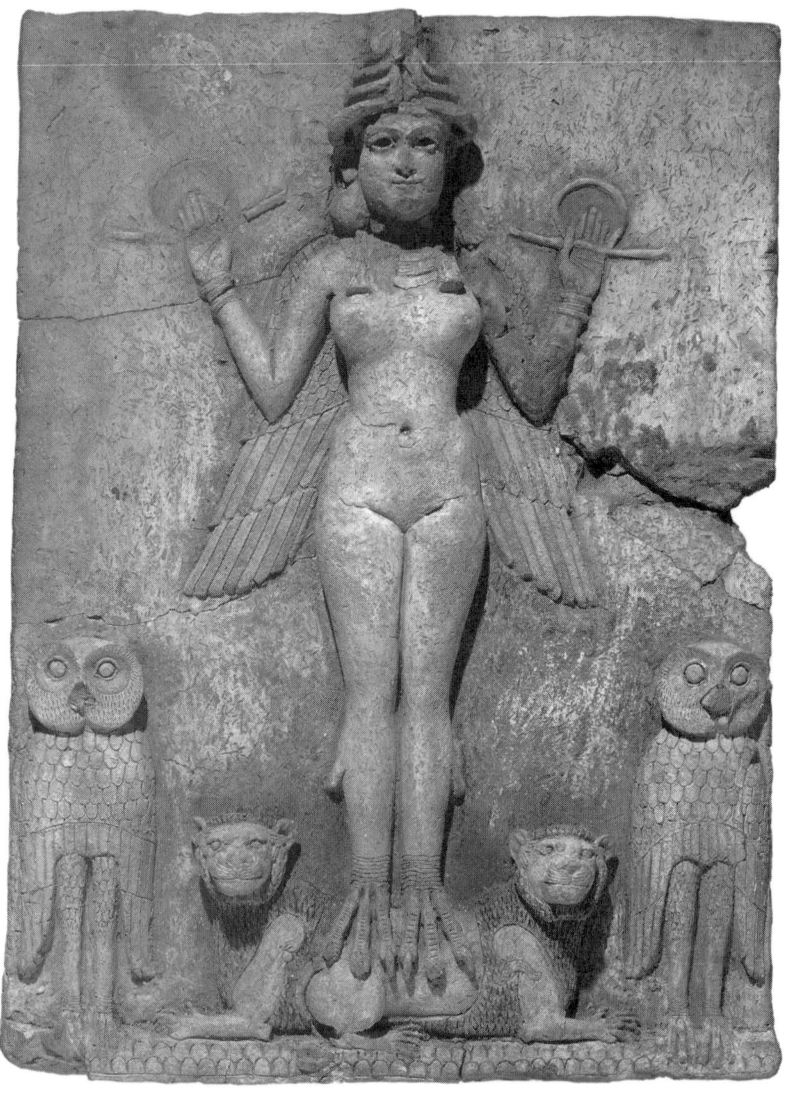

Ancient Babylonian goddess, possibly Ishtar [Inanna]. It might also represent Lilitu (called Lilith in the Bible), as seen from the bird-feet and accompanying owls. Plaque of baked straw-tempered clay. The goddess was originally painted red. c.1792 - 1750 BC.

7.
CONCLUDING THOUGHTS

WHEN SECOND-WAVE feminism began, it dismissed religion as irremediably sexist, and so spirituality was irrelevant. Secular feminists often think in that way still and consider feminists with an interest in spirituality to be "soft feminists." Nonetheless, for large numbers of their feminist sisters, both spirituality and religion are not only meaningful, but essential. Furthermore, the "soft feminists" who have remained inside Judaism, Christianity, and Islam are undertaking the difficult, unpopular, and sometimes dangerous task of bringing about in their traditions changes that, when in place, should transform them in ways that we can now only imagine. In addition, Feminist Goddess Worshippers are rejoicing in the creation of a new women's spirituality, which has already had a recognisable effect on feminism in the West and is in the process of altering the spiritual landscape of Western countries.

I did not start this book with a hypothesis in mind, but with the aim of describing the four religions I selected and the feminist theology they have produced. Therefore I have no theory to present, only observations and questions.

In a number of ways, the growth and development of Feminist Goddess Worship is very similar to the growth and development of the three monotheistic traditions we discussed above. This statement seems to apply especially to Christianity. The following parallels suggest some questions as well as possible topics for further research.

Like early Christians, Feminist Goddess Worshippers gather in small, independent groups which meet in private homes ("house churches"), a situation which, in early Christianity, appears to have contributed to women's leadership, but, in the case of Feminist Goddess Worship, probably stems *from* female leadership. Is smallness one condition for female spiritual self-realisation, including leadership? If the spiritual group is small and informal, like the early Christian "house church," is it more likely to be egalitarian? Undoubtedly, when the venue of Christian worship became large and public, men demanded and got exclusivity of leadership.

Feminist Goddess Worship is, like early Christianity, decentralized, but Feminist Goddess Worshippers appear to want their religion to remain so. It seems most unlikely that Feminist Goddess Worshippers would have any time for a leader and organiser such as Paul, even a female version of him. Feminist Goddess Worshippers have a deep distrust of hierarchy and a dread of institutional religion. Is centralisation a barrier to female leadership?

Like early Christianity, Feminist Goddess Worship focuses on ritual which is exciting, engrossing, and immensely effective. It has no "sacred book" and no fixed liturgy. "Ritual loves not paper." When ritual really works, its performance is spontaneous and depends on memory, imagination, and ability to innovate, none of which are sex specific. In cultures in which women were not educated, did not learn to read, as in the post-Diaspora Rabbinic Period, emphasis on being able to read sacred books and fixed liturgies effectively cuts women off from participation, let alone leadership. Is emphasis on doing ritual as opposed to reading sacred texts and fixed liturgy another factor that favours women's full participation as well as leadership?

Like early Christianity, Feminist Goddess Worship also has an ecstatic component, with possession and trance experiences quite normal. A spirit does not choose by sex the person to possess, and women are just as likely as men to have ecstatic, mystical experiences, to become prophets. Not surprisingly, religious groups that emphasise ecstatic experience are usually egalitarian and have female as well as male leaders. They also attract many women members. Focus on ecstatic experience certainly promotes the full participation of women. Is it also an element which strongly favours women's leadership?

Like Judaism, Christianity, and Islam, Feminist Goddess Worship traces its existence to a very powerful sacred story. At the beginning of the tradition, it was and is of utmost importance for all four religions that the sacred story is "history," that is, an account of what actually happened in the past, a history which informs and gives meaning to the present. Why is grounding in the historical, the "factual, so important for the three monotheistic traditions and, at least at its start, for Feminist Goddess Worship?

By its almost universal insistence on being a women-only religion, Feminist Goddess Worship easily differentiated itself from the three monotheistic traditions, New Age and Alternative spirituality, and most of Wicca, but it has only recently clearly differentiated itself from Dianic Wicca. One of the problems all new religions have in becoming distinct is borrowing or appropriation. In their early stages, Judaism, Christianity, and Islam all borrowed and appropriated elements from pagan traditions and from the preceding monotheistic tradition(s). At the same time they often reacted negatively to other contemporary religions.

In that regard, it is tempting to see some of the main tenets of Feminist Goddess Worship as a reaction against well-known values of the monotheistic traditions, particularly Christianity, for example, the repudiation by most devotees of Christian concepts of good and evil, sin, guilt, and its negative view of sexuality. In addition, there are elements in the understanding of (*the*) Goddess of Feminist Goddess Worship that seem like an imitation of the God of monotheism, especially Christianity. The Triple Goddess and the Trinity are a case in point. Worshippers who view the Goddess as the One and the Many could also be seen to be trying to accommodate (*the*) Goddess to monotheism. Would not polytheism with its basic commitment to the values of diversity be a more appropriate form of religion for feminists?

Revolutionary feminist theologians are trying to transform the monotheistic traditions that they do not want to leave by reviving, importing, and inventing goddesses, female aspects of the deity, female imagery.[1] What many of them are doing sometimes seems suspiciously like trying not only to put the Many back into the One, but, at the same time, make the One into the Many. That is why I questioned whether Judaism and Christianity would be themselves at all, if the Revolutionaries had their way. By definition they are monotheistic, and monotheism excludes even complementarity of deities, as those who worshipped Asherah and Yahweh together eventually found out. The question remains: Do Feminist Goddess Worshippers really serve the One Goddess? Are they really monotheists?

Not only has second-wave feminism ignored female spirituality, but so have most contemporary religious-studies scholars. The result is that we have only just begun to find out about it, and there is an enormous amount of research still to be done. Yet the fact remains that women have always expressed their spirituality in as full a fashion as their situations have allowed. It is, then, important that we listen to what women say about their spiritual experiences and about their own sense of what those experiences mean to them.

Feminist theologians are correct, therefore, to point to women's experience as the key. It is the key to our accepting and rejoicing at the satisfaction of a woman who stays in a fundamentalist religion, despite our feminist conviction that the religion is sexist and demeaning for women; her experience tells another story. Women's experiences are also the key to our understanding what it is about religions of complementarity between female and male that makes women inside them insist that they are egalitarian. And to women's experiences we must turn to seek the reason why, despite the obvious appeal of Feminist Goddess Worship, Jewish and Christian Revolutionaries stay in their contradictory and ambivalent positions of deep emotional commitment to sexist traditions. Finally, the empowering experiences of feminists who worship (*the*) Goddess speak to the validity of the new spirituality to nurture women and emphasize the necessity of our hearing its central myth for what it is.

However these various female and feminist spiritualities develop in the future, feminism can no longer ignore spirituality and religion. They are now legitimate parts of the feminist agenda, and they will have increasing influence on that agenda in the future. As Feminist Goddess Worshippers might say, the magic of spiritual and religious transformation is abroad in the land.

Notes

[1]As Mary Bednarowsky points out, there are "common themes and even methods in women's religious thought that cut across traditions..." (1999: 185).

GLOSSARY

Agunah, pl. *agunot* – means "one who is anchored or chained," a woman whose husband has refused to give her a *get*, a Jewish religious divorce.
Aisha (A'isha) – Muhammad's very young and favourite wife.
Ali – Muhammad's cousin and husband of his youngest daughter, Fatima, whose claim to the caliphate was denied and to whose line Shiite Muslims are committed.
Allah – the name of the One God of Islam, also the chief deity of the pre-Islamic Kaaba.
Allat – a pre-Islamic goddess of Arabia.
al-'Uzza – a pre-Islamic goddess of Arabia.
Apostle – either one of Jesus's chosen "Twelve Disciples" or an authoritative missionary of the early Christian Church. See Apostolic Succession.
Apostolic Succession – a Christian doctrine whereby bishops gain their authority from the tracing the line of descent of their office from an Apostle and so from Christ (Bowker 1997:82).
Ashkenazi(m) – descendants of Jews who, in the Diaspora, settled in eastern, northern, and central Europe.
Ayatollah – means "sign of God," a senior member of the Shiite Muslim *ulama*.

Baptism – in Christianity, immersion in or sprinkling with water by a priest. The ritual symbolically cleanses a person of sin and allows rebirth into a Christian life.
bar mitzvah – a coming-of-age ritual for a Jewish boy at thirteen years of age.

bat mitzvah – a coming-of-age ceremony for a Jewish girl.
BCE – Before Common Era. The same dates as B.C., "Before Christ," but without the Christian content.
Bris(milah), berit – ritual circumcision of a Jewish male baby at eight days after birth.
bishop – one of the highest of Christian offices.

c. – abbreviation for Latin *circa*, meaning "about, around."
caliph (***khalifa(h)***) – meaning "deputy, successor."
CEDAW – the United Nations' Convention on the Elimination of All Forms of Discrimination Against Women, came into force on 3 September 1981, produced during the United Nations Decade for Women (1975-1985).
CE – Common Era. The same dates as A.D., "Anno Domini," "in the Year of the Lord," but without the Christian content.
Christos – the "Anointed One," Greek for Hebrew "Messiah."
circle – a small Feminist Goddess Worship group that meets to do ritual, also used by Wiccans for introductory and training meetings and for ritual sessions with large numbers of participants.
circumcision – the removal of the prepuce or foreskin of the penis of a male or the clitoris and other parts of the genitals of a female.
confirmation – a Christian ritual to make a person a full member of the community by calling down the Holy Spirit again on those who have already been baptised (Bowker 1997:230-231).
coven – a tightly knit, small Wiccan worship group of no more than thirteen persons, usually led by a priestess (Starhawk 1989b).
Covenant – originally an agreement between God and Abraham on behalf of the people and re-affirmed under Moses. In return for God's attention to them as His special concern and His giving them the land of Canaan, the Israelites, later the Jews, were to obey the Ten Commandments and the other laws of God as set out in the Torah. Judaism normally construes the teachings in the Talmud as elaboration of the Torah and interpretation of the Covenant in the light of new circumstances.

Dianic Wicca – usually refers to women-only Wicca, worship o female, not male deities. Originally, term "Dianic" was usedby Zsuzsanna Budapest for her feminist witchcraft. Today the term

"Dianic Wicca" often refers to lesbian Witches (Eller1993:60).
Diaspora – the Roman dispersal of the Jewish people from Judah, and Jerusalem in the year 70 of our era, when the Romans destroyed the Second Temple and the Holy City. The Romans re-located them all over their empire. The period following the "Babylonian Exile," when many people chose not to return to Judah is often called the first Diaspora.

Eucharist – also called the Breaking of the Bread, the Lord'sSupper, and Holy Communion, commemorates or renews the LastSupper of Jesus and His twelve disciples and Jesus'ssacrifice on the Cross. A priest consecrates bread and wine, as, at least symbolically, the body of Jesus and the blood of Jesus and administers them to the baptised.
"Evening of Power or Destiny" – in the month of Ramadan, when Muhammad had his first ecstatic experience and began to recite the Qur'an at the dictation of the Angel Gabriel.
Exodus – the liberation of the Israelites from slavery in Egypt, a pivotal event for Judaism.The Exodus symbolises God's caring for the people of Israel and His liberating nature and function.

Fatima – the Prophet Muhammad's youngest daughter, mother of his grandsons, Hasan and Hussein.
female – as used in this book, an adjective describing biological sex.
feminine – as used in this book, describing a set of human characteristics that are culturally assigned to those of the female sex; gender characteristics; also a grammatical term in languages that are gendered.
First Communion – a person's first partaking of the Christian sacrament of Holy Communion or the Eucharist, usually after Confirmation.
first-wave feminism – the feminism of the late nineteenth and early twentieth centuries.
fitna – Arabic, chaos or disorder.
Fundamentalism – the adherence to the basic and core "truths and practices of a religion" (Bowker 1997: 360).
gender – a set of characteristics culturally ascribed according to

biological sex, "femininity" or "masculinity"; adjectives "feminine" and "masculine."

get – proof of religious divorce in Judaism.
goddess culture – usually in pre-historic times, one that worshipped *The* Goddess and in which women were highly valued, even ruled, possibly a matriarchy; and culture in which a goddess or goddesses were supreme.
Great Goddess – or *The* Goddess, the supreme deity of Feminist Goddess Worship, often identified with Nature; also a deity of Wiccans and other Pagans.

hadith, pl. ***ahadith*** – a saying, narrative, or tradition of theProphet Muhammad.
Haggadah – the liturgy for Passover in Judaism.
Halakha(h) – the rabbinic law of Judaism.
Hasan – one of the Prophet's two grandsons.
Hasidism – from Hebrew *hasid* meaning "pious" (Epstein 1990: 271). *Hasidim* observe rabbinic law, *halakha(h)*, strictly, but they are even more devoted to ecstatic experience.
hijab – Arabic, meaning "any partition which separates two things," but usually the veil of a Muslim woman.
Hijra(h) – the journey in 622 CE of the Prophet and his followers from Mecca to Medina. The *hijra* marks the beginning of the Muslim era and of the lunar Muslim calendar.
Hussein – one of the Prophet's two grandsons, who, in 680, as heir of Ali, attempted to take the caliphate, but died at the battle of Karbala, a martyr according to Shiite Muslims.

imam – meaning "guide," for Shiite Muslims a leader descended in direct line from Ali, Muhammad's son-in-law.
Islamic feminism – seeks female empowerment from inside "a rethought Islam." Islamic feminists plan to achieve their goal mainly through appeal to the rights that Islam grants women.
Islamist – Muslim fundamentalist or "revivalist," applied to movements that advocate "the reinstitution of the laws and practices set forth in the core Islamic discourses" (Ahmed 1992: 2). Islamist governments usually enforce adherence to such laws and prac-

tices, as does the Taliban regime in Afghanistan, and they repress women especially.

Jihad – effort, struggle; war
Judea, Judaea – the Roman province encompassing ancient Judah.

Kaaba (*Ka'ba*) – the cube-shaped shrine at Mecca, toward which-Muslims face when they pray and around which they circle asone of the rites they perform during the pilgrimage to Mecca.
Kabbalah – a Jewish mystical tradition which was extremely popular in the eleventh, twelfth, and thirteenth centuries (Matt 1995: 2,15-16). There is revival of interest in Kabbalism today.
Karbala – the battle in 680 CE at which Hussein, one of Prophet's two grandsons, died, when, as heir of Ali, he attempted to take the caliphate.
***Kashrut*, kosher** – Jewish dietary laws (Bowker 1997: 281-282).
Khadija(h) – the Prophet Muhammad's first wife.
kosher – see *kashrut*.

male – as used in this book, an adjective describing biological sex.
Manat – a pre-Islamic goddess of Arabia.
masculine – as used in this book, describing a set of human characteristics that are culturally assigned to those of the male sex; gender characteristics; also a grammatical term in languages that are gendered.
mass – in Roman Catholicism and High Anglicanism (Anglo-Catholicism), the usual name of the Eucharist.
matriarchy – literally, "rule by mother(s), now generally "female dominance."
matrilineal, matriliny – tracing descent in the female line.
menarche – first menstruation.
Messiah – means "the Anointed One," in Greek *Christos*: For Jews, both Davidic king, restorer of political Israel, and this worldly saviour; for Christians, Jesus Christ; for some Muslims, the *Mahdi* (Bowker 1997: 637).
mikveh – a ritual bath in Judaism.

minyan – in Judaism, a prayer quorum of ten adult males.
Mishnah – the code of Jewish law, part of the Talmud.
mitzvah, pl.*mitzvot* – a commandment or obligation which observant Jews must carry out on a daily basis.
Mizrahi(m) – descendants of Jews who remained in the Middle East and North Africa throughout Jewish history.
Monarchy – the kingdom(s) of Israel in the north, Judah in the south, c.1000-586 BCE.
monotheism – belief that there is one god and only one.
Moses – leader of the Exodus, a pivotal event for Judaism, and reputed author of the Torah.
mujtahid – in Shiite Islam, a scholar-jurist capable independently of interpreting the Law. All Shiites are expected to be guided by a *mujtahid*, who becomes a role model.

New Testament – the Christian scriptures.

Old Testament – the Christian name for the Hebrew Bible.

Pagan, pagan – from Latin *paganus* meaning country dweller, English equivalent "heathen," a dweller on the heath; today a member of a usually polytheistic nature religion based on older pagan traditions, a Pagan, often called Neo-Pagan.
Palestine – original Roman name for what is now Israel and Lebanon.
patriarchy – literally, "rule by father(s)," now in general usage signifying "male dominance."
patrilineal, patriliny – tracing descent in the male line.
Pentecost – ten days after Jesus's Ascension, the Holy Spirit descended on the apostles (Acts 2), from Greek *pentecostos* "fifty," because it fell exactly fifty days after Jesus's Resurrection. It occurred at the conclusion of a Jewish festival that takes place fifty days after Passover (Bowker 1997:744).
The Prophet – Muhammad, to whom God sent the revelations that became the Qur'an, the sacred book of Islam.

***Qur'an*, Quran, Koran** – Islam's sacred book, "the eternal unmediated Word of God" (Ruthven 1997: 5).

rabbi – a Jewish "teacher." A rabbi's authority does not come from heredity, but from a congregation's recognition that arabbi is a scholar and authentic interpreter of Torah [the Law].
Ramadan – the ninth lunar month, in which Muslims practise total abstinence by day.
Resurrection – the Christian belief that Jesus Christ, having died on the Cross, rose from the dead three days later.
Rosh Hashanah – the Jewish New Year.

Sabbath – the seventh day of the week, when Jews do no work. Jewish households celebrate weekly, from dusk on Friday to dusk on Saturday.
Second Temple – re-building in Jerusalem completed in 516 BCE, destroyed by the Romans in 70 CE.
second-wave feminism – the feminism that began in the 1960s.
Sephardi(m) – descendants of Jews from Spain and Portugal, expelled in 1492 and scattered to North Africa (especially Morocco), Western Europe, the Balkans and Greece, Asia Minor (Turkey), India, and China.
Septuagint – the Greek translation of the Hebrew Bible.
sex – as used in this book, a biological term, either of two divisions of organisms distinguished as female or male; adjectives "female" and "male."
Sharia(h) – Islamic law.
Shekhinah – the rabbinic idea of "divine immanence," which was developed by Kabbalists until it became "the feminine half of God..." (Matt 1995: 1).
Shiite Muslims – a minority of Muslims, who believe that spiritual leadership belongs only to direct descendants of Muhammad's son-in-law, Ali, whose line was cheated of its rights. There are a number of branches of Shiism (Bowker 1997: 889).
shiva – in Judaism, the period of seven days of mourning after a funeral.
Solomonic Temple – built in Jerusalem by Solomon, king of Judah and Israel c.967-c.928 BCE, destroyed in 586 BCE by the Babylonians.
Sunna(h) – "practice or custom," contains collections of the sayings and deeds, as well as "unspoken approvals and disapprovals," of

the Prophet Muhammad and of his Companions.
Sunni Muslims – the majority of Muslims, who adhere to the Qur'an and the Sunna (Bowker 1997: 929).
synagogue – a special place where Jews gathered together for worship, festivals, community functions, and instruction (Epstein 1990: 79,112). Also a congregation or the totality of a Jewish community as a political and social entity (Kraemer 1993: 118).

Talmud – contains the code of Jewish law, the *Mishnah*, and commentaries on it. The Talmud explains and amplifies theTorah in sixty-three volumes.
Targum – an Aramaic version of the Hebrew Bible.
Torah – the first five books of the Hebrew Bible, traditionally ascribed to Moses.
Transubstantiation – the Christian ritual whereby a priest consecrates bread and wine, and they become, at least symbolically, the body of Jesus and the blood of Jesus.
Twelve Disciples or Twelve Apostles – the band of twelve male followers that Jesus is said to have selected as intimates. They were Simon Peter, Andrew, Philip, Matthew, "Doubting" Thomas, Bartholemew, Thaddeus, Simon the Zealot, James son of Alphaeus, James son of Zebedee, James's brother John, and Judas Iscariot (Mark 3:14).

ulama – "learned men," the religious scholar-jurists of Islam.
umma(h) – the Islamic community.

Virgin Birth – the Christian belief that a virgin, Mary, conceived Jesus by the Holy Spirit and gave birth to Him.

Wicca, Wiccan – contemporary Witchcraft, Witch (Starhawk 1989b).

Yom Kippur – the Jewish "Day of Atonement."

BIBLIOGRAPHY

Abu-Lughod, Lila. 1993. *Writing Women's Worlds: Bedouin Stories.* Berkeley, CA: University of California.

Abu-Odeh, Lama. 1996. "Crimes of Honour and the Construction of Gender in Arab Societies." *Feminism and Islam: Legal and Literary Perspectives.* Ed. Mai Yamani. London: Ithaca. 141-194.

Adams, Carol J., ed. 1993. *Ecofeminism and the Sacred.* New York: Continuum.

Adelman, Penina V. 1994. "A Drink from Miriam's Cup: Invention of Tradition among Jewish Women," *Journal of Feminist Studies in Religion* 10 (2): 151.

Adelman, Penina V. 1990 (1986). *Miriam's Well: Rituals for Jewish Women around the Year.* New York: Biblio.

Adler, Margot. 1986 [1979]. *Drawing Down the Moon: Witches, Druids, Goddess-Worshippers, and Other Pagans in America Today.* Boston: Beacon.

Afshar, Haleh. 1996. "Islam and Feminism: An Analysis of Political Strategies." *Feminism and Islam: Legal and Literary Perspectives.* Ed. Mai Yamani. London: Ithaca. 197-216.

Afshar, Haleh, ed. 1993. *Women in the Middle East.* London: Macmillan.

Aharoni, Y. 1982. *The Archaeology of the Land of Israel.* Philadelphia: Westminster.

Ahmed, Leila. 1992. *Women and Gender in Islam: Historical Roots of a Modern Debate.* New Haven: Yale University Press.

Al-Ali, Nadje. 2000. *Secularism, Gender and the State in the Middle East: The Egyptian Women's Movement.* Cambridge: Cambridge University.

Alam, S. M. Shamsul. 1998. "Women in the Era of Modernity and Islamic Fundamentalism: The Case of Taslima Nasrin." *Signs* 23 (1): 429-461.

Ali, Yasmin. 1992. "Muslim Women and the Politics of Ethnicity and

Culture in Northern England." *Refusing Holy Orders: Women and Fundamentalism in Britain*. Eds. Gita Sahgal and Nira Yuval-Davis. London: Virago. 101-123.

Allen, Paula G. 1991. *Grandmothers of the Light: A Medicine Woman's Sourcebook*. Boston: Beacon.

Allen, Paula G. 1986. *The Sacred Hoop: Recovering the Feminine in American Indian Traditions*. Boston: Beacon.

Alpert, Rebecca. 1997. *Like Bread on the Seder Plate: Jewish Lesbians and the Transformation of Tradition*. New York: Columbia University Press.

Alpert, Rebecca and Goldie Milgram. 1996. "Women in the Reconstructionist Rabbinate." *Religious Institutions and Women's Leadership: New Roles Inside the Mainstream*. Ed. Catherine Wessenger. Columbia, SC: University of South Carolina Press. 291-310.

Altomare, Kareema. 2000. "A Partial List of Organizations for Muslim Women's Rights, Advocacy, and Higher Islamic Education in the United States." *Windows of Faith: Muslim Women Scholar-Activists in North America*. Ed. Gisela Webb. Syracuse, NY: Syracuse University Press. 249-257.

Alvi, Sajida, Homa Hoodfar, and Sheila McDonough. 2006. *The Muslim Veil in North America: Issues and Debates*. Toronto: Women's Press.

Anderson, Grace M. 1990. *God Calls, Man Chooses: A Study of Women in Ministry*. Burlington, ON: Trinity.

Ann, Martha and Dorothy Myers Imel. 1993. *Goddesses in World Mythology: A Biographical Dictionary*. Oxford: Oxford University.

Anon. 1993. "On Being Orthodox and Lesbian." *Neshama* 5: 4-5, 8.

Anon. 1901. *Assyrian and Babylonian Literature: Selected Translations*. New York: Appleton.

Antonelli, Judith S. 1995. *In the Image of God: A Feminist Commentary on the Torah*. New York: Aronson.

Anwar, Etin. 2006. *Gender and Self in Islam*. London: Routledge.

Aquino, Maria P., Daisy L. Machada, and Jeanette Rodriguez, eds. 2002. *A Reader in Latina Feminist Theology: Religion and Justice*. Austin: University of Texas Press.

Azzam, Maha. 1996. "Gender and the Politics of Religion in the Middle East." *Feminism and Islam: Legal and Literary Perspectives*. Ed. Mai Yamani. London: Ithaca. 217-230.

Badran, Margot. 1995. *Islam and Nation: Gender and the Making of Modern Egypt*. Princeton, NJ: Princeton University Press.

Balka, Christie and Andy Rose, eds. 1989. *Twice Blessed: On Being Lesbian, Gay, and Jewish*. Boston: Beacon.

Barclay, E. and Y. Jaeger. 2004. *Guidelines: Questions and Answers about the Laws of Family Purity*. Southfield, MI: Targum.

Barger, Lilian C. 2003. *Eve's Revenge: Women and the Spirituality of the*

Body. Grand Rapids, MI: Brazos, Baker Book House.

Baring, Anne and Jules Cashford. 1991. *The Myth of the Goddess: Evolution of an Image.* London: Viking Arkana.

Barlow, Rebecca and Shahram Akbarzadeh. 2008. "Prospects for Feminism in the Islamic Republic of Iran." *Human Rights Quarterly* 30: 21-40.

Barstow, Anne L. 1994. *Witchcraze: A New History of the European Witch Hunts.* San Francisco: Harper Collins Pandora.

Baskin, Judith R. 2002. *Midrashic Women: Formations of the Feminine in Rabbinic Literature.* Hanover, NH: Brandeis University Press.

Baskin, Judith. 1985. "The Separation of Women in Rabbinic Judaism." *Women, Religion, and Social Change.* Eds. Yvonne Yazbeck Haddad and Ellison Banks Findly. Albany, NY: State University of New York Press. 3-18.

Bauer, Janet L. 1997. "Conclusion: The Mixed Blessings of Women's Fundamentalism: Democratic Impulses in a Patriarchal World." *Mixed Blessings: Gender and Religious Fundamentalism Cross Culturally.* Eds. Judy Brink and Joan Mencher. New York: Routledge. 221-254.

Beattie, Tina. 1999, "Global Sisterhood or Wicked Stepsisters: Why Don't Girls with God-Mothers Get Invited to the Ball?" Is *There a Future for Feminist Theology?* Eds. Deborah F. Sawyer and Diane M. Collier. Sheffield, UK: Sheffield Academic. 115-125.

Beauvoir, Simone de. 1970 [1949]. *The Second Sex.* New York: Bantam.

Beck, Evelyn T., ed. 1982. *Nice Jewish Girls: A Lesbian Anthology.* Watertown, MA: Persephone.

Beck, Lois and Nikki Keddie, eds. 1978. *Women in the Muslim World.* Cambridge, MA: Harvard University Press.

Bednarowsky, Mary F. 1999. *The Religious Imagination of American Women.* Bloomington: Indiana University Press.

Bell, Diane. 1993. *Daughters of the Dreaming.* 2nd ed. Minneapolis: University of Minnesota Press.

Berger, Pamela. 1985. *The Goddess Obscured: Transformation of the Grain Goddess from Goddess to Saint.* Boston: Beacon.

Berriozábal, Maria Antonietta 1992. Paper in "Roundtable Discussion: *Mujeristas*: Who We Are and What We Are About." *Journal of Feminist Studies in Religion* 8 (1): 116-120.

Betteridge, Anne H. 1989. "The Controversial Vows of Urban Muslim Women in Iran." *Unspoken Worlds: Women's Religious Lives.* 2nd ed. Eds. Nancy A. Falk and Rita M. Gross. Belmont, CA: Wadsworth. 102-111.

Black, Naomi. 1989. *Social Feminism.* Ithaca: Cornell University Press.

Blohm, Uta. 2005. *Religious Traditions and Personal Stories: Women-Working as Priests, Ministers, and Rabbis.* New York: Lang.

Bolen, Jean S. 1984. *Goddesses in Everywoman: A New Psychology of Women*. New York: Harper Colophon.

Borresen, Kari. 1981. *Subordination and Equivalence: The Nature and Role of Women in Augustine and Thomas Aquinas*. Washington, DC: University Press of America

Bova, Cherie. 1997. "The Writings of Julian of Norwich as Accommodation and Subversion." *Canadian Woman Studies/les cahiers de la femme* 17 (1) (Winter): 22-25.

Bowker, John, ed. 1997. *The Oxford Dictionary of World Religions*. Oxford: Oxford University Press.

Brettschneider, Marla, and Dawn R. Rose. 2004. "Engaging Jewish Feminist Diversity Issues: Seven Concepts and Several Questions." *Nashim: Journal of Jewish Feminist Studies and Gender Issues* 8: 180-188.

Brettschneider, Marla and Dawn R. Rose. 2003. "Meeting at the Well: Multiculturalism and Jewish Feminism. Introduction."*Journal of Feminist Studies in Religion* 19 (1): 85-90.

Briffault, Robert. 1927. *The Mothers: A Study of the Origins ofSentiments and Institutions*. 3 vols. New York: Macmillan.

Brin, Deborah and Liane Sharkey. 1992. "Jewish Women Creating Ritual." *Fireweed* (Spring): 35.

Brink, Judy and Joan Mencher, eds. 1997. *Mixed Blessings: Gender and Religious Fundamentalism Cross Culturally*. New York:Routledge.

British and Foreign Bible Society. 1962. *He Kaine Diatheke: TextWith Critical Apparatus [The Greek New Testament]*. London:British and Foreign Bible Society.

Brooten, Bernadette. 1982. *Women Leaders in the Ancient Synagogue*. Chico, CA: Scholars.

Brower, Ruth C. 2002. *Modern Women Modernizing Men: The Changing Missions of Three Professional Women in Asia and Africa, 1902-69*. Vancouver: University of British Columbia

Brouwer, Ruth C. 1990. *New Women for God: Canadian Presbyterian Women and India Missions*. Toronto: University of Toronto Press.

Brown, Joanne and Carol Bohn, eds. 1989. *Christianity, Patriarchy, and Abuse: A Feminist Critique*. New York: Pilgrim.

Burkert, Walter. 1987. *Ancient Mystery Cults*. Cambridge, MA: Harvard University Press.

Butler, Judith. 2001. "Contingent Foundations: Feminism and the Question of "Postmodernism." *Feminism in the Study of Religion: A Reader*. Ed. Darlene M. Juschka. New York: Continuum. 629-647.

Butler, Becky, ed., 1990. *Ceremonies of the Heart: Celebrating Lesbian Unions*. Seattle: Seal.

Buturovic, Amila. 1997. "Spiritual Empowerment Through Spiritual Submission: *Sufi* Women and Their Quest for God." *Canadian Woman Studies/Les cahiers de la femme* 17 (1): 53-56.

Bynum, Caroline W., Stevan Harrell, and Paula Richman, eds. 1986. *Gender and Religion: On the Complexity of Symbols*. Boston: Beacon.

Campbell, Ena 1982. "The Virgin of Guadalupe and the Female Self-Image: A Mexican Case History." *Mother Worship: Themes and Variations*. Ed. James J. Preston. Chapel Hill: University of North Carolina Press. 5-24.

Campbell, Joseph. 1965 (1964). *The Masks of God: Occidental Mythology*. New York: Viking.

Campbell, Joseph. 1964 (1949). *The Hero with a Thousand Faces*. New York: World Meridian.

Cantor, Aviva. 1979. "A Jewish Woman's Haggadah." *Womanspirit Rising: A Feminist Reader in Religion*. Eds. Carol P. Christ and Judith Plaskow. New York: Harper and Row. 185-192.

Carley, Kathleen E. 2002. *Women and the Historical Jesus: Feminist Myths of Christian Origins*. Santa Rosa, CA: Polebridge.

Carmody, Denise L. 1995. *Christian Feminist Theology: A Constructive Interpretation*. Oxford: Blackwell.

Carmody, Denise L. 1989. *Women and World Religions: 2nd ed.* Englewood Cliffs, NJ: Prentice Hall.

Carmody, Denise and John Carmody. 1993. "Homosexuality and Roman Catholicism." *Homosexuality and World Religions*. Ed. Arlene Swidler. Valley Forge, PA: Trinity International. 135-148.

Caron, Charlotte. 1993. *To Make and Make Again: Feminist Ritual Thealogy*. New York: Crossroad.

Carson, Anne. 1992. *Goddesses and Wise Women: The Literature of Feminist Spirituality 1980-1992. An Annotated Bibliography*. Freedom, CA: Crossing.

Carson, Anne. 1986. *Feminist Spirituality and the Feminine Divine: An Annotated Bibliography*. Trumansburg, NY: Crossing.

Chadwick, Henry. 1993. "The Early Christian Community." *The Oxford History of Christianity*. Ed. John McManners. Oxford: Oxford University Press. 21-69.

Chadwick, Owen. 1993. "Great Britain and Europe." *The Oxford History of Christianity*. Ed. John McManners. Oxford: Oxford University Press. 349-395.

Chafets, Zev. 2009. "Obama's Rabbi." *New York Times Magazine* April 5: 34-39.

Chesler, Phyllis and Rivka Haut, eds. 2003. *Women of the Wall: Claiming Sacred Ground at Judaism's Holy Site*. Woodstock, VT: Jewish Lights.

Christ, Carol P. 2003. *She Who Changes: Re-Imagining the Divine in the World*. New York: Palgrave Macmillan.

Christ, Carol P. 1997. *Rebirth of the Goddess: Finding Meaning in Feminist Spirituality*. Reading, MA: Addison-Wesley.

Christ, Carol P. 1995. *Odyssey with the Goddess: A Spiritual Quest in Crete*. New York: Continuum.

Christ, Carol P. 1987. *Laughter of Aphrodite: Reflections on a Journey to the Goddess*. San Francisco: Harper and Row.

Christ, Carol P. 1983. "Symbols of Goddess and God in Feminist Theology." *The Book of the Goddess, Past and Present: An Introduction to Her Religion*. Ed. Carl Olson. New York: Crossroad. 231-251.

Christ, Carol P. 1979. "Spiritual Quest and Women's Experience." *Womanspirit Rising: A Feminist Reader in Religion*. Eds. Carol P. Christ and Judith Plaskow. New York: Harper and Row. 228-245.

Christ, Carol P. and Judith Plaskow, eds. 1979. *Womanspirit Rising: A Feminist Reader in Religion*. New York: Harper and Row.

Chuvin, Pierre 1990. *A Chronicle of the Last Pagans*. Cambridge, MA: Harvard University Press.

Clark, Elizabeth and Herbert Richardson. 1977a. "Augustine: Sinfulness and Sexuality Selections from 'On Marriage and Concupiscence'." *Women and Religion: A Feminist Sourcebook of Christian Thought*. Eds. Elizabeth Clark and Herbert Richardson. New York: Harper and Row. 69-77.

Clark, Elizabeth and Herbert Richardson. 1977b. "Jerome: The Exaltation of Christian Virginity Selections from Letter 22 ('To Eustochium') and from Against Jovinian." *Women and Religion: A Feminist Sourcebook of Christian Thought*. Eds. Elizabeth Clark and Herbert Richardson. New York: Harper and Row. 53-68.

Clark, Elizabeth and Herbert Richardson. 1977c. "Luther and the Protestant Reformation: From Nun to Parson's Wife." *Women and Religion: A Feminist Sourcebook of Christian Thought*. Eds. Elizabeth Clark and Herbert Richardson. New York: Harper and Row. 131-148.

Cleary, Thomas, ed. 1993. *The Essential Koran: The Heart of Islam*. San Francisco: HarperSanFrancisco.

Cleverdon, Catherine L. 1974. *The Woman Suffrage Movement in Canada*. Toronto: University of Toronto Press.

Cohen, Debra H. 1997. "Chasm between Orthodoxy and Feminism Closing." *Canadian Jewish News* February 27: 49.

Cohen, Judith. 1996. "A Bosnian Sephardic Woman in Kahnewake, Quebec." *Canadian Woman Studies/les cahiers de la femme* 16 (4):112-113.

Cohler-Esses, Dianne. 2003. "A Common Language between East and West." *Journal of Feminist Studies in Religion* 19 (1): 111-118.

Coleman, Kristy S. 2005. "Who's Afraid of 'the Goddess Stuff'?" *Feminist Theology* 13: 217-237.

Collins, Patricia Hill. 1990. *Black Feminist Thought: Knowledge, Consciousness, and the Politics of Empowerment*. London: HarperCollins.

Collins, Sheila. 1974. *A Different Heaven and Earth*. Valley Forge, PA: Judson.

Collinson Patrick. 1993. "The Late Medieval Church and its Reformation (1400-1600)." *The Oxford History of Christianity*. Ed. John McManners. Oxford: Oxford University Press. 243-276.

Coleman, Monica A. 2006. "Must I Be a Womanist?" *Journal of Feminist Studies in Religion* 22: 85-95

Connors, Jane. 1996. "The Women's Convention in the Muslim World." *Feminism and Islam: Legal and Literary Perspectives*. Ed. Mai Yamani. London: Ithaca. 351-371.

Conway, Sheila. 1987. *A Woman and Catholicism: My Break with the Roman Catholic Church*. Toronto: Paperjacks.

Cooey, Paula M., William R. Eakin, and Jay B. McDaniel, eds. 1997 (1991). *After Patriarchy: Feminist Transformations of the World Religions*. Maryknoll, NY: Orbis.

Cook, Ramsay. 1974. "An Introduction." *The Woman Suffrage Movement in Canada*. Catherine L. Cleverdon. Toronto: University of Toronto Press. vi-xxvi.

Cooke, Miriam. 2002. "Multiple Critique: Islamic Feminist Rhetorical Strategies." *Postcolonialism, Feminism and Religious Discourse*. Eds. Laura E. Donaldson and Kwok Pui-lan. New York: Routledge. 142-160.

Cooke, Miriam. 2001. *Women Claim Islam: Creating Islamic Feminism Through Literature*. New York: Routledge.

Crespin, Debra R. and Sarah Jacobus, eds. 1997-1998. "Sephardi and Mizrahi Women Write About Their Lives" Issue. *Bridges: A Journal for Jewish Feminists and Our Friends* 7 (1).

Curb, Rosemary and Nancy Monahan, eds. 1985. *Lesbian Nuns: Breaking Silence*. Tallahassee, FL: Naiad.

Daly, Mary. 1985 (1968). *The Church and the Second Sex: With the Feminist Postchristian Introduction and New Archaic Afterwords*. Boston: Beacon.

Daly, Mary. 1978. *Gyn/Ecology: The Metaethics of Radical Feminism*. Boston: Beacon.

Daly, Mary. 1974 (1973). *Beyond God the Father: Toward a Philosophy of Women's Liberation*. Boston: Beacon.

Dashu, Max. 2005. "Knocking Down Straw Dolls: A Critique of Cynthia Eller's The Myth of Matriarchal Prehistory." *Feminist Theology* 13: 185-216.

Davidman, Lynn. 1991. *Tradition in a Rootless World: Women Turn to Orthodox Judaism*. Berkeley: University of California Press.

Davis, Elizabeth G. 1972 (1971). *The First Sex*. Baltimore, MD: Penguin.

Davis, Minerva. 1992. *The Wretched of the Earth and Me*. Toronto: Lugus.

Dever, William G. 2005. *Did God Have a Wife? Archaeology and Folk*

Religion in Ancient Israel. Grand Rapids, MI: Eerdmans.

Dever, William G. 2003. *Who Were the Early Israelites and Where Did They Come From?* Grand Rapids, MI: Eerdmans.

Donaldson, Laura E. and Kwok Pui-lan, eds. 2002. *Postcolonialism, Feminism and Religious Discourse*. New York: Routledge.

Douglass, Jane Dempsey. 1974. "Women and the Continental Reformation." Religion and Sexism: Images of Women in the Jewish and Christian Traditions. Ed. Rosemary Radford Reuther. New York: Simon and Schuster. 292-318.

Driver, Tom F. 1998. *Liberating Rites: Understanding the Transformative Power of Ritual*. Boulder, CO: Westview.

Duncan, Carol B. 2008. *This Spot of Ground: Spiritual Baptists in Toronto*. Waterloo, ON: Wilfred Laurier University Press.

Duncan, Carol B. 1997a. "So Carnally, So Spiritually: Spiritual Baptist Women Speak of Mothering." *Vox Feminarum: The Canadian Journal of Feminist Spirituality* 1 (4): 54-56.

Duncan, Carol B. 1997b. "'This Spot of Ground': Migration, Community, and Identity among Spiritual Baptists in Toronto." *Canadian Woman Studies/Les cahiers de la femme* 17 (1): 32-35.

Dunne, Bruce W. 1990. "Homosexuality in the Middle East: An Agenda for Historical Research." *Arab Studies Quarterly* 12 (3): 55-82.

Duran, Khalid. 1993. "Homosexuality and Islam." *Homosexuality and World Religions*. Ed. Arlene Swidler. Valley Forge, PA: Trinity International. 181-198.

Dyke, Doris J. 1991. *Crucified Woman*. Toronto: United Church.

Eisler, Riane 1987. *The Chalice and the Blade: Our History, OurFuture*. San Francisco: Harper and Row.

Eller, Cynthia. 2000. *The Myth of Matriarchal Prehistory: Why an Invented Past Won't Give Women a Future*. Boston: Beacon.

Eller, Cynthia. 1993. *Living in the Lap of the Goddess: The Feminist Spirituality Movement in America*. New York: Crossroad.

Elliger, K. and W. Rudolph, eds. 1977. *Biblia Hebraica Stuttgartensia*. Stuttgart: Deutsche Bibelstiftung.

Ellison, Marvin M. 1993. "Homosexuality and Protestantism." *Homosexuality and World Religions*. Ed. Arlene Swidler. Valley Forge, PA: Trinity International. 135-148.

El-Nimr, Raga'. 1996. "Women in Islamic Law." *Feminism and Islam: Legal and Literary Perspectives*. Ed. Mai Yamani. London: Ithaca. 87-102.

El-Saadawi, Nawal, ed. 1980. *The Hidden Face of Eve: Women in the Arab World*. London: Zed.

Elwell, Sue Levi. 1996. "Women's Voices: The Challenge of Feminism to Judaism." *Religious Institutions and Women's Leadership: New Roles Inside the Mainstream*. Ed. Catherine Wessenger. Columbia, SC:

University of South Carolina Press. 331-344.

Eron, Lewis John. 1993. "Homosexuality and Judaism." *Homosexuality and World Religions*. Ed. Arlene Swidler. Valley Forge, PA: Trinity International. 103-134.

Eugene, Toinette M. 1992. "To Be of Use." *Journal of Feminist Studies in Religion* 8 (2): 138-147.

Fakhro, Munira. 1996. "Gulf Women and Islamic Law." F*eminism and Islam: Legal and Literary Perspectives*. Ed. Mai Yamani. London: Ithaca. 251-262.

Falk, Marcia. 2003. "My Father's Riddle, Or Conflict andReciprocity inthe Multicultural (Jewish) Self." *Journal of Feminist Studies in Religion* 19 (1): 97–103.

Falk, Marcia. 1996. *The Book of Blessings: New Jewish Prayers for Daily Life, the Sabbath, and the New Moon Festival*. San Francisco: HarperSanFrancisco.

Falk, Nancy A. and Rita M. Gross, eds. 1989. *Unspoken Worlds: Women's Religious Lives*. 2nd ed. Belmont, CA: Wadsworth.

Fargis, Paul and Sheree Bykofsky, eds. 1989. *The New York Public Library Desk Reference*. New York: Webster's New World.

Feldman, Ron H. 2003. "'On Your New Moons': The Feminist Transformation of the Jewish New Moon Festival." *Journal of Women and Religion* 19/20: 26-51.

"Female Spirituality" Issue. 1997. *Canadian Woman Studies/Les cahiers de la femme* 17 (1) (Winter).

Fernea, Elizabeth W., ed. 1985. *Women and the Family in the Middle East: New Voices of Change*. Austin: University of Texas Press.

Fernea, Elizabeth W. and Basima Q. Bezirgan, eds. 1977. *Middle Eastern Muslim Women Speak*. Austin: University of Texas Press.

Fine, Irene. 1988. *Midlife—A Rite of Passage: The Wise Woman—A Celebration*. San Diego, CA: Women's Institute for Continuing Jewish Education.

Finkelstein, Israel. 1988. *The Archaeology of the Israelite Settlement*. Jerusalem: Israel Exploration Society.

Finson, Shelley D. 1995. *A Historical Review of the Development of Feminist Liberation Theology*. Ottawa: Canadian Research Institute for the Advancement of Women (CRIAW/ICREF).

Finson, Shelley D. 1991. *Women and Religion: Bibliographic Guide to Christian Feminist Liberation Theology*. Toronto: University of Toronto Press.

Fiorenza, Elizabeth Schüssler. 2001. *Wisdom Ways: Introducing Feminist Biblical Interpretation*. Maryknoll, NY: Orbis.

Fiorenza, Elizabeth Schüssler. 1992 (1983). *In Memory of Her: A Feminist Theological Reconstruction of Christian Origins*. New York: Crossroad.

Fiorenza, Elisabeth. 1979. "Feminist Spirituality, Christian Identity, and Catholic Vision." *Womanspirit Rising: A Feminist Reader in Religion*. Eds. Carol P. Christ and Judith Plaskow. New York: Harper and Row. 136-148.

Firestone, Shulamith. 1970. *The Dialectic of Sex*. New York: Morrow.

Fletcher-Marsh, Wendy. 1995. *Beyond the Walled Garden: Anglican Women and the Priesthood*. Dundas, ON: Artemis.

Foley, Helene P., ed. 1994. *The Homeric Hymn to Demeter: Translation, Commentary, and Interpretive Essays*. Princeton, NJ: Princeton University Press.

Frankiel, Tamar. 1990. *The Voice of Sarah: Feminine Spirituality and Traditional Judaism*. San Francisco: HarperSanFrancisco

Freedman, Debbie. 2000. *Timbrels and Torahs: Celebrating Women's Wisdom*. Berkeley, CA: Jot of Wisdom. Video.

Freeman, James M. 1989. "The Ladies of Lord Krishna: Rituals of Middle-Aged Women in Eastern India." *Unspoken Worlds: Women's Religious Lives*. 2nd ed. Eds. Nancy A. Falk and Rita M. Gross. Belmont, CA: Wadsworth. 82-92.

Friedan, Betty. 1963. *The Feminine Mystique*. Harmondsworth, Mdsx., UK: Penguin.

Friedl, Erika. 1989. "Islam and Tribal Women in a Village in Iran." *Unspoken Worlds: Women's Religious Lives*. 2nd ed. Eds. Nancy A. Falk and Rita M. Gross. Belmont, CA: Wadsworth. 125-133.

Friedman, Richard E. 1987. *Who Wrote the Bible?* New York: Harper and Row Perennial.

Frymer-Kensky, Tikva. 1992. "Deuteronomy." *The Women's Bible Commentary*. Eds. Carol Newsom and Sharon H. Ringe. Louisville, Ky: Westminster John Knox. 52-62.

Frymer-Kensky, Tikva. 1994. "The Bible and Women's Studies." *Feminist Perspectives on Jewish Studies*. Eds. Lynn Davidman and Shelly Tenenbaum. New Haven: Yale University Press. 16-39.

Frymer-Kensky, Tikva. 1992. *In the Wake of the Goddesses: Women, Culture, and the Biblical Transformation of Pagan Myth*. New York: Free.

Gaard, Greta, ed. 1993. *Ecofeminism: Women, Animals, Nature*. Philadelphia: Temple University Press.

Gadon, Elinor W. 1989. *The Once and Future Goddess: A Symbol for Our Time*. San Francisco: Harper and Row.

Garay, Kathleen. 1997. "'She Swims and Floats in Joy': Marguerite Porete, an 'Heretical' Mystic of the Later Ages." *Canadian Woman Studies/les cahiers de la femme* 17 (1) (Winter): 18-21.

Gardner, Gerald B. 1959. *The Meaning of Witchcraft*. London: Aquarian.

Gauch, Suzanne. 2007. *Liberating Shahrazad: Feminism, Postcolonialism,*

and Islam. Minneapolis: University of Minnesota Press.
Giese, Rachel. 2003. "Out of the Koran: A Conference for Queer Muslims Is a Step toward Liberation." *Xtra* June 12: 15.
Gimbutas, Marija. 1991. *The Civilization of the Goddess: The World of Old Europe*. San Francisco: HarperSanFrancisco.
Gimbutas, Marija. 1989. *The Language of the Goddess: Unearthing the Hidden Symbols of Western Civilization*. San Francisco: HarperSanFrancisco.
Gimbutas, Marija. 1974. *The Goddesses and Gods of Old Europe, 6500 to 3500* BC. Berkeley: University of California Press.
Gleason, Judith. 1987. *Oya: In Praise of the Goddess*. Boston: Shambhala.
Glory, Morning and Otter G'Zell. 1996. "Who on Earth Is the Goddess?" *Magical Religion and Modern Witchcraft*. Ed. James R. Lewis. Albany, NY: State University of New York. 25-34.
Glückel. 1977 (1932). *The Memoir of Glückel of Hameln*. New York: Schocken.
"God Decentralized: A Special Issue." 1997. *The New York Times Magazine* 7 December.
Goldberg, Aviva R. 1997. "Jewish Women's Spirituality: A Critical Analysis." Unpublished Master's Research Paper. Graduate Programme in Women's Studies, York University, Toronto.
Goldberg, Aviva R. 2002. *Re-awakening Deborah: Locating the Feminist in the Liturgy, Ritual, and theology of contemporary Jewish Renewal*. Unpublished Ph.D. dissertation, York University, Toronto.
Goldenberg, Naomi R. 2007. "What's God Got to Do with It? A Call for Problematizing Basic Terms in the Feminist Analysis of Religion," *Feminist Theology* 15: 275-288.
Goldenberg, Naomi R. 1979. *Changing of the Gods: Feminism and the End of Traditional Religions*. Boston: Beacon.
Goldman, Karla. 2007. "Women in Reform Judaism: Between Rhetoric and Reality." *Women Remaking American Judaism*. Ed. Riv-Ellen Prell. Detroit, MI: Wayne State University. 109-134.
Goldstein, Elyse, ed. 2009. *New Jewish Feminism: Probing the Past, Forging the Future*. Woodstock, VT: Jewish Lights.
Goldstein, Elyse. 2000. *The Women's Torah Commentary: New Insights from Women Rabbis on the 54 Weekly Torah Portions*. Woodstock, VT: Jewish Lights.
Goldstein, Elyse. 1990. "Who Has Made Me a Woman." *Lilith* (Spring): 32.
Gottlieb, Lynn. 1995. *She Who Dwells Within: A Feminist Vision of a Renewed Judaism*. San Francisco: HarperSanFrancisco.
Gottschall, Marilyn. 2000. "The Mutable Goddess: Particularity and Eclecticism within the Goddess Public." *Daughters of the Goddess:*

Studies of Healing, Identity and Empowerment. Ed. Wendy Griffin. Walnut Creek, CA: AltaMira. 59-72.

Grant, Jacquelyn. 1993. "'Come to My Help, Lord, For I'm in Trouble': Womanist Jesus and the Mutual Struggle." *Reconstructing the Christ Symbol: Essays in Feminist Christology*. Ed. Maryanne Stevens. Mahwah, NJ: Paulist. 54-71.

Grant, Jacquelyn. 1989a. *White Women's Christ and Black Women's Jesus: Feminist Christology and Womanist Response*. Atlanta, GA: Scholars.

Grant, Jacquelyn. 1989b. "Womanist Theology: Black Women's Experience as a Source for Doing Theology; with Special Reference to Christology." *African American Religious Studies: An Interdisciplinary Anthology*. Ed. Wilmore Gayraud. Durham, NC: Duke University Press. 208-227.

Grant, Jacquelyn. 1982. "Black Women and the Church." *All the Women Are White, All the Blacks Are Men, But Some of Us Are Brave: Black Women's Studies*. Eds. Gloria T. Hull, Patricia Bell Scott and Barbara Smith. New York: Feminist Press. 141-152.

Graves, Robert. 1961. *The White Goddess: A Historical Grammar of Poetic Myth*. London: Faber and Faber.

Greenberg, Blu. 1981. *On Women and Judaism: A View from Tradition*. Philadelphia: Jewish Publication Society of America.

Green-McCreight, Kathryn. 2000. *Feminist Reconstructions of Christian Doctrines: Narrative Analysis and Appraisal*.New York: Oxford University Press.

Griffin, Wendy. 2004. "The Goddess Net." *Religion Online: Finding Faith on the Internet*. Eds. Lorna L. and Douglas E. Cowan. New York: Routledge. 189-203.

Griffin, Wendy. 2003. "Goddess Spirituality and Wicca." *Her Voice, Her Faith: Women Speak on World Religions*. Eds. Arvind Sharma and Katerine Young. Boulder, CO: Westview. 243-281.

Griffin, Wendy, ed. 2000. *Daughters of the Goddess: Studies of Healing, Identity and Empowerment*. Walnut Creek, CA: AltaMira.

Gross, Rita M. 2000. "Roundtable: Feminist Theology and Religious Diversity." *Journal of Feminist Studies in Religion* 16: 73-131.

Gross, Rita M. 1983. "Steps Toward Feminine Imagery of Deity in Jewith Theology." *On Being a Jewish Feminist*. [1983]. Ed. Susannah Heschel. New York: Schocken. 234-247.

Gross, Rita M. 1996. *Feminism and Religion: An Introduction*. Boston: Beacon.

Gross, Rita M. 1989. "Menstruation and Childbirth as Ritual and Religious Experience among Native Australians." *Unspoken Worlds: Women's Religious Lives*. 2nd ed. Eds. Nancy A. Falk and Rita M. Gross. Belmont, CA: Wadsworth. 257-266.

Gross, Rita M. 1979. "Female God Language in a Jewish Context." *Womanspirit Rising: A Feminist Reader in Religion*. Eds. Carol P. Christ and Judith Plaskow. New York: Harper and Row. 167-173.

Haar, Sandra. 1996. "Seeds of Doubt: Constructing a Sephardi Identity." *Canadian Woman Studies/Les cahiers de la femme* 16 (4): 63-68.

Haddad, Yvonne Y. and John L. Esposito, eds. 2001. *Daughters of Abraham: Feminist Thought in Judaism, Christianity, and Islam*. Gainesville: University of Florida.

Haddad, Yvonne Y., Jane I. Smith, and Kathleen M. Moore, eds. 2006. *Muslim Women in America: The Challenge of Islamic Identity Today*. New York: Oxford University Press.

Haker, Hille, Susan Ross, and Marie-Therese Wacker, eds. 2006. *Women's Voices in World Relgions*. London: SCM Press.

Halpern, Baruch. 1983. *The Emergence of Israel in Canaan*. Chico, CA: Scholars.

Hamadeh, Najla. 1996. "Islamic Family Legislation: The Authoritarian Discourse of Silence." *Feminism and Islam: Legal and Literary Perspectives*. Ed. Mai Yamani. London: Ithaca. 331-349.

Hamson, Daphne. 1996. *After Christianity*. Valley Forge, PA: Trinity International.

Hamson, Daphne 1990. *Theology and Feminism*. Oxford: Blackwell.

Harris, Lis. 1985. *Holy Days: The World of a Hasidic Family*. New York: Summit.

Harrison, Victoria S. 2007. "Representing the Divine: Feminism and Religious Anthropology." *Feminist Theology* 16 (1): 128-146.

Hartman, Tova. 2007. *Feminism Encounters Traditional Judaism: Resistance and Accomodation*. Waltham, MA: Brandeis University Press.

Haskins, Susan. 1993. *Mary Magdalene: Myth and Metaphor*. New York: Harcourt Brace.

Hassan, Riffat. 2003. "Islam." *Her Voice, Her Faith: Women Speak on World Religions*. Eds. Arvind Sharma and Katherine Young. Boulder, CO: Westview. 215-242.

Hassan, Riffat. 1997. "Muslim Women and Post-Patriarchal Islam." *After Patriarchy: Feminist Transformations of the World Religions*. Eds. Paula M. Cooey, William R. Eakin and Jay B. McDaniel. Maryknoll, NY: Orbis. 39-64.

Hauptman, 1974. "Images of Women in the Talmud." *Religion and Sexism: Images of Women in the Jewish and Christian Traditions*. Ed. Rosemary Reuther. New York: Simon and Schuster. 184-212.

Hawley, John S. 1994. *Fundamentalism and Gender*. New York: Oxford University Press.

Hayes, John H. and J. M. Miller, eds. 1977. *Israelite and Judaean History*. Philadelphia: Westminster.

Helms, Barbara Lois. 1992. "Rabi'ah as Mystic, Muslim, and Woman."

The Annual Review of Women in World Religions. Volume III. Eds. Arvin Sharma and Katherine K. Young. Albany, NY: State University of New York. 1-87.

Henry, Sondra and Emily Taitz. 1990. *Written out of History: Jewish Foremothers.* New York: Biblio.

Hermansen, Marcia K. 1992. "The Female Hero in the Islamic Religious Tradition." *The Annual Review of Women in World Religions. Volume II: Heroic Women, eds.* Arvin Sharma and Katherine K. Young. Albany, NY: State University of New York. 111-143.

Herrera, Marina. 1993. "Who Do You Say Jesus Is? Christological Reflections from a Hispanic Woman's Perspective." *Reconstructing the Christ Symbol: Essays in Feminist Christology*. Ed. Maryanne Stevens. Mahwah, NJ: Paulist. 72-94.

Heschel, Susannah. 2004. "Gender and Agency in the Feminist Historiography of Jewish Identity." *Journal of Religion* 84 (4): 580-591.

Heschel, Susannah. 2003. "Judaism." *Her Voice, Her Faith: Women Speak on World Religions.* Eds. Arvind Sharma and Katerine Young. Boulder, CO: Westview. 145-168.

Heschel, Susannah, ed. 1983. *On Being a Jewish Feminist.* New York: Schocken.

Heywood, Isabel Carter. 1989a. *Speaking of Christ: A Lesbian Feminist Voice.* Ed. Ellen C. Davis. New York: Pilgrim.

Heywood, Isabel Carter. 1989b. *Touching Our Strength: The Erotic as Power and the Love of God.* San Francisco: Harper and Row.

Heywood, Isabel Carter. 1984. *Our Passion for Justice: Images of Power, Sexuality and Liberation.* New York: Pilgrim.

Holladay, John, Jr. 1987. "Religion in Israel and Judah under the Monarchy: An Explicitly Archaeological Approach." *Ancient Israelite Religion.* Eds. P. D. Miller, P. D. Hanson, and S. D. McBride. Philadelphia: Fortress. 249-299.

The Holy Bible Containing the Old and New Testaments: Revised Standard Version. 1952. Camden, NJ: Nelson.

hooks, bell. 1984. *Feminist Theory: From Margin to Center.* Boston: South End.

hooks, bell. 1981. *Ain't I a Woman? Black Women and Feminism.* Boston: South End.

Hurwitz, Sara. 2009. "Orthodox Women in Rabbinic Roles." *New Jewish Feminism: Probing the Past, Forging the Future.* Ed. Elyse Goldstein. Woodstock, VT: Jewish Lights. 144-154.

Hourani, Albert. 1991. *A History of the Arab Peoples.* Cambridge, MA: Harvard University Belknap.

Human Edge. 1990. "Hidden Faces." Television Ontario (TVO) film.

Hurtado, Larry, ed. 1990. *Goddesses in Religions and Modern Debate.* Atlanta, GA: Scholars.

Imam, Ayesha. 1997. "The Muslim Religious Right ('Fundamentalists') and Sexuality." *Women Living Under Muslim Laws*. Dossier 17: 725 (Boit postale 23, 3479, Gravelle, France).

Isasi-Díaz, Ada María 1996. *Mujerista Theology: A Theology for the Twenty-First Century*. Maryknoll, NY: Orbis.

Isasi-Díaz, Ada María. 1996a."The Task of Hispanic Women's Liberation Theology—*Mujeristas:* Who We Are and What We Are About.." *Feminist Theology from the Third World: A Reader*. Ed. Ursula King. Maryknoll, NY: Orbis. 88-102.

Isasi-Díaz, Ada María. 1993. "Defining Our *Proyecto Historico*: *Mujerista* Strategies for Liberation." *Journal of Feminist Studies in Religion* 9 (1-2): 17-27.

Isherwood, Lisa, ed. 2005. Special Issue of *Feminist Theology* (on Feminist Goddess Worship) 13.

Isherwood, Lisa and Dorothea McEwan, eds. 2001. *Introducing Feminist Theology: 2nd ed.* Sheffield, UK: Sheffield Academic.

Jacobson, Doranne. 1989. "Golden Handprints and Red-Painted Feet: Hindu Childbirth Rituals in Central India." *Unspoken Worlds: Women's Religious Lives*. 2nd ed. Eds. Nancy A. Falk and Rita M. Gross. Belmont, CA: Wadsworth. 59-71.

Jamali, Umarah. 2007. "Muslim Groups Press India to Expel Author." *The Globe and Mail* August 28: A13.

Jamzadeh, Laai and Margaret Mills. 1986. "Iranian Sofreh: From Collective to Female Ritual." *Gender and Religion:On the Complexity of Symbols*. Eds. Caroline W. Bynum, Stevan Harrell, and Paula Richman. Boston: Beacon. 23-65.

Janowitz, Naomi and Maggie Wenig. 1979. "Sabbath Prayers for Women." *Womanspirit Rising: A Feminist Reader in Religion*. Eds. Carol P. Christ and Judith Plaskow. New York: Harper and Row. 1979. 174-178.

Jewish Publication Society. 1985. *Tanakh, The Holy Scriptures: The New JPS Translation According to the Traditional Hebrew Text*. Philadelphia: Jewish Publication Society.

"Jewish Women" Issue. 1992. *Fireweed* 35 (Spring).

"Jewish Women in Canada" Issue. 1996. *Canadian Woman Studies/Les cahiers de la femme* 16 (4) (Fall).

Johnson, Elizabeth A. 1997 (1993). *She Who Is: The Mystery of God in Feminist Theological Discourse*. New York: Crossroad

Johnson, Marilyn. 1997. "The Presence of Mother Earth in Women's Ceremonies: Observations of an Ojibway Medicine Woman/Wiccan Practitioner." *Canadian Woman Studies/Les cahiers de la femme* 17 (1): 121-122

Jones, Alan. 1996. "Introduction." *The Koran*. Trans. J. M. Rodwell. London: Dent Everyman. xi-xxvii.

Joseph, Suad. 1998. "Comment on Majid's 'The Politics of Feminism in Islam': Critique of Politics and the Politics of Critique." *Signs* 23 (2): 363-369.

Joseph, Norma Baumel. 2007. "Women in Orthodoxy: Conventional and Contentious." *Women Remaking American Judaism*. Ed. Riv-Ellen Prell. Detroit, MI: Wayne State University. 181-210.

Jung, Carl Gustav. 1959. *The Basic Writings of C.G. Jung*. New York: Modern Library.

Juschka, Darlene M., ed. 2001. *Feminism in the Study of Religion: A Reader.* New York: Continuum.

Kamenetz, Rodger. 1997. "Unorthodox Jews Rummage Through the-Orthodox Tradition." *The New York Times Magazine*, Special Issue, "God Decentralized." December 7: 84-87.

Kaplan, Dara E. 2003. *American Reform Judaism: An Introduction.*New Brunswick, NJ: Rutgers University Press.

Karkala-Zorba, Katerina. 2006. "Women and the Church: A Greek Orthodox Perspective." *Women's Voices in World Relgions*. Eds. Hille Haker, Susan Ross and Marie-Therese Wacker. London: SCM Press. 36-45.

Karmi, Ghada. 1996. "Women, Islam and Patriarchalism." *Feminism and Islam: Legal and Literary Perspectives*. Ed. Mai Yamani. London: Ithaca. 181-210.

Kaufman, Debra R. 1991. *Rachel's Daughters: Newly Orthodox Jewish Women*. New Brunswick, NJ: Rutgers University Press.

Katoppo, Marianne. 1996. "The Concept of God and the Spirit from the Feminist Perspective." *Feminist Theology from the Third World: A Reader*. Ed. Ursula King. Maryknoll, NY: Orbis. 244-250.

Katoppo, Marianne. 1980 (1979). *Compassionate and Free: An Asian Woman's Theology*. Maryknoll, NY: Orbis

Keddie, Nikki R. 2007. *Women in the Middle East: Past and Present.* Princeton, NJ: Princeton University Press.

Kee, H. C. 1970. *Jesus in History: An Approach to the Gospels*. New York: Harcourt, Brace and World.

Keller, Rosemary S. and Rosemary R. Reuther, eds. 2006. *Encyclopedia of Women and Religion in North America*. Bloomington: Indiana University Press.

Khan, Shahnaz. 2002. "Muslim Women: Negotiations in the Third Space." *Gender, Politics, and Islam*. Eds. Therese Saliba, Carolyn Allen, and Judith A. Howard. Chicago: The University of Chicago Press. 305-336.

Khanum, Saeeda. 1992. "Education and the Muslim Girl." *Refusing HolyOrders:Women and Fundamentalism in Britain*. Eds. Gita Sahgal and Nira Yuval-Davis. London:Virago. 124-140.

Kien, Jenny. 2000. *Reinstating the Divine Woman in Judaism*. Florida: Universal.

Kim, Nami. 2005. "'My/Our' Comfort *Not* at the Expense of 'Somebody Else's': Toward a Critical global Feminist Theology." *Journal of Feminist Studies in Religion* 21: 75-94.

King, Ursula, ed. 2000. *Religion and Gender*. Oxford: Blackwell.

King, Ursula, ed. 1996 [1994]. *Feminist Theology from the Third World: A Reader*. Maryknoll, NY: Orbis.

King, Ursula. 1989. *Women and Spirituality: Voices of Protest and Promise*. New York: New Amsterdam.

Kinsley, David. 1989. *The Goddesses' Mirror: Visions of the Divine from East and West*. Albany, NY: State University of New York.

Kittredge, Cherry and Zalmon Sherwood, eds. 1995. *Equal Rites: Lesbian and Gay Worship, Ceremonies, and Celebrations*. Louisville, KY: Westminster John Knox.

Klapheck, Elisa. 2006. "'House of Renewal': A New Form of Judaism." *Women's Voices in World Relgions*. Eds. Hille Haker, Susan Ross and Marie-Therese Wacker. London: SCM Press. 20-26.

Kletter, Raz . 1996. *The Judean Pillar-Figurines and the Archaeology of Asherah*. British Archaeological Reports International Series 636. London: Tempus Reparatum.

Klirs, Tracy G., ed. 1992. *The Merit of Our Mothers: A BilingualAnthology of Jewish Women's Prayers*. Cincinnati, OH: Hebrew Union College.

Kraemer, Ross S. 1993. *Her Share of the Blessings: Women's Religions among Pagans, Jews, and Christians in the Greco-Roman World*. New York: Oxford University Press.

Kraemer, Ross S. and Mary R. D'Angelo 1999. *Women and Christian Origins*. New York: Oxford University Press.

Kramer, Heinrich and James Sprenger. 1971. *The Malleus Maleficarum*. Trans. M. Summers. New York: Dover.

Kwok, Pui-lan. 1996. "The Future of Feminist Theology: An Asian Perspective." *Feminist Theology from the Third World: A Reader*. Ed. Ursula King. Maryknoll, NY: Orbis. 63-75.

Kwok, Pui-lan. 2000. *Introducing Asian Feminist Theology*. Cleveland, OH: Pilgrim.

Kwok, Pui-lan 1992. "Speaking from the Margins." *Journal of Feminist Studies in Religion* 8 (2): 102-105.

Laffey, Alice L. 1988. *An Introduction to the Old Testament: AFeminist Perspective*. Philadelphia: Fortress

Lateef, Shahida. 1990. *Muslim Women in India: Political and Private Realities*. London: Zed.

Lebans, Gertrude. 1994. *Gathered by the River: Reflections and Essays of Women Doing Ministry*. Toronto: United Church.

Legge, Marilyn J. 1992. *The Grace of Difference: A CanadianFeminist Theological Ethic*. Atlanta, GA: Scholars.

"Lesbians and Religion" Issue. 1994-1995. *Sinister Wisdom: Journal of Words and Pictures for the Lesbian Imagination of All Women.*

Levine, Amy-Jill. 2003. "Multiculturalism, Women's Studies, and Anti-Judaism." *Journal of Feminist Studies in Religion* 19 (1): 119–128.

Levine, Amy-Jill. 2001. "Settling at Beer-lahai-roi." *Daughters of Abraham: Feminist Thought in Judaism, Christianity, and Islam.* Eds. Yvonne Y. Haddad and John L. Esposito. Gainesville, FL: University of Florida. 12-34.

Lewis, James R., ed. 1996. *Magical Religion and ModernWitchcraft.* Albany, NY: State University of New York.

Lindner, Eileen W., ed. 2007. *Yearbook of American and Canadian-Churches.* Nashville, TN: Abingdon.

Lit(wo)man, Jane. 1988. "On Being a Jewish Witch." *Genesis 2* 19 (1): 2, 42.

Longman, Chia. 2007. "`Not Us, but You Have Changed!'Discourses of Difference and Belonging among *Haredi* Women." *Social Compass* 54: 77-95.

Lorde, Audre. 1989. "Uses of the Erotic: The Erotic as Power." *Weaving the Visions: New Patterns in Feminist Spirituality.* Eds. Judith Plaskow and Carol P. Christ. San Francisco: Harper and Row. 208-213.

Low, Alaine and Soraya Tremayne, eds. 2001. *Sacred Custodians of the Earth? Women, Spirituality, and the Environment.* New York: Berghahn.

Mack, B. L. 1995. *Who Wrote the New Testament?* San Francisco: HarperSanFrancisco.

Magee, Penelope M. 2000 [1995]. "Disputing the Sacred: Some Theoretical Approaches to Gender and Religion." *Religion and Gender.* Ed. Ursula King. Oxford: Blackwell. 101-120.

Majid, Anouar 1998. "The Politics of Feminism in Islam," *Signs* 23 (2): 321-361.

Makdisi, Jean Said. 1996. "The Mythology of Modernity: Women and Democracy in Lebanon." F*eminism and Islam: Legal and Literary Perspectives.* Ed. Mai Yamani. London: Ithaca. 231-250.

Mandell, Nancy, ed. 1997. *Feminist Issues: Race, Class, and Sexuality.* 2nd ed. Scarborough, Ontario: Prentice Hall Canada.

Manji, Irshad 2003. *The Trouble with Islam: a Wake-Up Call for Honesty and Change.* New York: Random House.

Manning, Christel J. 1999. *God Gave Us the Right: Conservative Catholic, Evangelical Protestant, and Orthodox Jewish Women Grapple with Feminism.* New Brunswick, NJ: Rutgers University Press.

Marcus, Julie. 1992. *A World of Difference: Islam and Gender Hierarchy in Turkey.* London: Zed.

Marder, Janet R. 1996. "Are Women Changing in Rabbinate? A Reform Perspective." *Religious Institutions and Women's Leadership: New Roles Inside the Mainstream.* Ed. Catherine Wessenger. Columbia, SC:

University of South Carolina Press. 271-290.
Mariechild, Diane. 1988 (1981). *Mother Wit: A Guide to Healing and Psychic Development*. Freedom, CA: Crossing.
Marron, Kevin. 1989. *Witches, Pagans, and Magic in the New Age*. Toronto: Seal.
Marshall, Gül A. 2005. "Ideology, Progress, and Dialogue: A Comparison of Feminist and Islamist Women's Approaches to the Issue of Head covering and Work in Turkey." *Gender and Society* 19: 104-120.
Marsot, Afaf el-Sayyid. 1996. "Entrpreneurial Women in Egypt." *Feminism and Islam: Legal and Literary Perspectives*. Ed. Mai Yamani. London: Ithaca. 33-47.
Marty, M. E. and R. S. Appleby, eds. 1991. *Fundamentalism Observed*. Chicago: University of Chicago Press.
Masenya, Madipoane J. 1995. "African Womanist Hermeneutics: A Suppressed Voice from South Africa Speaks." *Journal of Feminist Studies in Religion* 11 (1): 149-155.
Maslow, Abraham H. 1968. *Toward a Psychology of Being: 2nd ed.* New York: Van Nostrand Reinhold.
Matt, Daniel C. 1995. *The Essential Kabbalah: The Heart of Jewish Mysticism*. San Francisco: HarperSanFrancisco.
Matter, E. Ann. 1983. "The Virgin Mary: A Goddess?" *The Book of the Goddess, Past and Present: An Introduction to Her Religion*. Ed. Carl Olson. New York: Crossroad. 80-96.
Matthews, Caitlin. 1991. *The Elements of the Goddess*. Shaftesbury, Dorset: Element.
Matthews, Caitlin. 1989. *The Elements of Celtic Tradition*. Shaftesbury, Dorset: Element.
Matza, Diane, ed. 1997. *Sephardic-American Voices: Two Hundred Years of a Literary Legacy*. Waltham, MA: Brandeis University.
Maumoon, Dunya. 1999. "Islamism and Gender Activism: Muslim Women's Quest for Autonomy," *Journal of Muslim Minority Affairs* 19: 269-283.
Mayer, Ann Elizabeth. 1998. "Comment on Majid's 'The Politics of Feminism in Islam'." *Signs* 23 (2): 369-377.
Mayr-Harting, Henry. 1993. "The West: The Age of Conversion (700-1050)." *The Oxford History of Christianity*. Ed. John McManners. Oxford: Oxford University Press. 101-129.
McClung, Nellie L. 1980. *In Times Like These*. Toronto: University of Toronto Press.
McGinty, Anna M. 2007. "Formation of Alternative Femininities through Islam: Feminist Approaches among Muslim Converts in Sweden." *Women's Studies International Forum* 30: 474-485
McManners, John, ed. 1993. *The Oxford History of Christianity*. Oxford: Oxford University Press.

McRay, John. 1991. *Archaeology and the New Testament*. Grand Rapids, MI: Baker.

Medjuck, S. 1993. "If I Cannot Dance to It, It's Not my Revolution: Jewish Women and Feminism in Canada." *The Jews in Canada*. Eds. Robert J. Brym, William Shaffir, and Morton Weinfeld. Toronto: Oxford University Press. 328-343.

Mernissi, Fatima. 1993 [1990]. *The Forgotten Queens of Islam*. Minneapolis, MN: University of Minnesota Press.

Mernissi, Fatima. 1991. *Women and Islam: An Historical and Theological Inquiry*. Oxford: Blackwell.

Mernissi, Fatima. 1989. "Women, Saints, and Sanctuaries in Morocco." *Unspoken Worlds: Women's Religious Lives*. 2nd ed. Eds. Nancy A. Falk and Rita M. Gross. Belmont, CA: Wadsworth. 112-121.

Mernissi, Fatima. 1987 [1975]. *Beyond the Veil: Male-Female Dynamics in Modern Muslim Society*. Bloomington: Indiana University Press.

Meyer, Marvin W., ed. 1987. *The Ancient Mysteries, a Sourcebook: Sacred Texts of the Mystery Religions of the Ancient Mediterranean World*. San Francisco: Harper and Row.

Meyers, Carol 1988. *Discovering Eve: Ancient Israelite Women in Context*. New York: Oxford University.

Meyers, Carol L. 1992. "Everyday Life: Women in the Period of the Hebrew Bible." *The Women's Bible Commentary*. Eds. Carol Newsom and Sharon H. Ringe. Louisville, KY: Westminster John Knox. 244-251.

Millen, Rochelle L. 2007. "Her Mouth Is Full of Wisdom": Reflections on Jewish Feminist Theology" *Women Remaking American Judaism*. Ed. Riv-Ellen Prell. Detroit, MI: Wayne State University. 27-50.

Millett, Kate. *Sexual Politics*. New York: Avon.

Minces, Juliette. 1982. *The House of Obedience: Women in Arab Society*. London: Zed.

Mir-Hosseini, Ziba. 1996. "Stretching the Limits: A Feminist Reading of the Shari'a in Post-Khomeini Iran." *Feminism and Islam: Legal and Literary Perspectives*. Ed. Mai Yamani. London: Ithaca. 285-319.

Moghadam, Valentine M. 2002. "Islamic Feminism and Its Discontents: Toward a Resolution of the Debate." *Signs* 27: 1135-1171.

Moghissi, Haideh. 1999. *Feminism and Islamic Fundamentalism: The Limits of Postmodern Analysis*. London: Zed.

Moghissi, Haideh, ed. 2006. *Muslim Diaspora: Gender, Culture, and Identity.* New York: Routledge.

Mohagheghi, Hamideh. 2006. "Emerging Women's Moveents in Muslim Communities in Germany." *Women's Voices in World Relgions*. Eds. Hille Haker, Susan Ross and Marie-Therese Wacker. London: SCM Press. 63-71.

Moody, Linda A. 1996. *Women Encounter God: Theology across the Boundaries of Difference*. Maryknoll, NY: Orbis.

Moore, Deborah Dash and Andres Bush. 2007. "Mitzvah, Gender, and Reconstructionist Judaism." *Women Remaking American Judaism*. Ed. Riv-Ellen Prell. Detroit, MI: Wayne State University. 135-152.

Moore, Tracy, ed. 1995. *Lesbiot: Israeli Lesbians Talk About Sexuality, Feminism, Judaism and their Lives*. London: Cassell.

Moraga, Cherrie and Gloria Anzaldua, eds. 1983. *This Bridge Called My Back: Writings By Radical Women of Color*. New York: Kitchen Table.

Morris, Colin. 1993. "Christian Civilization (1050-1400)." *The Oxford History of Christianity*. Ed. John McManners. Oxford: Oxford University Press. 205-242.

Motz, Lotte 1997. *The Faces of the Goddess*. New York: Oxford University Press.

Muir, Elizabeth G. 1991. *Petticoats in the Pulpit: The Story of Early Nineteenth-Century Methodist Women Preachers in Upper Canada*. Toronto: United Church.

Muir, Elizabeth G. and Marilyn F. Whiteley, eds. 1995. *Changing Roles of Women within the Christian Church in Canada*. Toronto: University of Toronto Press.

Mumtaz, Khawar and Farida Shaheed. 1987. *Women of Pakistan: Two Steps Forward. One Step Back?* London: Zed.

Musallam, B. F. 1989. *Sex and Society in Islam: Birth Control Before the 19th Century*. Cambridge: Cambridge University.

Myers, Jody and Jane RachelLitman. 1995. "The Secret of Jewish Femininity: Hiddenness, Rower, and Physicality in the Theology of Orthodox Women in the Contemporary World." *Gender and Judaism: The Transformation of Tradition*. Ed. T. M. Rudavsky. New York: New York University. 51-77.

Nadell, Pamela S. 1998. *Women Who Would Be Rabbis: A History of Women's Ordination*. Boston: Beacon.

Nadell, Pamela S. and Jonathan D. Sarna, eds. 2001. *Women and American Judaism: Historical Perspectives*. Hanover, NH: Brandeis University Press.

Naipaul, V. S. 1998. *Beyond Belief: Islamic Excursions Among theConverted Peoples*. New York: Random House.

Neudel, Marian Henriquez. 1989. "Innovation and Tradition in a Contemporary Midwestern Jewish Congregation." *Unspoken Worlds: Women's Religious Lives*. 2nd ed. Eds. Nancy A. Falk and Rita M. Gross. Belmont, CA: Wadsworth. 179-188.

Neumann, Erich. 1971 (1954). *The Origins and History of Consciousness*. Princeton, NJ: Princeton University Bollingen.

Neumann, Erich. 1970 (1955). *The Great Mother: An Analysis of the Archetype*. Princeton, NJ: Princeton University Bollingen.

Newsom, Carol and Sharon H. Ringe, eds. 1992. *The Women's Bible*

Commentary. Louisville, Ky: Westminster John Knox.

Northup, Leslie. 1997. *Ritualizing Women: Pattern of Spirituality.* Cleveland, OH: Pilgrim.

Northup, Leslie, ed. 1993. *Women and Religious Ritual.* Washington, DC: Pastoral.

Oduyoye, Mercy A. 2004 (2002). *Beads and Strands: Reflections of an African Woman on Christianity in Africa.* Maryknoll, NY: Orbis.

Oduyoye, Mercy A. 2001. *Introducing African Women's Theology.* Cleveland, OH: Pilgrim.

Olazagasti-Segovia, Elena. 1992. Paper in "Roundtable Discussion: *Mujeristas*: Who We Are and What We Are About." *Journal of Feminist Studies in Religion* 8 (1): 109-112.

Olson, Carl, ed. 1983. *The Book of the Goddess, Past and Present: An Introduction to Her Religion.* New York: Crossroad.

Olyan, Saul M. 1988. *Asherah and the Cult of Yahweh in Israel.* Atlanta, GA: Scholars.

Orenstein, Debra, ed. 1994. *Lifecycles: Vol. 1. Jewish Women on LifePassages and Personal Milestones.* Woodstock, VT: JewishLights.

Orenstein, Debra and Jane R. Litman, eds. 1994. *Lifecycles: Vol. 2. Jewish Women on Biblical Themes in Contemporary Life.*Woodstock, VT: Jewish Lights.

Osman, Ghada. 2003. "Back to Basics: The Discourse of Muslim Feminism in Contemporary Egypt." *Women and Language* 26: 73-78.

Pagels, Elaine. 1979. *The Gnostic Gospels.* New York: Random House.

Paper, Jordan. 2005. *The Deities Are Many: A Polytheistic Theology.* Albany: State University of New York.

Paper, Jordan. 1997. *Through the Earth Darkly: Female Spirituality in Comparative Perspective.* New York: Continuum.

Patai, Raphael. 1990. *The Hebrew Goddess: Third Enlarged Edition.* Detroit, MI: Wayne State University.

Pemberton, Carrie. 2003. *Circle Thinking: African Women Theologians in Dialogue with the West.* Leiden: Brill.

Perera, Sylvia B. 1981. *Descent to the Goddess: A Way of Initiation for Women.* Toronto: Inner City.

Plaskow, Judith. 2003. "Dealing with Difference Without andWithin." *Journal of Feminist Studies in Religion* 19 (1): 91-95.

Plaskow, Judith. 1997 [1991]. "Transforming the Nature ofCommunity: Toward a Feminist People of Israel." *After Patriarchy: Feminist Transformations of the World Religions.* Eds. P. M. Cooey, W. R. Eakin, and J. B. McDaniel. Maryknoll, NY: Orbis. 87-105.

Plaskow, Judith. 1994. "Jewish Theology in Feminist Perspective." *Feminist Perspectives on Jewish Studies.* Eds. Lynn Davidman and Shelly Tenenbaum. New Haven: Yale University Press. 62-84.

Plaskow, Judith. 1991. "Feminist Anti-Judaism and the Christian God."

Journal of Feminist Studies in Religion 7/2: 99-108.
Plaskow, Judith. 1990. *Standing Again at Sinai: Judaism from a Feminist Perspective*. San Francisco: Harper and Row.
Plaskow, Judith. 1983. "The Right Question is Theological." *On Being a Jewish Feminist*. Ed. Susannah Heschel. New York: Schocken. 223-233.
Plaskow, Judith. 1980/5741. "Blaming Jews for Inventing Patriarchy." *Lilith* 7: 11-12.
Plaskow, Judith. 1979. "Bringing a Daugther into the Covenant." *Woman spirit Rising: A Feminist Reader in Religion*. Eds. Carol P. Christ and Judith Plaskow. New York: Harper and Row. 179-184.
Plaskow, Judith and Carol P. Christ, eds. 1989. *Weaving the Visions: New Patterns in Feminist Spirituality*. San Francisco: Harper and Row.
Plaskow, Judith, with Donna Berman, ed. 2005. *The Coming of Lilith: Essays on Feminism, Judaism, and Sexual Ethics*. Boston: Beacon.
Pollack, Rachel. 1997. *The Body of the Goddess: Sacred Wisdom in Myth, Landscape and Culture*. Shaftesbury, Dorset, UK: Element.
Parvey, Constance. 1974. "The Theology and Leadership of Women in the New Testament." *Religion and Sexism: Images of Women in the Jewish and Christian Traditions*. Ed. Rosemary Radford Reuther. New York: Simon and Schuster. 117-149.
Preisand, Sally. 1975. *Judaism and the New Woman*. New York: Behrman.
Prell, Riv-Ellen, ed. 2007. *Feminism and the Remaking of American Judaism*. Detroit, MI: Wayne State University.
Prentice, Alison, Paula Bourne, Gail Cuthbert Brandt, Beth Light, Wendy Mitchison, and Naomi Black. 1996. *Canadian Women: A History*. 2nd ed. Toronto: Harcourt Brace.
Preston, James J., ed. 1982. *Mother Worship: Themes and Variations*. Chapel Hil: University of North Carolina Press.
Pritchard, James B., ed. 1991. *The Harper Concise Atlas of the Bible*. New York: Harper Collins.
Procter-Smith, Marjorie and Janet R. Walton, eds. 1993. *Women at Worship: Interpretations of North American Diversity*. Louisville, KY: Westminster John Knox.
Prusak, Bernard P. 1974. "Woman: Seductive Siren and Source of Sin?" *Religion and Sexism: Images of Women in the Jewish and Christian Traditions*. Ed. Rosemary Radford Reuther. New York: Simon and Schuster. 89-116.
Rankka, Kristine M. 1998. *Women and the Value of Suffering: An Aw(e)ful Rowing Toward God*. Collegeville, MN: Liturgical.
Raphael, Melissa. 2003. *The Female Face of God in Auschwitz: A Jewish Feminist Theology of the Holocaust*. London: Routledge.
Raphael, Melissa. 2000. *Introducing Thealogy: Discourse on the Goddess*. Cleveland, OH: Pilgrim.

Reed, Donna, dir. 1990. *The Burning Times*. Montreal: Studio D, National Film Board of Canada.

Reed, Donna, dir. 1989. *Goddess Remembered*. Montreal: Studio D, National Film Board of Canada.

Reuther, Rosemary Radford. 2005. *Goddesses and the Divine Feminine: A Western Religious History*. Berkeley: University of California Press.

Reuther, Rosemary Radford. 2001. "Christian Feminist Theology: History and Future." *Daughters of Abraham: Feminist Thought in Judaism, Christianity, and Islam*. Eds. Yvonne Y. Haddad and John L. Esposito. Gainesville, FL: University of Florida. 65-80.

Reuther, Rosemary Radford. 1993. "Can Christology Be Liberated From Patriarchy?" *Reconstructing the Christ Symbol: Essays in Feminist Christology*. Ed. Maryanne Stevens. Mahwah, NJ: Paulist. 7-29.

Reuther, Rosemary Radford. 1992. *Gaia and God: An Ecofeminist Theology of Earth Healing*. San Francisco: HarperSanFrancisco.

Reuther, Rosemary Radford. 1985. *Women-Church: The Theology and Practice of Feminist Liturgical Communities*. New York: Harper and Row.

Reuther, Rosemary Radford. 1983. *Sexism and God-Talk: Toward a Feminist Theology*. Boston: Beacon.

Reuther, Rosemary Radford, ed. 1974. *Religion and Sexism: Images of Women in the Jewish and Christian Traditions*. New York: Simon and Schuster.

Reuther, Rosemary Radford. 1974a. "Misogynism and Virginal Feminism in the Fathers of the Church." *Religion and Sexism: Images of Women in the Jewish and Christian Traditions*. Ed. Rosemary Radford Reuther. New York: Simon and Schuster. 150-183.

Riccetti, Angela J. 2005. "A Break in the Path: Lesbian Relationships and Jewish Law." *Marriage, Sex, and the Family in Judaism*. Eds. M. J. Broyde and M. Ausubel. Langham, MY: Rowman and Littlefield. 262-294.

Rich, Adrienne 1976. *Of Woman Born: Motherhood as Experience and Institution*. New York: Norton

Rodwell, J. M., tr. 1996 (1909). *The Koran*. Ed. Alan Jones. London: Dent Everyman.

Rogow, Faith. 1990. "Why Is This Decade Different From All Other Decades? A Look at the Rise of Jewish Lesbian Feminism." *Bridges* 1: 62-79.

Rosenberg, Lisa. 1996. "Determination and Despair: Agunot Speak About Their Chains." *Canadian Woman Studies/les cahiers de la femme* 16 (4) (Fall): 69-74.

Ross, Tamar. 2004. *Expanding the Palace of Torah: Orthodoxy and Feminism*. Hanover, NH: Brandeis University Press.

Ross, Tamar and Judith Plaskow. 2007. "Gender Theory and Gendered Realities: An Exchange between Tamar Ross and Judith Plaskow."

Nashim: A Journal of Jewish Women's Studies and Gender Issues 13: 207-251.

Rudavsky, T. M., ed. 1995. *Gender and Judaism: The Transformation of Tradition*. New York: New York University.

Rudhardt, Jean. 1994. "Hymn to Demeter." Trans. Lavinia Lorch and Helene P. Foley. *The Homeric Hymn to Demeter: Translation, Commentary, and Interpretive Essays*. Ed. Helene P. Foley. Princeton, NJ: Princeton University Press. 198-211.

Runesson, Anders 2001.*The Origins of the Synagogue: A Socio-Historical Study.* Stockholm: Almqvist and Wiksell.

Russell, Letty M. and J. Shannon Clarkson, eds. *Dictionary of Feminist Theologies*. Louisville, KY: Westminster John Knox.

Rutherford, Myra. 2002. *Women and the White Men's God: Gender and Race in the Canadian Mission Field.* Vancouver: University of British Columbia Press.

Ruthven, Malise. 2004. *Fundamentalism: The Search for Meaning*. Oxford: Oxford University Press.

Ruthven, Malise. 1997. *Islam: A Short History*. Oxford: Oxford University Press.

Sahgal, Gita and Nira Yuval-Davis, eds. 1992. *Refusing HolyOrders: Women and Fundamentalism in Britain*. London:Virago.

Saiving, Valerie. 1979. "The Human Situation: A Feminine View." *Womanspirit Rising: A Feminist Reader in Religion*. Eds. Carol P. Christ and Judith Plaskow. New York: Harper and Row. 25-42.

Saliba, Therese, Carolyn Allen and Judith A. Howard, eds. 2002. *Gender, Politics, and Islam*. Chicago: The University of Chicago Press.

Salomonsen, Jone. 2002. *Enchanted Feminism: Ritual, Gender and-Divinity among the Reclaiming Witches of San Francisco*. NewYork: Routledge.

Sanday, Peggy R. 1981. *Female Power and Male Dominance: On the Origins of Sexual Inequality*. Cambridge: Cambridge University Press.

Sansarian, Eliz. 1992. *The Women's Rights Movement in Iran: Mutiny, Appeasement, and Repression from 1900 to Khomeini*. New York: Praeger.

Sarah, Elizabeth. 1993. "Judaism and Lesbianism: A Tale of Life on the Margins of the Text." *Jewish Quarterly* 40: 20-23.

Sawyer, Deborah F. and Diane M. Collier, eds. 1999. *Is There a Future for Feminist Theology?* Sheffield, UK: Sheffield Academic.

Schaberg, Jane. 1992. "Luke." *The Women's Bible Commentary*. Eds. Carol Newsom and Sharon H. Ringe. Louisville, KY: Westminster John Knox. 275-292.

Schneer, David and Karyn Aviv, eds. 2002. *Queer Jews*. New York: Routledge.

Schulman, Sydell Ruth. 1996. "Faithful Daughters and Ultimate Rebels:

The First Class of Conservative Jewish Women Rabbis." *Religious Institutions and Women's Leadership: New Roles Inside the Mainstream.* Ed. Catherine Wessenger. Columbia, SC: University of South Carolina Press. 311-330.

Schwartz, Shuly Rubin. 2007. "The Tensions That Merit Our Attention: Women in Conservative Judaism." *Women Remaking American Judaism.* Ed. Riv-Ellen Prell. Detroit, MI: Wayne State University. 153-180.

Sered, Susan S. 1994. *Priestess, Mother, Sacred Sister: ReligionsDominated by Women.* New York: Oxford University Press.

Sered, Susan S. 1992. *Women as Ritual Experts: The Religious Lives of Elderly Jewish Women in Jerusalem.* New York: Oxford University Press.

Sered, Susan S. 1988. "Food and Holiness: Cooking as a Sacred Act among Middle-Eastern Jewish Women." *Anthropological Review* 61 (3): 129-140.

Setta, Susan M. 1989. "When Christ Is a Woman: Theology and Practice in the Shaker Tradition." *Unspoken Worlds: Women's Religious Lives.* 2nd ed. Eds. Nancy A. Falk and Rita M. Gross. Belmont, CA: Wadsworth. 221-232.

Shalvi, Alice."The Geopolitics of Jewish Feminism." *Gender and Judaism: The Transformation of Tradition.* Ed. T. M. Rudavsky. New York: New York University. 231-242.

Sharawi, Huda. 1986. *Harem Years: The Memoirs of an Egyptian Feminist (1879-1924).* London: Virago.

Sharma, Arvind and Katerine Young, eds. 2003. *Her Voice, Her Faith: Women Speak on World Religions.* Boulder, CO: Westview.

Sharp, Carolyn. 1996. "The Emergence of Francophone Feminist Theology." *Studies in Religion* 25 (4): 397-407.

Shimony, Annemarie. 1989. "Women of Influence and Prestige among the Native American Iroquois." *Unspoken Worlds: Women's Religious Lives.* 2nd ed. Eds. Nancy A. Falk and Rita M. Gross. Belmont, CA: Wadsworth. 201-211.

Shirali, Kishwar Ahmed. 1997. "Madness and Power in India,"*Canadian Woman Studies/Les cahiers de la femme* 17 (1): 66-71.

Silberman, Neil A. 1992. "Who Were the Israelites?" *Archaeology* 45 (2): 22-30.

Silverblatt, Irene 1987. *Moon, Sun, and Witches: Gender Ideologies and Class in Inca and Colonial Peru.* Princeton, NJ: Princeton University Press.

Sjöö, Monica and Barbara Mor. 1987. *The Great Cosmic Mother: Rediscovering the Religion of the Earth.* San Francisco: Harper and Row.

Smith, Margaret. 1994. *Rabi'a: The Life and Work of Rabi'a and Other Women Mystics in Islam.* Oxford: Oneworld.

Smith, Morton. 1993 (1978). *Jesus the Magician*. New York: Barnes and Noble.

Spiegel, Marcia C. 1996. "Spirituality for Survival: Jewish Women Healing Themselves." *Journal of Feminist Studies in Religion* 12 (2): 121-137.

Spretnak, Charlene, ed. 1982. *The Politics of Women's Spirituality: Essays on the Rise of Spiritual Power within the Feminist Movement*. Garden City, New York: Doubleday Anchor.

Stanton, Elizabeth Cady. 1974 (1895 and 1898). *The (Original) Feminist Attack on the Bible (The Woman's Bible)*. New York: Arno.

Starhawk (Miriam Simos). 2002. *Webs of Power: Notes from the Global Uprising*. Gabriola, BC: New Society.

Starhawk (Miriam Simos). 1989a (1982). *Dreaming the Dark: Magic, Sex and Politics*. Boston: Beacon.

Starhawk (Miriam Simos). 1989b (1979). *The Spiral Dance: A Rebirth of the Ancient Religion of the Great Goddess*. San Francisco: Harper and Row.

Starhawk (Miriam Simos). 1987a. "On Being a Jewish Witch." *Genesis 2* 18 (4): 38-39.

Starhawk (Miriam Simos). 1987b. *Truth or Dare: Encounters with Power, Authority, and Mystery*. San Francisco: Harpet and Row.

Steele, Betty. 1987. *The Feminist Take Over: Patriarchy to Matriarchy in Two Decades*. Richmond Hill, ON: Irwin.

Steichen, Donna. 1985. "From Convent to Coven: Catholic Neo-Pagans at the Witches' Sabbath." *Fidelity* 5 (1): 27-37.

Stein, Judith. 1984. *A New Haggadah: A Jewish Lesbian Seder*. Cambridge, MA: Bebbeh Meiseh.

Stevens, Maryanne, ed. 1993. *Reconstructing the Christ Symbol: Essays in Feminist Christology*. Mahwah, NJ: Paulist.

Stone, Merlin. 1984 (1979). *Ancient Mirrors of Womanhood: A Treasury of Goddess and Heroine Lore from Around the World*. Boston: Beacon.

Stone, Merlin. 1977 (1976). *The Paradise Papers*. (U.S. title *When God Was a Woman*). London: Virago.

Strong-Boag, Veronica. 1972. "Introduction." *In Times Like These*. Nellie L. McClung. Toronto: University of Toronto. vii-xxii.

Stowasser, Barbara. 1994. *Women in the Qur'an: Traditions and Interpretations*. New York: Oxford University.

Stuckey, Johanna H. 1998. *Feminist Spirituality: An Introduction to Feminist Theology in Judaism, Christianity, Islam, and Feminist Goddess Worship*. Toronto: Centre for Feminist Research, York University.

Stuckey, Johanna H. 1997. "Priestesses and 'Sacred Prostitutes' in the Ancient Eastern Mediterranean." *Canadian Woman Studies/Les cahiers de la femme* 17 (1): 6-9.

Swidler, Arlene, ed. *Homosexuality and World Religions.* Valley Forge, PA: Trinity International.

Tabari, A. and N. Yeganeh. 1982. *In the Shadow of Islam: The Women's Movement in Iran.* London: Zed .

Taieb-Carlen, Sarah. 1997. "Trials and Tribulations in the First Year of a 'Mixed Sephardi/Ashkenazi Marriage'." *Celebrating the Lives of Jewish Women: Patterns in a Feminist Sampler.* Eds. Rachel J. Siegal and Ellen Cole. New York: Haworth. 81-93.

Taieb-Carlen, Sarah. 1996. "Les femmes séphardes et leur intégration à Toronto." *Canadian Woman Studies/Les cahiers de la femme* 16 (4): 91-94.

Taitz, Emily, Sondra Henry, and Cheryl Tallan. 2003. *The JPS Guide to Jewish Women: 600 BCE-1900 CE.* Philadelphia: Jewish Publication Society.

Teish, Luisa. 1985. *Jambalaya: The Natural Woman's Book of Personal Charms and Practical Rituals.* San Francisco: Harper and Row.

Teubal, Savina J. 1990. *Hagar the Egyptian: The Lost Tradition of the Matriarchs.* San Francisco: HarperSanFrancisco.

Teubal,Savina J. 1984. *Sarah the Priestess: The First Matriarch of Genesis.* Athens, OH: Ohio University Swallow.

Torjesen, Karen Jo. 1993. *When Women Were Priests: Women's Leadership in the Early Church and the Scandal of their Subordination in the Rise of Christianity.* San Francisco: HarperSanFrancisco.

Townes, Emilie M. 1995. *In a Blaze of Glory: Womanist Spirituality as Social Witness.* Nashville, TN: Abingdon.

Trible, Phyllis. 1984. *Texts of Terror: Literary-Feminist Readings of Biblical Narratives.* Philadelphia: Fortress.

Trible, Phyllis. 1979. "Eve and Adam: Genesis 2-3 Reread." *Womanspirit Rising: A Feminist Reader in Religion.* Eds. Carol P. Christ and Judith Plaskow. New York: Harper and Row. 74-83.

Trible, Phyllis. 1978. *God and the Rhetoric of Sexuality.* Philadelphia: Fortress.

Troyer, Kristen de, Judith A. Herbert, Judith A. Johnson, and Anne-Marie Korte, eds. 2003. *Wholly Woman, Holy Blood: A Feminist Critique of Purity and Impurity.* London: T. And T. Clark International.

Tubb, Jonathan N. 1998. *Canaanites.* Norman: University of Oklahoma Press.

Tucker, Judith E. 1985. *Women in Nineteenth-Century Egypt.* Cambridge: Cambridge University Press.

Umansky, Ellen. 1995. "Foreword." *She Who Dwells Within: A Feminist Vision of a Renewed Judaism.* Lynn Gottlieb. San Francisco: HarperSanFrancisco. xi-xv.

Umansky, Ellen and Diana Ashton, eds., 1992. *Four Centuries ofJewish Women's Spirituality: A Sourcebook.* Boston: Beacon.

Vargas, Alicia. 2007. "The Construction of Latina Christology: An Invitation to Dialogue." *Currents in Theology and Mission* 34: 271-277.

Wadley, Susan S. 1989. "Hindu Women's Family and Household Rites in a North Indian Village." *Unspoken Worlds: Women's Religious Lives*. 2nd ed. Eds. Nancy A. Falk and Rita M. Gross. Belmont, CA: Wadsworth. 72-81.

Wadud, Amina. 1999 [1992]. *Qur'an and Women: Rereading the SacredText from a Woman's Perspective*. New York: Oxford University Press.

Wadud, Amina. 2000. "Alternative Qur'anic Interpretation and the Status of Muslim Women." *Windows of Faith: Muslim Women Scholar-Activists in North America*. Ed. Gisela Webb. Syracuse, NY: Syracuse University Press. 3-21.

Wadud, Amina. 2006. *Inside the Gender Jihad: Women's Reform in Islam*. Oxford: Oneworld.

Walker, Alice 1983. *In Search of Our Mothers' Gardens: Womanist Prose*. San Diego, CA: Harcourt Brace Jovanovich

Walker, Barbara G. 1990. *Women's Rituals: A Sourcebook*. San Francisco: Harper and Row.

Wall, Kathleen. 1990. "Healing the Divisions: Goddess Figures in Two Works of Twentieth Century Literature." *Goddesses in Religions and Modern Debate*. Ed. Larry Hurtado. Atlanta, GA: Scholars. 205-226.

Walther, Wiebke. 1995 [1981, 1993]. *Women in Islam: From Medieval to Modern Times*. Princeton, NJ: Wiener.

Ware, Timothy. 1997. *The Orthodox Church: New Edition*. London: Penguin.

Ware, Kallistos. 1993. "Eastern Christendom." *The Oxford History of Christianity*. Ed. John McManners. Oxford: Oxford University Press. 131-166.

Warne, Randi R. 1993. *Literature as Pulpit: The Christian Social Activism of Nellie L. McClung*. Waterloo, Ontario: Wilfred Laurier University Press.

Warner, Marina. 1991 (1981). *Joan of Arc: The Image of Female Heroism*. London: Vintage.

Warner, Marina. 1983 (1976). *Alone of All Her Sex: The Myth and Cult of the Virgin Mary*. London: Vintage.

Webb, Gisela, ed. 2000. *Windows of Faith: Muslim Women Scholar-Activists in North America*. Syracuse, NY: Syracuse University Press.

Webster's Encyclopedic Unabridged Dictionary of the English Language. 1996 [1987]. New York: Gramercy.

Wegner, Judith Romney.1992. "Leviticus." *The Women's Bible Commentary*. Eds. Carol Newsom and Sharon H. Ringe. Louisville, KY: Westminster John Knox. 36-44.

Weissler, Chava. 2007. "Meanings of Shekhinah in the 'Jewish Renewal' Movement." *Women Remaking American Judaism*. Ed. Riv-Ellen Prell. Detroit, MI: Wayne State University. 51-82.

Wessenger, Catherine, ed. 1996. *Religious Institutions and Women's Leadership: New Roles inside the Mainstream*. Columbia, SC: University of South Carolina Press.

Wikan, Unni. 1991. *Behind the Veil in Arabia: Women in Oman*. Chicago: University of Chicago Press.

Wiles, Maurice. 1993. "What Christians Believe." *The Oxford History of Christianity*. Ed. John McManners. Oxford: Oxford University Press. 571-586.

Williams, Delores. 1993. *Sisters in the Wilderness: The Challenge of Womanist God-Talk*. Maryknoll, NY: Orbis.

Williams, Delores. 1985. "Black Women's Literature and the Task of Feminist Theology." *Immaculate and Powerful: The Female in Sacred Image and Social Reality.* Eds. C. W. Atkinson, C. H. Buchanan, and M. R. Miles. Boston: Beacon. 88-110.

Wilson, Bryan. 1993. "New Images of Christian Community." *The Oxford History of Christianity*. Ed. John McManners. Oxford: Oxford University Press. 597-617.

Winter, Bronwyn. 2001. "Fundamental Misunderstandings: Issues in Feminist Approaches to Islam." *Journal of Women's History* 13: 9-41.

Wordelman, Amy L. 1992. "Everyday Life: Women in the Period of the New Testament." *The Women's Bible Commentary*. Eds. Carol Newsom and Sharon H. Ringe. Louisville, KY: Westminster John Knox. 390-396.

Yamani, Mai, ed. 1996. *Feminism and Islam: Legal and Literary Perspectives*. London: Ithaca.

Young, Katherine K. and Arvind Sharma. 1974. *Images of the Feminine—Mythic, Philosophic and Human—in the Buddhist, Hindu, and Islamic Traditions: A Bibliography of Women in India*. Chico, CA: New Horizons.

Zanotti, Barbara, ed. 1986. *A Faith of One's Own: Explorations by-Catholic Lesbians*. New York: Crossing.

Zuckerman, Francine, ed. 1992. *Half the Kingdom: Seven Jewish Feminists*. Montreal: Véhicule.

SELECTED INTERNET RESOURCES

Bibliography on Women and Religion at Roman Catholic Notre Dame University <www.nd.edu/~archives/lau_bib.html>.

Covenant of the Goddess, umbrella organization for Goddess worshippers <www.cog.org>.

Christian Lesbians provides links, a chat room, devotionals, etc. <www.christianlesbians.com>.
Grace Unfolding/SisterFriends Together, site for lesbian, Gay, bisexual, and transgenedered people <www.sisterfriends-together.org>.
Jewish Orthodox Feminist Alliance <www.jofa.org>.
Karámah, meaning "Dignity," an organization of Muslim womenlawyers who deal with human-rights issues <www.karamah.org>.
Women and Gender Studies <www.libr.org/wss/wsslinks/index.html>.
Women in Islam, an association dealing with advocacy and education about human rights and social justice <www.womeninislam.org>.

ADDITIONAL BIBLIOGRAPHY

African Religions

Binford, Martha R. 1989, "Julia: An East African Diviner." *Unspoken Worlds: Women's Religious Lives*. 2nd ed. Eds. Nancy A. Falk and Rita M. Gross. Belmont, CA: Wadsworth. 3-14.
Gleason, Judith. 1987. *Oya: In Praise of the Goddess*. Boston: Shambhala.
Gleason, Judith. 1971. *Orisha: The Gods of Yorubaland*. New York: Atheneum.
Lincoln, Bruce. *Emerging from the Chrysalis: Studies in Rituals of Women's Initiation*. Cambridge, MA: Harvard University Press.
Murphy, Joseph M. 1983. "Oshun the Dancer." *The Book of the Goddess, Past and Present: An Introduction to Her Religion*. Ed. Carl Olson. New York: Crossroad. 190-201.
Murphy, James M. And Mei-Mei Sanford, eds. 2001. *Oshun Across the Waters: A Yoruba Goddess in Africa and the Americas*. Bloomington: University of Indiana Press.
McCall, Daniel F. 1982. "Mother Earth: The Great Goddess of West Africa." *Mother Worship: Themes and Variations*. Ed. James J. Preston. Chapel Hill: University of North Carolina Press. 304-323.
Paper, Jordan. 1997. *Through the Earth Darkly: Female Spirituality in Comparative Perspective*. New York: Continuum.
Sered, Susan S. 1994. *Priestess, Mother, Sacred Sister: Religions Dominated by Women*. New York: Oxford University Press.
Swidler, Arlene, ed. 1993. *Homosexuality and World Religions*. Valley Forge, PA: Trinity International.

African American Religions

Brown, Karen M. 1991. *Mama Lola: A Vodou Priestess in Brooklyn*.

Berkeley: University of California Press.

Murphy, James M. and Mei-Mei Sanford, eds. 2001. *Oshun Across the Waters: A Yoruba Goddess in Africa and the Americas*. Bloomington: University of Indiana Press.

Murphy, Joseph M. 1994. *Working the Spirit: Ceremonies of the African Diaspora*. Boston: Beacon.

Murphy, Joseph M. 1988. *Santería: African Religion in America*. Boston: Beacon.

Olmos Fernández, Marguerite and Lizabeth Paravisini-Gebert, eds. 2000. *Sacred Possessions: Vodou, Santería, Obeah, and the Caribbean*. New Brunswick, NJ: Rutgers.

Paper, Jordan. 1997. *Through the Earth Darkly: Female Spirituality in Comparative Perspective*. New York: Continuum.

Sered, Susan S. 1994. *Priestess, Mother, Sacred Sister: Religions Dominated by Women*. New York: Oxford University Press.

Swidler, Arlene, ed. 1993. *Homosexuality and World Religions*. Valley Forge, PA: Trinity International.

Teish, Luisa. 1985. *Jambalaya: The Natural Woman's Book of Personal-Charms and Practical Rituals*. San Francisco: Harper and Row.

Buddhism

Cabezon, Jose, ed. 1992. *Buddhism, Sexuality, and Gender*. Albany, NY: State University of New York.

Dresser, Marianne, ed. 1996. *Buddhist Women on the Edge: Contemporary Perspectives from the Western Frontier*. Berkeley, CA: North Atlantic.

Falk, Nancy A. 1989. "The Case of the Vanishing Nuns: The Fruits of Ambivalence in Ancient Indian Buddhism." *Unspoken Worlds: Women's Religious Lives*. 2nd ed. Eds. Nancy A. Falk and Rita M. Gross. Belmont, CA: Wadsworth. 155-165.

Gross, Rita M. 1993. *Buddhism After Patriarchy: A Feminist History, Analysis, and Reconstruction of Buddhism*. Albany, NY: State University of New York.

Haker, Hille, Susan Ross, and Marie-Theres Wacker, eds. 2006. *Women's Voices in World Religions*. London: SCM Press.

Kinsley, David 1989. *The Goddesses' Mirror: Visions of the Divine from East and West*. Albany, NY: State University of New York

Klein, Anne C. 1995. *Meeting the Great Bliss Queen: Buddhists, Feminists, and the Art of the Self*. Boston: Beacon.

Paul, Diane Y. 1983. "Kuan-yin, Savior and Savioress in Chinese Pure Land Buddhism." *The Book of the Goddess, Past and Present: An Introduction to Her Religion*. Ed. Carl Olson. New York: Crossroad. 161-173.

Paul, Diane Y. 1979. *Women in Buddhism: Images of the Feminine in the Mahayana Tradition*. Berkeley, CA: Asian Humanities

Swidler, Arlene, ed. 1993. *Homosexuality and World Religions.* Valley Forge, PA: Trinity International.

Young, Katherine K. and Arvind Sharma. 1974. *Images of the Feminine—Mythic, Philosophic and Human—in the Buddhist, Hindu,and Islamic Traditions: A Bibliography of Women in India.* Chico, CA: New Horizons.

Chinese Religion

Ahern, Emily. 1973. *The Cult of the Dead in a Chinese Village.*Stanford, CA: Stanford University Press.

Jordan, David K. 1972. *Gods, Ghosts, and Ancestors: The Folk Religion of a Taiwanese Village.* Berkeley: University of California Press.

Kinsley, David. 1989. *The Goddesses' Mirror: Visions of the Divine from East and West.* Albany, NY: State University of New York.

Paper, Jordan. 1997. "Female Rituals and Female Priestly Roles in Traditional Chinese Religion." *Canadian Woman Studies/Les cahiers de la femme* 17 (1): 96-99.

Paper, Jordan. 1997. *Through the Earth Darkly: Female Spirituality in Comparative Perspective.* New York: Continuum.

Paper, Jordan. 1995. *The Spirits Are Drunk: Comparative Approaches to Chinese Religion.* Albany, NY: State University of New York.

Swidler, Arlene, ed. 1993. *Homosexuality and World Religions.* Valley Forge, PA: Trinity International .

Wolf, Margery and Roxanne Witke, eds. 1975. *Women in Chinese Society.* Stanford, CA: Stanford University Press.

Hinduism

Freeman, James M. 1989. "The Ladies of Lord Krishna: Rituals of Middle-Aged Women in Eastern India." *Unspoken Worlds: Women's Religious Lives.* 2nd ed. Eds. Nancy A. Falk and Rita M. Gross. Belmont, CA: Wadsworth. 82-92.

Haker, Hille, Susan Ross, and Marie-Theres Wacker, eds. 2006. *Women's Voices in World Religions.* London: SCM Press.

Jacobson, Doranne. 1989. "Golden Handprints and Red-Painted Feet: Hindu Childbirth Rituals in Central India." *Unspoken Worlds: Women's Religious Lives.* 2nd ed. Eds. Nancy A. Falk and Rita M. Gross. Belmont, CA: Wadsworth. 59-71.

Jacobson, Doranne and Susan S. Wadley, eds. 1977. *Women in India: Two Perspectives.* Delhi: Manohar.

Kinsley, David. 1986. *Hindu Goddesses: Visions of the Divine Feminine in the Hindu Religious Tradition.* Berkeley: University of California Press.

Manushi, a feminist periodical on women in India, published in New Delhi.

O'Flaherty, Wendy D. 1980. *Women, Androgynes, and Other Mythical Beasts.* Chicago: University of Chicago Press.

Shirali, Kishwar A. 1989. "Madness and Power in India." *Canadian Woman Studies/Les cahiers de la femme* 17 (1): 66-71.

Swidler, Arlene, ed. 1993. *Homosexuality and World Religions.* Valley Forge, PA: Trinity International .

Wadley, Susan S. 1989. "Hindu Women's Family and Household Ritesin a North Indian Village." *Unspoken Worlds: Women'sReligious Lives.* 2nd ed. Eds. Nancy A. Falk and Rita M. Gross. Belmont, CA: Wadsworth. 72ff.

Wadley, Susan S. 1980. *The Powers of Tamil Women.* New York: Syracuse University Press.

Young, Katherine K. and Arvind Sharma. 1974. *Images of the Feminine—Mythic, Philosophic and Human—in the Buddhist, Hindu, and Islamic Traditions: A Bibliography of Women in India.* Chico, CA: New Horizons.

Japanese Religion

Blacker, Carmen. 1975. *The Catalpa Bow.* London: Allen and Unwin.

Brock, Ruth N. 1989. "On Mirrors, Mist, and Murmurs: Toward an Asian American Thealogy." *Womanspirit Rising: A Feminist Reader in Religion.* Eds. Carol P. Christ and Judith Plaskow. New York: Harper and Row. 234-243.

Kinsley, David. 1989. *The Goddesses' Mirror: Visions of the Divine from East and West.* Albany, NY: State University of New York.

Nakamura, Kyoko M. 1989. "No Women's Liberation: The Heritage of a Woman Prophet in Modern Japan," 134-144 in *Unspoken Worlds: Women's Religious Lives.* 2nd ed. eds. Nancy A. Falk and Rita M. Gross. Belmont, CA: Wadsworth.

Nakamura, Kyoko M. 1983. "The Significance of Amaterasu in Japanese Religious History." *The Book of the Goddess, Past and Present: An Introduction to Her Religion.* Ed. Carl Olson. New York: Crossroad. 176-189.

Paper, Jordan. 1997. *Through the Earth Darkly: Female Spirituality in Comparative Perspective.* New York: Continuum.

Swidler, Arlene, ed. 1993. *Homosexuality and World Religions.* Valley Forge, PA: Trinity International.

Korean Religion

Harvey, Youngsook Kim. 1989. "Possession Sickness and Women Shamans in Korea." *Unspoken Worlds: Women's Religious Lives*. 2nd ed. Eds. Nancy A. Falk andRita M. Gross. Belmont, CA: Wadsworth. 37-44.

Harvey, Youngsook Kim. 1979. *Six Korean Women: The Socialization of Shamans*. St. Paul, MN: West

Kendall, Laurel. 1985. *Shamans, Housewives and Other Restless Spirits*. Honolulu: University of Hawaii Press.

Paper, Jordan. 1997. *Through the Earth Darkly: Female Spirituality in Comparative Perspective*. New York: Continuum.

Sered, Susan S. 1994. *Priestess, Mother, Sacred Sister: Religions Dominated by Women*. New York: Oxford University Press.

Native American Religions

Allen, Paula G. 1986. *The Sacred Hoop: Recovering the Feminine inAmerican Indian Traditions*. Boston: Beacon.

Hungry Wolf, Beverley. 1980. *The Ways of My Grandmothers*. New York: Morrow.

Johnson, Marilyn. 1997. "The Presence of Mother Earth in Women's Ceremonies: Observations of an Ojibway Medicine Woman/Wiccan Practitioner." *Canadian Woman Studies/Les cahiers de la femme* 17 (1): 121-122.

Merkur, Daniel. 1991. *Powers Which We Do Not Know: The Gods and Spirits of the Inuit*. Moscow, ID: University of Idaho Press.

Paper, Jordan. 1997. *Through the Earth Darkly: Female Spirituality in Comparative Perspective*. New York: Continuum.

Paper, Jordan. 1988. *Offering Smoke: The Sacred Pipe and Native American Religion*. Moscow, ID: University of Idaho.

Shimony, Annemarie. 1989. "Women of Influence and Prestige among the Native American Iroquois." *Unspoken Worlds: Women's Religious Lives*. 2nd ed. Eds. Nancy A. Falk and Rita M. Gross. Belmont, CA: Wadsworth. 201-211.

Talamantez, Inez. 1989. "The Presence if Isanaklesh: A Native American Goddess and the Path of Pollen." *Unspoken Worlds: Women's Religious Lives*. 2nd ed. Eds. Nancy A. Falk and Rita M. Gross. Belmont, CA: Wadsworth. 246-256.

INDEX

Johanna H. Stuckey, Ph.D. (Yale), University Professor Emerita in Humanities, Women's Studies, and Religious Studies, York University, taught ancient goddess worship, feminist theology, and female spirituality at York University and at the School of Continuing Studies at the University of Toronto. For six years she wrote quarterly articles on ancient goddesses for *Matrifocus* (www.matrifocus.com). At present she is working on a book on Ancient Eastern Mediterranean goddesses and "dying gods."